Supplementary Volume no.

JEWS AND GOD-FEARERS AT APHRODISIAS

GREEK INSCRIPTIONS WITH COMMENTARY

JOYCE REYNOLDS AND ROBERT TANNENBAUM

TEXTS FROM THE EXCAVATIONS AT
APHRODISIAS
CONDUCTED BY
KENAN T. ERIM

THE CAMBRIDGE PHILOLOGICAL SOCIETY
1987

© CAMBRIDGE PHILOLOGICAL SOCIETY

ISBN 0 906014 08 5

DS
135
.T82
A637
1987

Printed in Great Britain by the University Press, Cambridge

CONTENTS

		page
LIST OF ILLUSTRATIONS		iv
PREFACE AND ACKNOWLEDGMENTS		v
BIBLIOGRAPHICAL ABBREVIATIONS		vii
EPIGRAPHIC CONVENTIONS		ix
INTRODUCTION		1
I	THE PRINCIPAL INSCRIPTION: THE STONE AND ITS TEXTS	3
II	THE PRINCIPAL INSCRIPTION: DATE AND PURPOSE	19
III	COMMENTARY: THE JEWISH INSTITUTIONS	25
IV	HISTORICAL SIGNIFICANCE	78
V	COMMENTARY: THE PERSONAL NAMES	93
VI	COMMENTARY: THE TRADE-DESIGNATIONS	116
VII	THE SOCIETY AND ECONOMY OF APHRODISIAS	124
APPENDIX: OTHER JEWISH INSCRIPTIONS AND GRAFFITI AT APHRODISIAS		132
INDEX OF GREEK WORDS USED IN THE INSCRIPTIONS		147

LIST OF ILLUSTRATIONS

1. The stone, showing faces *a* and *b* — 15
2. The stone, showing faces *b* and *c* — 16
3. Face *a*, the text — 16
4. Face *b*, the text — 17
5. Face *b*, the text: upper list — 18
6. Face *b*, the text: lower list — 18
7. Appendix 1*a* — 141
8. Appendix 1*b* — 141
9. Appendix 2 — 142
10. Appendix 3 — 142
11. Appendix 4 — 143
12. Appendix 5 — 143
13. Appendix 7*a* — 144
14. Appendix 7*b* — 144
15. Appendix 8 — 145
16. Appendix 9 — 145
17. Appendix 10 — 146
18. Appendix 11, face *a* — 146
19. Appendix 11, face *b* — 146

PREFACE AND ACKNOWLEDGMENTS

We publish here as our main text an important but controversial inscribed stone from Aphrodisias in Caria, which we believe to be Jewish, although it carries no statement or symbol to demonstrate it and includes elements which could as well be Christian. The case for its Judaic content rests essentially on the many biblical names that it presents, approximately half of them in the indeclinable Septuagint form, and on its use of the word προσήλυτος on face *a*, ll. 13, 17, 22, rather in the manner of a status-designation; for προσήλυτος is the characteristic Greek word for a convert to Judaism, and while it can be used in Christian texts (see Lampe, *A lexicon of patristic Greek s.v.*) it does not there perform the same function of categorisation. It seems to us to be a unique document, unparalleled so far in the evidence from the Western diaspora, and the more difficult therefore to interpret precisely because of its unusual importance. It is obvious that the distinction implied on face *a* between Jews, proselytes and *theosebeis*, and on face *b* between Jews and *theosebeis*, is new evidence which, for the first time, offers clear light on the meaning of the term *theosebeis*; but we think that there is new information here on many other points, and we have sought to draw attention to as much as possible. We think also that this new information will interest several different categories of reader, to each of which some points may be obscure that are familiar to others; and with the aim of meeting the needs of all, in so far as we could foresee them, we have given more explanation than we should have thought necessary for any one category. In preparing our commentary, we divided the work so that Reynolds is mainly responsible for sections 1, 2, 5–7 and the appendix, Tannenbaum for sections 3 and 4. We have not tried to secure uniformity of style; and we have retained some repetitions which seemed to us likely to help readers with particular points.

We had hoped that Olivier Masson of Paris would write sections 5 and 6; in the event he was unable to do so, but has been most generous in contributing ideas and in answering questions – we are now aware that we have not asked as often as we should have done. We have had help from many others too. Reynolds would like to record debts to the Princeton Institute for Advanced Study and the Tübingen Theological Seminar; we are jointly under obligation to Luisa Abramowski, Elisabeth Alföldi, Mary Berry, Glen Bowersock, John Chadwick, Gershon Cohen, Jeremy Cohen, Richard Duncan-Jones, John

Gager, Frank Gilliam, Anthony and Louise Grafton, Christian Habicht, Martin Hengel, Hildebrecht Hommel, G. Hütternmeister, A. T. Kraabel, Nicholas de Lange, Gert Lüderitz, Fergus Millar, Hugh Plommer, Tessa Rajak, Mossman and Charlotte Roueché, Michael Speidel, Homer Thompson and Geza Vermes, all of whom have given time to us and none of whom should be held in any way responsible for our product. For help in turning a difficult manuscript into a respectable typescript we are grateful to Yvonne Lee, Sandy Lafferty and Dr Neil-Ann Levine in Princeton and very especially to Iris Hunter in Cambridge and Z. Abramovitz-Ratner and G. Stephens-Clark in London, who, at very much the last minute, added much of the Greek and almost all the Hebrew, together with some final revisions of the English. Finally we acknowledge our great debt to the Cambridge Philological Society and to the patience of its editors and printers.

Since our work went to press, a revised edition of Schürer III, part 1 (edited by G. Vermes, F. Millar, M. Goodman) has appeared. This refers to our text, with discussion at some points overlapping with ours (25–6, 166, 190–8).

The concluding stage of preparation of the manuscript was shadowed by the death of Professor Louis Robert. We had written in expectation of being read by his critical eye; we had made proposals, especially in the interpretation of *theosebeis*, that differ from his published views, hoping that our evidence would interest him. We are sad that he will not see it, and that we shall not have the benefit of his comment; more to the point that all epigraphists have lost the outstanding scholar in the field.

December 1985 J. M REYNOLDS
Newnham College, Cambridge

R. F. TANNENBAUM
New York

BIBLIOGRAPHICAL ABBREVIATIONS

References to classical authors are normally those of *LSJ*[9] or *The Oxford Classical Dictionary*[2] (1970); to classical journals those of *L'Année Philologique*; to collections of Greek and Latin inscriptions those of *Supplementum Epigraphicum Graecum* (*SEG*), see the lists of abbreviations in vols. XXIX (1979), XXX (1980), with a few supplements given below; references to Aphrodisian inscriptions as yet unpublished are to texts found during the excavations of Kenan T. Erim and in process of being edited – for the late antique and Byzantine periods by C. M. Roueché (ready for press), for the classical period (with the exception of documents emanating from Rome, for which see Reynolds, *Aphrodisias*), by J. M. Reynolds and C. M. Roueché (in active preparation).

References to pseudepigraphic and New Testament sources and journals follow those of G. Kümmel, *Introduction to the New Testament* (1975); references to rabbinical sources those of Schürer–Vermes–Millar I (see below).

Avi-Yonah = M. Avi-Yonah, *Abbreviations in Greek inscriptions* (Quarterly of the Department of Antiquities in Palestine, Supp. to IX (1940) 33f.), repr. in Al. N. Oikonomides (ed.), *Abbreviations in Greek inscriptions* (1974).
Beth She'arim = M. Schwabe and B. Lifshitz, *Beth She'arim* II, *The Greek inscriptions* (1967).
CIJ = J. B. Frey, *Corpus Inscriptionum Iudaicarum* I, *Europe* (1936) (see also *s.v.* Lifshitz); II, *Asie-Afrique* (1952).
Donateurs = B. Lifshitz, *Donateurs et fondateurs dans les synagogues juives* (1967).
Goodenough = E. R. Goodenough, *Jewish symbols in the Greco-Roman period*, II (1953), IV (1954).
IGCA = H. Grégoire, *Recueil d'inscriptions grecques-Chrétiennes de l'Asie Mineure* (1922).
IGCEg = G. Lefebvre, *Recueil des inscriptions grecques-Chrétiennes d'Egypte* (1907).
Juster = J. Juster, *Les Juifs dans l'Empire romain* (1914).
Kajanto *LC* = I. Kajanto, *The Latin cognomina* (1965).
    OS = id., *Onomastic studies in the early Christian inscriptions of Rome and Carthage* (1963).
    Supernomina = id., *Supernomina; a study in Latin epigraphy* (1966).

Leon, *Jews* = H. J. Leon, *The Jews of ancient Rome* (1960).
Lifshitz, *Prolegomenon* = B. Lifshitz, *Prolegomenon* to the *Corpus of Jewish Inscriptions*, I (Reprint of *CIJ*, New York 1975).
Lüderitz, *Cyrenaika* = G. Lüderitz, *Corpus jüdischer Zeugnisse aus der Cyrenaika* (1983).
Moore, *Judaism* = G. F. Moore, *Judaism in the first centuries of the Christian era, the age of the Tannaim* (1946).
Poland, *Vereinswesens* = F. Poland, *Geschichte des griechischen Vereinswesens* (1909).
Pape-Benseler = W. Pape, bearb. G. E. Benseler, *Wörterbuch der griechischen Eigennamen*² (1875).
Reynolds, *Aphrodisias* = Joyce Reynolds, *Aphrodisias and Rome* (1982).
Robert, *NIS* = L. Robert, *Nouvelles inscriptions de Sardes* (1964).
    Noms Indigènes = id., *Noms indigènes de l'Asie Mineure Gréco-Romaine* (1963).
Safrai/Stern = S. Safrai and M. Stern (eds.), *The Jewish people in the first century*, I (1974), II (1976).
Schürer = E. Schürer, *The history of the Jewish people in the age of Jesus Christ*, III (4th edition, 1909).
Schürer–Vermes–Millar = *id.*, a new English version revised and edited by Geza Vermes and Fergus Millar, I (1973), II (1979).
Solin, *GP* = H. Solin, *Die griechische Personennamen in Rom; ein Namenbuch* (1982).
    OL = id., *Chronologie des Cognomens* in H. G. Pflaum and N. Duval (eds.) *L'Onomastique Latine* (1977).
Zgusta, *KP* = L. Zgusta, *Kleinasiatische Personennamen* (1964).

EPIGRAPHIC CONVENTIONS

Brackets: ( ) enclose the resolution of an abbreviation or the addition of a letter omitted on the stone; a question mark shows that it is tentative.
    [ ] enclose a restoration; a question mark shows that it is tentative.
    Underdotting marks a letter incompletely preserved and reasonably, but not always certainly, interpreted.
    Underlining with a continuous line marks letters erased in antiquity but still legible.
    Underlining with a broken line marks letters added on the stone in a hand different from that in which the original text was cut.
    A box around letters indicates that they have been cut over an erasure.
    Measurements are all in metres; for monuments they are given in the order width × height × depth.
    Inventory numbers are normally assigned only to stones brought into the museum by the excavator; where numbers have been so assigned they are cited in the introductory accounts.

INTRODUCTION

Aphrodisias was a city of ancient Caria, now part of western Turkey, standing at about 140 km east of Ephesus (Selçuk), beside a tributary of the river Maeander (Büyük Menderes) whose valley provided one of the major east/west routes across Asia Minor. Settlement there is known to go back to the neolithic period, but the development of a city seems to be comparatively late (perhaps in the second century B.C.), although the sanctuary of Aphrodite, from whom it took its name, must be much older. Its city fathers seem to have favoured Roman intervention in Asia Minor; and in the first century B.C. they built a special relation with Rome, and in due course also one with Julius Caesar and the party of Octavian/Augustus his heir, on the identification of their Aphrodite with Venus the mother of Aeneas, from whom legend derived both Romulus the founder of Rome and Iulus the ancestor of the family of Caesar. They fought against Rome's enemies, and against Caesar's; and were rewarded in 39 B.C. with grants of *eleutheria* (freedom) and *ateleia* (exemption from all Roman taxation and levies), privileges which the city retained until at least the late third century A.D., when it became the metropolis of a new province, Phrygia-Caria. In the shelter of the peace substantially maintained by the Roman emperors it was a prosperous place; the crops of its fertile and well-watered fields included flax from which linen was woven, the sheep pastured on its hillsides gave wool for woollen cloth production, the marble from its quarries encouraged fine sculpture and high quality stone-work; among other resources there was almost certainly iron. There were, in fact, many attractions there for immigrants.

It has been known for some time that by the early Byzantine period the immigrants included Jews (App. 1). The stone published here is the first evidence for their presence at an earlier date and shows them, as we believe, to have been a significant element in the population in the third century A.D. When they first came we do not know; but their coming cannot be regarded as surprising, for Jewish communities are attested in Caria, some as early as the second century B.C., and, a little later, in a number of neighbouring cities with which Aphrodisias was certainly in communication – for instance Laodicea ad Lycum, Hierapolis, Tralles, Ephesus, Smyrna. Our stone and its Jewish community has, therefore, a wider historical context than the city of Aphrodisias itself, although as yet one which can only be indicated in rather general terms.

It was found, along with other unattached stones, during construction of the Aphrodisias museum, in connection with the excavations on the site conducted by Professor K. T. Erim, sponsored by New York University and generously supported by the National Geographic Society. There can be no certainty that its findspot, east of what is now the entry to the museum, bears any relation to its original location, for although it may seem, at first sight, too large to be moved far, that is not a strong argument, given the size of a number of blocks demonstrably taken from the theatre of Aphrodisias for re-use in the city-walls in late antiquity (Reynolds, *Aphrodisias* xvii, 54–5). Nevertheless, there is a scatter of stones which are Jewish, or likely to be so (at least nos. 2–7 of the appendix and perhaps also nos. 9, 10), found in the area immediately north, east and south-east of the museum, which suggests a possibility that a Jewish quarter, with synagogue and related buildings, lay thereabouts. The discovery was reported by Professor Erim in *AJA* 81 (1977) 306, *AS* 27 (1977) 31. It has been referred to in print notably by A. T. Kraabel, *Numen* 28.2 (1981) 125–6, n. 26, B. J. Brooten, *Women leaders in the ancient synagogue* (1982) 151, Wayne Meeks, *The first urban Christians* (1983) 39, 207–8.

I THE PRINCIPAL INSCRIPTION: THE STONE AND ITS TEXTS

The stone carrying the principal inscription (excavation inventory no. 76.1) was a chance discovery, made during the preparations for construction of the Aphrodisias museum, and found lying loose. It is a block of marble, tapering a little towards the top (width across faces *a* and *c*, 0·45–0·43 m × ht. 2·80 × width across face *b*, 0·46–0·425), the surface carefully smoothed on faces *a*, *b* and *c* (but left roughly dressed only on face *d*). It is inscribed on two faces, *a* and *b* (which is to the right of *a* at right angles), the two main texts being in different hands, although supplemented in both cases by another hand or hands which may have worked on both faces. On faces *b* and *c* (which is to the right of *b* at right angles), there is a drafted margin or rebate down both sides (the right-hand margin overcut on face *b* by its inscription), and on face *a* a similar margin down the right side (overcut by the face *a* inscription) and a fillet with rough-dressed surface (*c*. 0·085 wide) down the left side (overcut when the face *a* inscription was supplemented). On face *a* there are two holes, almost square, approximately at the mid-point, one immediately to the right of the fillet and one near the centre of the face, clearly in order to attach something to the lower part of the face. Finally there has been quite extensive damage at the top and the bottom of the stone, severe chipping along all edges and scratching of all visible surfaces, much of it certainly later than the inscription, but some possibly earlier.

On face *a* the text is concentrated in the upper part of the stone, and initially respected the fillet, although it overcut the margin; but at some stage, likely to be quite soon after the original inscription, it was decided to add an entry to the left of ll. 9–17 (possibly removing it from ll. 26–7 which were then erased, see p. 10), and for this the fillet too was overcut. The whole text was laid out without the use of guide-lines and standardised letter-heights or forms. Letter-heights average 0·03 in ll. 1–5 and 0·02 thereafter; letters were apparently designed freehand, and include both angular and lunate *epsilon* and *sigma* (as well as lunate *omega*), *alpha* sometimes with a straight, sometimes with a dropped bar, and *omicron* frequently written small. The mason felt a strong compulsion to compress; hence ligatured *omega* and *nu* in l. 5 and many abbreviations, most of them marked by a sign – a supraschript bar, ⟩, s, ɔ or c (ll. 3–5, 13, 15, 17, 19, 21, 22) – or by raising the final inscribed letter above the text (l. 10).

The heading (l. 1) slants upwards from left to right, as if the designer had failed to mark his base line in correct horizontal relation to the stone. The first line of the preamble (l. 2) begins very formally with a capital letter (*omicron*) and its first three and last two letters are more or less correctly aligned, but between them the base line describes an arc, suggesting that such guideline as was used (? a stretched cord) ran along the top of the letters. The surprisingly large space between ll. 2 and 3 was probably dictated by the presence of an abbreviation mark above the last letter of l. 3. The rest of the preamble (ll. 3–8) shows rather more successful care for alignment and spacing, although still far from perfect. It is separated from what follows by a lightly incised line running across about one third of the width of the face; ll. 10 f. show rather less care; at l. 21 there may be a change of hand; at l. 22, where the alignment at the left side changes, it is quite clear that there has been, and that the standard of skill has dropped; ll. 26, 27 have been erased but are not quite illegible. The entry added to the left of ll. 9–17 is very gauchely cut, perhaps by the hand which cut ll. 22–5; but it must be said, in extenuation, that it cannot have been easy to work on the rough surface.

Approximately 1·13 m below this text, and at an angle to it, is a graffito in a different style from anything in the text (letter-heights, *c.* 0·06). It is so near the bottom of the stone that if the stone was upright when it was made the cutter must have been sitting on the ground, and even so cannot have worked at all comfortably.

On face *b* the text is arranged in two parts, separated by a sizeable vacant area (0·15 in height). At the top one line has probably been lost through damage, the second partly so, while the third has been efficiently erased. The letters are *c.* 0·02 high throughout, cut between guide-lines which are visible on inspection, and although not absolutely regular in height, are kept to a rough standard by those lines; they are also normally consistent in form, with lunate *epsilon*, *sigma* and *omega*, although *alpha* appears both with a straight and with a dropped bar. The style changes only where entries have been added in a different hand, sometimes over erasures (ll. 15, 20, 32, 39, 48), sometimes on the original surface (ll. 5, 8, 30, 58, 60–1). As on face *a* the mason has felt a compulsion to compress, so that there are many abbreviations, but it was comparatively rarely that he marked them by a sign; he has, however, put a downward-slanting stroke attached to the *rho* at the end of l. 23, round dots after the last inscribed letters in ll. 26, 27, 41, a slanting stroke attached to one in the middle of l. 48, probably s in l. 32 and c at the end of l. 56. Complete phrases are normally separated by stops in the form of small round circular dots or arrowheads, and once of a small circle (l. 53). There are also commonly two dots (occasionally

THE STONE AND TEXTS 5

one only) set above initial *iota* when it is followed by another vowel which is to be pronounced separately (diaeresis marks, ll. 5, 10, 13, 14, 26–28, 43). Both these last two features are common in official Aphrodisias inscriptions up to the third quarter of the third century (when the dated series at present fails for a time, before reviving in the fourth century); in these, however, the diaeresis marks are usually placed on either side of the letter that they distinguish.

In the following transcription indeclinable names are not accented.

Outspaced lines are shown as on the stone.

Face *a*
Col. (i) Θεὸς βοηθός, πατέλλᾳ? δο[. 1 *or* 2.]
Οἱ ὑποτεταγμέ-
νοι τῆς δεκαν(ίας)
τῶν φιλομαθῶ[ν]
5 τῶν κὲ παντευλογ(--ων)
εἰς ἀπενθησίαν
τῷ πλήθι ἔκτισα[ν]
ἐξ ἰδίων μνῆμα
Σα- Ἰαηλ προστάτης
μου 10 *v*. σὺν υἱῷ Ἰωσούᾳ ἄρχ(οντι?)
ηλ Θεόδοτος Παλατῖν(ος?) σὺν
πρεσ *v*. υἱῷ Ἱλαριανῷ *vac.*
βευ- Σαμουηλ ἀρχιδ(έκανος?) προσήλ(υτος)
τῆς Ἰωσῆς Ἰεσσέου *vacat*
Περ- 15 Βενιαμιν ψαλμο(λόγος?)
γε- Ἰούδας εὔκολος *vacat*
ούς Ἰωσῆς προσήλυ(τος)
Σαββάτιος Ἀμαχίου
Ἐμμόνιος θεοσεβ(ής) *v.v.*
20 Ἀντωνῖνος θεοσεβ(ής)
Σαμουηλ Πολιτιανοῦ
Εἰωσηφ Εὐσεβίου προσή(λυτος)
κα[ὶ] Εἰούδας Θεοδώρ(ου)
καὶ Ἀντιπέος Ἑρμή(ου?)
25 καὶ Σαβάθιος νεκτάρις
[?κα]ὶ Σαμο[υ]ηλ πρεσ-
βευτὴς ἱερεύς

Col. (ii) (at an angle to i and in a different hand)

If cut when the stele was standing: ΝΜΔ

If cut upside down to the main text: ΠWN

Face b   [? one line completely lost]
[.. c. 8 .. Σ]εραπίωνος v. [v.]
[one line completely erased]
['Ιωση]φ Ζήνωνος vacat
5 [Ζή]νων Ἰακωβ stop Μανασῆς Ἰωφ sic
Ἰούδας Εὐσεβίου vacat
Ἑορτάσιος Καλλικάρπου vacat
Βιωτικός stop Ἰούδας Ἀμφιανοῦ
Εὐγένιος χρυσοχόος vacat
10 Πραοίλιος stop Ἰούδας Πραοιλίου v.
Ῥοῦφος stop Ὀξυχόλιος γέρων
Ἀμάντιος Χαρίνου stop Μύρτιλος
Ἰακω πρυβαιυν(όμυς?) stop Σεβῆρυς vacat
Εὔοδος stop Ἰάσων Εὐόδου vacat
15 Εὐσαββάθιος λαχα(νοπώλης?) stop Ἀνύσιος
Εὐσαββάθιος ξένος stop Μίλων
Ὀξυχόλιος νεώτερος vacat
Διογένης stop Εὐσαββάθιος Διογέν(ους)
[Ἰού]δας Παύλου stop Θεόφιλος vac.
20 [Ἰ]α[κ]ωβ ὁ κὲ Ἀπελλί(ων?) stop Ζαχαρίας μονο(πώλης?)
[Λε]όντιος Λεοντίου stop Γέμελλος
[Ἰο]ύδας Ἀχολίου stop Δαμόνικος vacat
Εὐτάρκιος Ἰούδα stop Ἰωσηφ Φιληρ(?)
Εὐσαββάθιος Εὐγενίου vacat
25 Κύρυλλος stop Εὐτύχιος χαλκο(τύπος?)
Ἰωσηφ παστι(λλάριος?) stop Ῥουβην παστ(ιλλάριος?)
Ἰούδας Ὀρτασί(ου) stop Εὐτύχιος ὀρν(ιθοπώλης?)
Ἰούδας ὁ κὲ Ζωσι(?) stop Ζήνων γρυτ(οπώλης?)
Ἀμμιανὸς χιλᾶς stop Αἰλιανὸς Αἰλια(νοῦ)
30 Αἰλιανὸς ὁ καὶ Σαμουηλ Φίλανθος
Γοργόνιος Ὀξυ(χολίου) stop Ἑορτάσιος Ἀχιλλέ(ως)
Εὐσαββάθιος Ὀξυχ(ολίου) stop Παρηγόριος
Ἑορτάσιος Ζωτικοῦ Συμεών Ζην(?)
               vacat
Καὶ ὅσοι θεοσεβῖς stop Ζήνων βουλ(ευτής)

THE STONE AND TEXTS

35 Τέρτυλλος βουλ(ευτής) *stop* Διογένης βουλ(ευτής)
   Ὀνήσιμος βουλ(ευτής) *stop* Ζήνων Λονγι(ανοῦ?) βου(λευτής)
   Ἀντιπέος βουλ(ευτής) *stop* Ἀντίοχος βουλ(ευτής)
   Ῥωμανὸς βουλ(ευτής) *stop* Ἀπονήριος βουλ(ευτής)
   Εὐπίθιος πορφυρ(ᾶς) *stop* Στρατήγιος
40 Ξάνθος *vacat* Ξάνθος Ξάνθου *v.*
   Ἀπονήριος Ἀπον(ηρίου) *stop* Ὑψικλῆς Μελ(?) *stop*
   Πολυχρόνιος Ξάν(θου) *stop* Ἀθηνίων Αἰ(λιανοῦ?)
   Καλλίμορφος Καλ(λιμόρφου?) *stop* ΙΟΫΝΒΑΛΟΣ
   Τυχικὸς Τυχι(κοῦ) *stop* Γληγόριος Τυχι(κοῦ) *v.*
45 Πολυχρόνιος βελ(?) *stop* Χρύσιππος
   Γοργόνιος χαλ(κοτύπος?) *stop* Τατιανὸς Ὀξυ(χολίου?)
   Ἀπελλᾶς Ἡγε(μονέως?) *stop* Βαλεριανὸς πενα(κᾶς?)
   Εὐσαββάθιος Ἡδ(υχρόος?) ?Μανικιος Ἀττά(λου?) *vac.*
   Ὁρτάσιος λατύ(πος?) *stop* Βραβεύς *vacat*
50 Κλαυδιανὸς Καλ(λιμόρφου?) *stop* Ἀλέξανδρος πυ(?)
   Ἀππιανὸς λευ(?) *stop* Ἀδόλιος ἰσικιάριος
   Ζωτικὸς ψελ(λός?) *stop* Ζωτικὸς γρύλλος
   Εὐπίθιος Εὐπι(θίου) *stop* Πατρίκιος χαλκο(τύπος)
   Ἐλπιδιανὸς ἀθλη(τής?) *stop* Ἡδυχροῦς *vacat*
55 Εὐτρόπιος Ἡδυχ(ρόος) *stop* Καλλίνικος *vac.*
   Βαλεριανὸς ἀρκά(ριος?) *stop* Εὔρετος Ἀθηναγ(όρου)
   Παράμονος ἰκονο(γράφος?) *stop vacat*
   Εὐτυχιανὸς γναφ(εύς) *stop* Προκόπιος τρα(πεζίτης?)
   Προυνίκιος γναφ(εύς) *stop* Στρατόνικος γναφ(εύς)
60 Ἀθηναγόρας τέκτω(ν) *vacat*
   Μελίτων Ἀμαζονίου *vacat*
            vacat   vacat

Readings, resolutions and supplements

Introductory notes. Except in face *a*, ll. 1–19 the abbreviated words all provide distinguishing additions to names. Where such additions survive in unabbreviated form and have a case ending they can be identified as: *patronymics* (19 cases: *a*, ll. 14, 18, 21, 22, *b*, ll. 2, 4, 6–8, 10, 12, 14, 21–4, 33, 40, 61); *second names* (3 cases, each introduced by ὁ καί, ὁ κέ: *b*, ll. 20, 28, 30); *designations of status, profession, craft or trade* (3 cases: *b*, ll 9, 51, 60); *other descriptions* (5 cases: *a*, ll. 16, 25, *b*. ll. 11, 16, 17). It is often clear, or reasonably so, to which category an abbreviated word, or one without a case ending, should be assigned: thus it seems right to take the two indeclinable names in *b*, l. 5, as well as a number of abbreviated names, e.g. in *a*, ll. 23, 24, as patronymics, and a considerable number of abbreviated words, e.g. in b, ll. 13, 15, 20, 25, which do not correspond to attested names, as trade designations. But there is sometimes doubt, since the abbreviations are often very sharp. We have normally interpreted as a patronymic when the inscribed letter-group coincides with the opening letters of a name which appears elsewhere in the inscription (preferably earlier), and as a description of some kind otherwise; but the argument for this procedure is not watertight, see for instance b, l. 47.

Face a, col. (i).
Line **1**, πατέλλᾳ; for the word division see p. 26.

δο̣[. 1 *or* 2.]; the circular letter, which is written small, is damaged above so that *omega* cannot be excluded; it may have been surmounted by a bar, and although what is visible is more probably a chip, there is a real possibility that the word was in abbreviation; there is certainly room for one more letter, possibly for two, after the 'circle'.

3. δεκαν(ίας): the abbreviation is marked by c above the final *nu*; δεκανία seems to be the only attested word which offers a likely meaning here; for the possible sense see pp. 28–30.

4. φιλομαθῷ[ν]: only the tops of the three strokes of lunate *omega* survive, surmounted by a bar which marks the abbreviation; there was no room to complete the word, probably because the edge of the stone was already chipped. The supplement seems inevitable in the context.

5. παντευλογ(?): *omicron* is written small, enough survives of the damaged letter that follows to make *gamma* highly likely; it is not clear whether there was an abbreviation mark. Since there is no suitable attested word to fit the data, unattested possibilities must be explored, see pp. 34–7.

6. ἀπενθησίαν: the reading is clear, but the word seems to be unattested, see p. 38.

9–17 (left margin). Σαμουηλ πρεσβευτὴς Περγεούς: in some lights the initial Π of the second title appears to be EI, but examination of the stone leaves no doubt that the upper horizontal covers the second upright as well as the first, and was intended to do so; while the central and lower ones are lighter and must, we think, be dismissed as unintentional. For discussion of the meaning see pp. 41–2; for the possible relation of these lines to the erasure on this face, see on ll. 26–7.

10. ἄρχ(οντι?): *chi* has been cut above *rho* (for this method of abbreviation see Avi-Yonah, 29–30); the abbreviated word is most unlikely to be a patronymic, for if Jael is a man, as argued on p. 101, it is he who was Joshua's father, and if Jael is a woman it would be unusual to refer to her husband in so oblique a manner; in any case (see also p. 43) a status-designation is more probable in this area of the list, where it seems that we have not yet reached the decany president (see l. 13) and need an explanation for the precedence given to these names (cf. the προστάτης in l. 9 and the πρεσβευτὴς Περγεούς in ll. 9–17 left margin). Of the possible titles, we have rejected any compound with ἀρχι-, since it should be so abbreviated as to include some element of the second part of the word, see L. Robert, *RPh* 32 (1958) 37, and cf. ἀρχισ(υνάγωγος) in *SEG* xx.462. For Jewish *archontes* see p. 42.

11. Παλατῖν(ος?): the abbreviation is marked by a slightly curved stroke rising obliquely from the right *hasta* of *nu*; a name exists to fit the data (Παλατῖνος, Palatinos), so that a patronymic is theoretically possible; but in this area of the list a status-designation is more appropriate, cf. on l. 10. For Παλατῖνος, Palatinus, as a name, see p. 103, and as a title, pp. 42–3.

13. ἀρχιδ(έκανος?): the abbreviation is marked by a small s above the *delta*; a name exists to fit the data (Ἀρχίδημος) so that a patronymic is theoretically possible, but so sharp an abbreviation of one that appears nowhere else on the stone is against it, when a status designation, very appropriate in the context, is available; in any case, as a proselyte, Samuel ought not to refer to his natural father (see p. 94); it must be admitted, however, that Joseph, the proselyte in l. 22, does do so. On the word chosen see p. 43.

προσήλ(υτος): the abbreviation is marked by a small s above the line between *eta* and *lambda*; see also ll. 17, 22, where the same word must be intended; no other attested noun fits the data. On the meaning see pp. 43–5.

15. ψαλμο(λόγος?): the abbreviation is marked by s above the line to the right of *omicron*; there can hardly be any doubt that a psalm-singer is intended, see p. 46, but the *omicron* is clear so that either there is a mis-spelling for the normal ψαλμῳ(δός) or the word used was ψαλμο(λόγος), which is not listed in *LSJ*[9] or Lampe's *Lexicon of patristic Greek*, but appears in *TLG* with reference to *V. Nili jun.* p. 40.4 (*PG* 120.52*b*), where it is used as an adjective.

17. προσήλυ(τος): the abbreviation is marked by c lightly cut to the right of *ypsilon*; see on l. 13.

19, 20. θεοσεβ(ής): the abbreviations are marked by s, high or above the line to the right of *beta*. While a patronymic, Θεοσεβ(οῦς), is theoretically possible, the heading at *b*, l. 34 (καὶ ὅσοι θεοσεβῖς) strongly suggests the categorising adjective here too; see further pp. 48–66.

22. προσή(λυτος): the abbreviation is marked by a slight raising of *eta* and an s placed to the right of it; see on l. 13.

23. Θεοδώρ(ου): it is not clear whether the abbreviation was marked; the line is badly set out so that the cutter was left without space in which to complete the patronymic.

24. Ἑρμῆ appears as a genitive of the name Ἑρμῆς in P. Oxy. 27.2480.46 of A.D. 565; but, although there is no abbreviation mark, an abbreviation was perhaps intended here, e.g. Ἑρμή(ου).

25. νεκτάρις for νεκτάριος as commonly in the *koine*; it may be a second name or a descriptive adjective, cf. εὔκολος in l. 16.

26, 27. Although there has been erasure here, the shadows of letters are visible and seem to yield a name and designations very like those of the man who was listed by the second cutter in the left margin, beside ll. 9–17, although apparently with ἱερεύς instead of the Περγεούς found there. It is tempting to conjecture that the two are identical – either with an error in l. 27 which has been corrected in the version beside ll. 9–17, or with an error made by the second hand (which was certainly that of a less careful and more ignorant man than the first). If so the entry may have been moved because Samuel's status was too high for the bottom of the list – or possibly because he was not in fact an Aphrodisian Jew and therefore perhaps not a member of the decany, see also p. 30.

Face a, Col. (ii). The graffito is not obviously meaningful.

Face b.

Line **2.** The first part of the line is wholly lost, and only the lower parts of the underdotted letters are visible, but if they are correctly interpreted this is a patronymic with space before it for one name only; that leaves only l. 1 for a heading, see further p. 19.

3. Very efficiently erased and subsequently also damaged.

5. The second entry is in a different hand, poorly cut and aligned, the patronymic perhaps incorrectly spelt, see p. 103, no. 47.

8. In the second entry the patronymic was originally abbreviated but was completed in a different hand.

9. χρυσοχόος; it is possible that the last two letters were added later. For the trade-designation 'goldsmith' see p. 119, no. 9.

10. The reading is clear, see p. 104.

13. Ἰακω: for this form of Ἰακωβ see p. 101.

προβατον(όμος?); since no known name fits the data, O. Masson proposes an unattested but plausible trade-designation, shepherd, sheep-rearer; see p. 118, no. 6.

15. Written *in rasura* except for the first and the last two letters.

λαχα(νοπώλης?): an erased *ypsilon* seems to be visible under the dot which concludes the entry; no obvious name fits the data and the trade-designation, 'green-grocer', is available and appropriate; for the several variants available see p. 118, no. 2.

19. [Ἰού]δας: the name is most naturally restored as proposed; there is no room for Θευδᾶς.

20. The first entry was written *in rasura* and subsequently damaged, but the supplements are obvious; for Jacob's second name see p. 98.

21. [Λε]όντιος: the supplement is obvious.
22. ['Ιο]ύδας: the supplement is obvious; see also on l. 19.
23. The first letter is defective, but can hardly be other than *epsilon* or *sigma*; neither gives a satisfactorily explicable name, see p. 100, list A, no. 25.

Φιληρ(?): the abbreviation is marked by a small line curving down and rightwards from the lower junction of the bowl with the *hasta* of *rho*; the few names that fit the data seem rather rare, see p. 104; on the other hand there is no obvious trade-designation available either.

25. χαλκο(τύπος?): names to fit the data are rare and the trade-designation, 'bronze-smith', is very suitable; for the several words available, see p. 118, no. 7.

26. παστι(λλάριος?), παστ(ιλλάριος?): the dot after ΠΑΣΤΙ is simply the divider between entries, but that after ΠΑΣΤ must be an abbreviation mark; names to fit the data are rare and the trade-designation, 'confectioner', suitable; but this is not the only possible form, see p. 118, no. 5.

27. Όρτασί(ου): clearly from a variant for Έορτάσιος, ll. 7, 31, 33, 49, and see p. 99.

ὀρν(ιθοπώλης?): the abbreviation is marked by a dot to the right of *nu*; since names to fit the data are comparatively rare we have tentatively proposed the trade-designation 'poulterer'; for the range of words available see p. 118, no. 4.

28. Ζώσι(μος?): a very common name, although Ζωσιμιανός, or another rarer but related name, is also possible; see p. 100.

γρυτ(οπώλης?): the abbreviation may be marked by a small s high in the line to the right of *tau*; no likely name fits the data and the trade-designation 'rag-picker, rag-dealer' is available and suitable, see p. 117, no. 1.

29. χιλᾶς: either a second name or a trade-designation, see p. 105, list A, no. 67 and pp. 118–19, no. 8.

Αἰλια(νοῦ); the resolution is obvious.

30. The last word is added in a second hand and surely best taken as an additional, single-name entry, despite the omission of a stop before it; Aelianus is unlikely to have had three names.

31. Ὀξυ(χολίου): the patronymic is deduced from ll. 11, 17, cf. l. 32.

Ἀχιλλέ(ως): the resolution is obvious.

32. The first entry written *in rasura*; the abbreviation is marked by a small s high in the line to the right of *ypsilon*; the patronymic is deduced from ll. 11, 17, 31.

33. The mason was short of space and omitted a stop between the entries.

Ζήν(ωνος?): the patronymic is deduced from ll. 4, 5, 28, but a related name, such as Ζηνόδοτος, is also possible.

34. After a *vacat* of c. 0·15 in height a second list is introduced by a heading, in which θεοσεβῖς shows a common enough spelling of the case-ending; for ὅσοι, presumably with an ellipse of εἰσιν, meaning 'as many as are *theosebeis* (*sc.* among those listed)', see Arndt and Gringrich, *A Greek English lexicon of the New Testament, sv.* ὅσος 2.

34–8. βουλ(ευτής), βου(λευτής): the abbreviations, especially the former, are not uncommon.

36. Λονγι(ανοῦ?): a patronymic was required to distinguish this Zenon from a homonymous bouleute (l. 34) senior to him, but space was short so that it had to be abbreviated; the name restored occurs elsewhere at Aphrodisias – a related name such as Λονγι(νοῦ) is also possible.

39. The first entry, written partly *in rasura*, is outspaced, clearly because the erased area was too short for it; the impression given is of the correction of an error (the cutter had perhaps omitted a letter or a syllable), rather than of the substitution of a new name for one previously there.

πορφυρ(ᾶς): there is little doubt but that the trade-designation 'purple-dealer, purple-dyer' stood here, but for the range of words available see p. 121, no. 14.

41. Ἀπον(ηρίου): resolution of the abbreviated patronymic is obvious.

Μελ(?); the abbreviation is marked by a dot to the right of *lambda*; a patronymic is possible, although nothing suitable occurs earlier in the list; if so perhaps Μελ(ίτωνος), cf. Μελίτων in l. 61; but a trade-designation such as μελανουργός, 'ink-maker', is not excluded, see p. 121, no. 12.

42. Ξάν(θου): the abbreviated patronymic is deduced from l. 40.

Αἰ(λιανοῦ): the abbreviated patronymic is deduced from ll. 29, 30, but the *alpha* could very well be a *lambda*, in which case a trade-designation λι(νουργός), 'linen-worker', would be quite likely, see p. 121, no. 11.

43. Καλ(λιμόρφου?): a patronymic from a homonymous father seems likely, although the trade-designation καλ(ιγάριος), 'boot-maker', remains a possibility, see p. 120, no. 7.

ΙΟΥΝΒΑΛΟΣ: there are diacritical marks above *iota*. It is not certain how the letters should be split up; one possibility is Ἰούν(ιος) Βαλος, giving a Roman citizen's nomenclature without the *praenomen*, which is frequently omitted by the third century; alternatively there may have been one, or less probably two, Semitic names (Ἰουνβαλος, Ἰουν Βαλος) see pp. 106, 108, list B, nos. 17, 35, 36, 37.

44. Τυχι(κοῦ): a patronymic from a homonymous father seems likely in the first entry; the same name is deduced therefrom in the second.

45. βελ(?): suitable names to fit the data are rare, so that a trade-designation seems possible, although there is none available in very common use; for βελ(οποιός), 'missile-maker', see p. 119, no. 3.

46. χαλ(κοτύπος?): see on l. 26, but the sharper abbreviation here should be

THE STONE AND TEXTS 13

noted and χαλ(ινουργός), 'harness-maker', must also be considered, see p. 122, no. 20.

47. Ἡγέ(μονος?)/Ἡγε(μονέως?): there is no suitable name elsewhere in the lists from which to deduce a patronymic, but also no obvious trade-designation to propose. Of the various attested names which would fit the data Ἡγεμονεύς is known from another (third century) text at Aphrodisias, see p. 108, list B, no. 33.

πενα(κᾶς?): a suitable name to fit the data is hard to find, so that O. Masson proposes an attested variant of the trade-designation 'maker of wooden tablets', see p. 121, no. 13.

48. The first entry is cut *in rasura*, in a different hand, and so later than ll. 54, 55, from which the patronymic Ἡδ(υχρόος) can be fairly deduced; the abbreviation seems to be marked by a small stroke slanting upwards and rightwards from the lower right angle of *delta*.

It is not quite certain how the second name should be interpreted; it was possibly a Roman citizen's name, Μ(ᾶρκος) Ἀνίκιος Ἄττα or Ἄττα(λος), but a non-Roman name is perhaps as likely, Μανικιος son of Ἄττας or Ἄτταλος, see pp. 105, 106, 109, list B, nos. 7, 15, 16, 43.

49. λατύ(πος?): there is no obvious name to fit the data, and the trade-designation 'stone-cutter' is particularly suitable at Aphrodisias, see p. 120, no. 8.

50. Καλ(λιμόρφου?): the patronymic is deduced from l. 43, but it may be worth considering the trade-designation καλ(ιγάριος), 'boot-maker', too, see on l. 43.

πυ(?): names to fit the data exist and several are attested in use at Aphrodisias (cf. Πύρρος, Πυθέας, *MAMA* VIII.409, 492) but not elsewhere in the lists; it may, therefore, be worth considering trade-designations too – thus πυ(λουρός), 'door-keeper' or, perhaps, 'customs-collector', πυ(ρηνᾶς), 'knob-turner', or πύ(κτης), 'boxer'; see pp. 121–2, nos. 15, 16, 17.

51. λευ(?): names to fit the data are known (e.g. Λεύκιος, cf. J. and L. Robert, *Bull. Ep.* 1984, 546, Λεύκιππος) but not much used at Aphrodisias, so that it may be worth considering the trade-designations λευ(κουργός), 'marble-worker', which would be particularly suitable, or λευ(κωτής), 'plasterer', see pp. 120–1, nos. 9, 10.

52. ψελ(λός?): Ψελλός seems not easily to be found as a name until the Byzantine period, see p. 111, but was certainly used as a descriptive tag, 'stutterer', cf. Josephus, *Vita* 1.3; it would also be possible to resolve here as a trade-designation, ψελ(οποιός), ψελ(ιοποιός), 'armlet-maker', see p. 122.

γρύλλος: Γρύλλος was certainly used as a name, but here may be a descriptive tag, 'comic character', see p. 107, rather than a second name.

54. ἀθλη(τής?): no suitable name to fit the data has been found and this professional designation, although a little surprising, see p. 119, no. 1, seems inevitable.

55. Ἡδυχ(ρόος): the patronymic is deduced from ll. 48, 54.

56. ἀρκά(ριος?): there are names to fit the data, including Ἀρκάθιος, which is found at Aphrodisias, *MAMA* VIII.536, but the comparatively common designation 'treasurer' seems to us very likely, see p. 119, no. 2.

Ἀθηναγ(όρου): the abbreviation is marked by c to the right of *gamma*; the resolution is obvious.

57. ἰκονο(γράφος?) or ἰκονο(ποιός?): there was no need to abbreviate since the second half of the line was left blank; a suitable name to fit the data is not easy to find and a trade-designation involving production of images is likely at Aphrodisias; for discussion of the words available see p. 120, no. 5.

58. γναφ(εύς): a suitable name to fit the data is not easy to find, so that the comparatively common trade-designation, 'fuller' or 'carder', seems very probable, see pp. 119–20, no. 4.

59. See on l. 58.

60, 61. Added in a different hand.

1. The stone, showing faces *a* and *b*.

2. The stone, showing faces *b* and *c*.

3. Face *a*, the text.

4. Face *b*, the text.

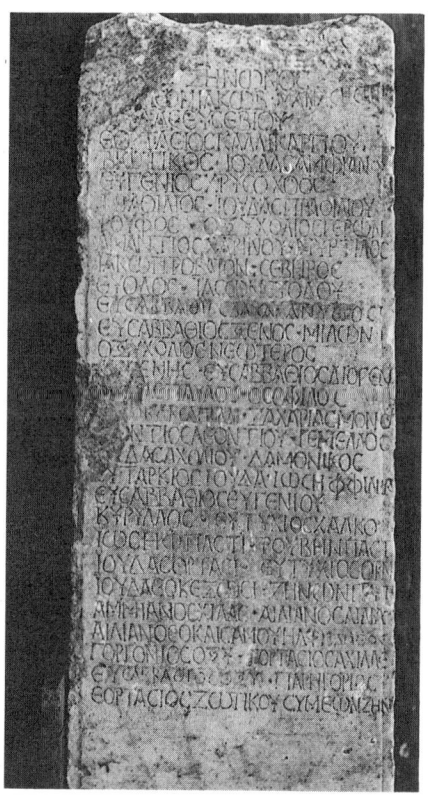 

5. Face *b*, the text: upper list.   6. Face *b*, the text: lower list.

II THE DATE AND PURPOSE OF THE INSCRIPTIONS

The stone appears to have had a long history and may not always have occupied the same position throughout. At first sight it looks suited to an architectural function, for instance as a door-jamb; but its taper, although slight, is not really consistent with anything except a pilaster or a free-standing stele. Since it is too deep to be easily interpreted as a pilaster, we conclude that it was probably prepared as a stele, although the fillet or *taenia* down the left side of face *a* is an unexpected and unexplained feature. It was, then, intended to stand with its fourth face against or facing a wall, and the face opposite that, *b* in our enumeration, presented to the viewer as the main one. But if it was in that position when face *b* was inscribed, a problem arises from the absence of a heading for the face *b* text as it has survived, and of space for restoration of an adequate one in the damaged area. It has a short and obviously subsidiary heading in l. 34, at the start of its second list, which presupposes one at the start of the first list; but although a very short one could be presumed in the lost l. 1, and a rather more extended one if we allow for a line or so cut on a crowning feature above (many Aphrodisian stelae known to us did in fact carry crowning capitals), this would be surprisingly high above eye-level, and still surprisingly restricted in area to offer an explanation that did justice to the long catalogues of persons which follow. It may be that the heading was so restricted; but there are two other possibilities. Either another stele, making a pair with this one, stood a short distance away to the left, carrying an explanatory text – we could perhaps suppose that they stood on either side of a doorway or the entrance to an apse, *naiskos* or similar feature; or the explanation was cut on the side of this stele to the left and at right angles to face *b*, in fact on face *a*, where there *is* an explanatory inscription whose sense would provide what is lacking, but one cut in a different hand. If we envisage the stele as placed to the left of an entry, face *a* would greet the visitor with an explanation of the feature that he was approaching and the names of the donors who initiated the construction, while he would see face *b* as he passed into the entry and could learn the names of others associated with it. That is an attractive and economical hypothesis. To assess it the dating evidence for each inscription must be examined in detail.

Neither text contains an explicit date nor any obvious feature within itself which proves it to belong to a particular era. Both are cut in styles which are outside the standard tradition of Aphrodisian public epigraphy. As already noted on pp. 4–5, however, face *b* has stops and diaeresis marks in common with public inscriptions of the second and third centuries in the city,[1] along with alignment and letter forms which seem consonant with the same period.[2] In that context the names it lists offer dating criteria – Αἰλιανός (ll. 29, 30, perhaps 42) is unlikely to be earlier than the reign of Hadrian, from whose *nomen*, Aelius, it derives, while the absence of any sign of the nomen Αὐρήλιος, or its derivatives, suggests that the lists were drawn up before the Antonine Constitution of 212 gave Roman citizenship to virtually all inhabitants of the Roman Empire, and produced a large-scale dissemination of the emperor's *nomen* Aurelius, often combined with his *praenomen* to give Marcus Aurelius. In a late second- or early third-century setting some other features of the text would fit well – the names in -ιος and -ιανος for which a long period of popularity had just begun,[3] the nine city-councillors among the *theosebeis* who may seem, on social grounds, to be symptomatic of the difficulty of recruiting councillors at that time.[4] The number of indeclinable biblical names for Jews might fit somewhat less well in the third century, but the history of their usage is far from clear, see p. 111, n. 1 and they cannot be regarded as a serious obstacle. Moreover if an early third-century date is rejected, the text must be put much later, when Roman citizen nomenclature, widely adopted after 212, had been abandoned for a single-name system;[5] perhaps as late as the late fourth or fifth centuries, since a few M. Aurelii probably continue to appear at Aphrodisias in inscriptions of the fourth century[6] and with them some Flavii who derived a new *nomen* from that of the emperor under whom they served (App. 9 and notes). But with a date in the late fourth or fifth centuries it is difficult to reconcile the letter forms and still more the layout of face *b*. The only alternative is to suppose that within the community of Jews and *theosebeis* Roman citizen nomenclature was entirely dropped, which seems inconsistent with the evidence for awareness of status which these lists seem to show in other respects.

Face *a*, however, is in a different hand and a different style, laid out with much less feeling for symmetry and cut with much less skill than face *b*, declining in quality steadily as it proceeds; but it should be noted that at its best it is as good, and sometimes better, than the work of the second hand on face *b*, which can only have been marginally later than the first hand.[7] Its appearance certainly makes a much poorer impression on modern observers than that of face *b*; indeed some of its epigraphical features have suggested a date in the fifth or even the sixth centuries, particularly the variation of letter sizes and forms, the poor alignment, the failure to calculate the space needed for an entry, which has led to large empty areas in some lines and squeezed letters or uncompleted words in others, the many abbreviation marks and the variety of methods used for showing abbreviations. We do not see anything in it, however, which cannot

DATE AND PURPOSE 21

be paralleled earlier and explained as the lapse of a poor craftsman and/or, perhaps, of one working from a draft in a cursive hand; notably the abbreviation marks, which at first sight seem very Byzantine, are all attested in use by the third century, although more freely in papyri than in inscriptions.[8] Of the names listed almost the same can be said as of those on face *b* – 'Αντωνῖνος (l. 20) provides a probable *terminus post quem* in the reign of Antoninus Pius; the absence of Marci Aurelii and of names related to Aurelius is complete – and again not easily explicable after 212, since again we seem to have a status-conscious group in which the omission of any status-symbol, even within a club-list, would seem surprising. Since there is a possibility of a much later date for this inscription it must be admitted that the name *Aurelius* seems to have left a weaker mark than might have been expected on the nomenclature of late antiquity[9] so that there would be nothing so striking about its absence from a small group of 23 names (at the most 27) in or after the late fourth century, as there would be in the case of the much longer list on face *b*. Nevertheless the impression, for what it is worth, is rather of a combination of the names of an earlier period.

There are on face *a* several other elements which might have been diagnostic, but none seems in fact to offer probative clues. Thus a psalm-singer (l. 15) is sometimes said to be a Byzantine feature in Jewish liturgy, but one is possible, we believe, already in the third century, see p. 46; proselytes (ll. 13, 17, 22), while unexpected in an inscription at any time after Hadrian's ban on circumcision (unless, perhaps, during the reign of Heliogabalus), see p. 43–4, may be explained at any date on one of a series of hypotheses (that the laws against circumcision were not adopted in Aphrodisias, that the Aphrodisian Jews accepted baptism without circumcision as sufficient for conversion, that if the date was later than the Constantinian legislation on proselytism these men converted from paganism, not Christianity, and were therefore not liable under the law of the Christian Empire), so that again no date can be deduced; *theosebeis* are known as late as the sixth century, see p. 65.

The case is far from certain, but on balance there seems to be a reasonable possibility that face *a* too is of the third century. In favour of that one may point to some parallels between its letters and those on an Aphrodisian statue-base likely to be of the third century; also those of a probably third-century text in the synagogue at Sardis;[10] there is the fact that it shares with face *b* one otherwise unattested and odd name, 'Αντιπέος (*a*, l. 24, *b*, l. 37, see pp. 97–8, list A, no. 6), a peculiarity which looks very like the product of the same time as well as the same place – certainly something more acceptable if the two texts are at least approximately contemporary rather than two centuries apart.

There are indications in the spelling and syntax to be taken into account too, although with some caution since the differences between the work of the first and of the second hands show that the original text was drafted with a care which did not exactly reflect the spelling used by all members of the community. There is, however, comparatively little iotacism, no gemination of consonants and only one simplification of a doubled consonant (l. 25), while the dative case is retained and used correctly.[11]

The absence of Hebrew, and of any indication of a knowledge of Hebrew, provides yet another reason for preferring the earlier date. It is clear that a knowledge of Hebrew became widespread, and may have been compulsory, in the western diaspora from c. A.D. 400 (for evidence from papyri, inscriptions and a *novella* of Justinian, see pp. 82–4).[12] Face *a* of our inscription, however, suggests strongly that the Aphrodisian Jews who composed it were wholly ignorant of Hebrew. Not even the formulaic invocation is in Hebrew, all institutional terms are translated very freely (with the exception of πάτελλα), or else are terms developed in the Hellenistic period apparently as parallels for Palestinian equivalents (see p. 79). This does not rule out, but does appear to reduce, the possibility that the text was written by Jews living in an increasingly hebraizing age.

In the circumstances it seems that a third-century date can be proposed for the face *a* text as well as for the face *b* text, and that the features of its lettering and layout which suggest a later date can be attributed to the poor quality of the workmanship. If that is so, it can be assigned to the same time-range as the face *b* text, so that there is no obstacle to treating the two as contemporary, face *a* being the introduction to face *b*. The position is not, unfortunately, susceptible of proof. It may be wrong; but it seems to us likely.

If face *b* is a continuation of face *a* we think it reasonable to suppose that the members of the decany named on face *a* were the initiators and major donors of the monument described, while those on face *b* also contributed to it. If face *b* is not such a continuation its purpose needs discussion.

It has been suggested to us, in fact, that the intention on face *b* was to list all synagogue members or, if it is accepted that the *theosebeis* are judaizing gentiles (see pp. 48–66), all synagogue members, followed by all regularly attending associates. The probably total absence of women is not a valid argument against this; the total absence of synagogue officials, and of persons with titles of honour like πατὴρ τῆς συναγωγῆς, cannot be pressed against it either, since they should appear at the head of the list, and if the opening lines of the face *b* text were cut on an adjacent stele standing to the left, see p. 19, they are lost to us with that stele. Moreover the very formal status, almost enrolment, which would be implied for *theosebeis* need not surprise, for it is paralleled in principle at Panticapaeum, see p. 54. There are some demographic objections, however, which may be worth considering. We should not, of course, expect the list of *theosebeis* to show very strong evidence of family units, since the adherence of a *theosebes* to the synagogue might follow from a personal choice which took him out of his family context; but in a complete list of Jews there ought to be quite a number of family groups recorded, father/son pairs, and even perhaps quite a number of fathers with more than one son. The evidence here is, of course, very restricted, for family relationships can only be deduced where patronymics are given (even then not always with complete certainty); and patronymics are given with only twenty-three out of the fifty-five surviving names of Jews and with not more than nineteen out of the fifty-two names of *theosebeis* on face *b*. But it may nevertheless be significant that at the outside there are seven possible father/son pairs detectable among the Jews and one possible pair of brothers, in fact seven possible family groups in all, most consisting of two recorded members, one perhaps of three; while among the *theosebeis* there are at the outside five possible father/son pairs and four possible pairs of brothers, in fact five possible family groups in all, three consisting of two recorded members, two perhaps of three.[13] The difference between the two totals is negligible and for the Jews the number seems remarkably low. We suggest therefore that what was inscribed on face *b* was a list that contained only a section of the Jewish male community. The most obvious explanation for it – and one which covers, as it must, the *theosebeis* as well as the Jews – is that here, too, is a list of donors. On the hypothesis from which we are now arguing (that there is no connection between face *a* and face *b*), these donors contributed to a monument different from the one described on face *a*; which seems most unlikely. This hypothesis of two separate lists should, then, be abandoned. The most economical solution seems to be that the two groups listed on face *b* contributed to the same object as the decany of face *a*, the decany providing the initiative.

We do not think that the evidence allows useful speculation on the reason why these groups consist wholly of men, when women are often named as contributors to Jewish donations elsewhere.[14]

NOTES

1. See Reynolds, *Aphrodisias*, pl. v.1, l. 4 for the circle as stop, pl. xiv.1, l. 1 for diaeresis marks above a vowel, both in public inscriptions of the third century.
2. For partial parallels see T. B. Mitford, *The inscriptions of Kourion* (1971) 174, no. 93, 179, no. 96, both early third century.
3. Cf. L. Robert, *NIS* 40; H. Solin, *OL* 139, 140.
4. Cf. A. H. M. Jones, *The Greek city* (1940) 182f.
5. Cf. L. Robert, *NIS* 52.
6. For M. Aurelii in the fourth century see perhaps *MAMA* viii.586; there are other unpublished examples likely to be as late.
7. That must be true at least for the completion of the patronymic in *b*, l. 8; and is probable for all the additions.
8. For some partial parallels in inscriptions see e.g. *TAM* v.1, pl. xii, no. 136, L. Robert, *NIS*, pl. vi, no. 7 (but the dates of inscriptions in the Sardis synagogue are under review, see p. 53,

n. 221); for the earliest dates at which the relevant abbreviation marks are attested see Avi-Yonah, 43–4.
9 Cf. the name index to *ICVR* I, where it is recorded only 178 times in 4091 texts.
10 The Aphrodisian inscription, on a base for a statue of the *Demos* erected by the *Boule*, is as yet unpublished; for the Sardian one see n. 8.
11 On the history of the dative case see J. Humbert, *La disparition du datif en Grec du premier au dixième siècle* (1930) esp. 101–84; Humbert cited inscriptions of Asia Minor, as showing, like the ostraca and papyri of Egypt, that while the substitution of the genitive, more rarely of the accusative, for the dative occurred occasionally in the third century, it gained ground markedly in the fourth and thereafter.
12 De Boer, *VT* 1 (1951), 49ff.; for the date, see 57, n. 1.
13 **Jews**: father/son pairs, Αἰλιανὸς Αἰλιανοῦ, l. 29, perhaps father of Αἰλιανὸς ὁ καὶ Σαμουηλ, l. 30; Διογένης, l. 18, probably father of Εὐσαββάθιος Διογένους in the same line; Εὐγένιος χρυσοχόος, l. 9, possibly father of Εὐσαββάθιος Εὐγενίου, l. 24; Εὔοδος, l. 24, probably father of Ἰάσων Εὐόδου in the same line; Ἰούδας Ἀχολίου, l. 23, perhaps father of Εὐτάρκιος Ἰούδα, l. 24; one of the two Ὀξυχόλιοι, ll. 11, 17, perhaps father of Γοργόνιος Ὀξυ(χολίου), l. 31, and/or of Εὐσαββάθιος Ὀξυ(χολίου), l. 32; Πραοίλιος, l. 10, probably father of Ἰούδας Πραοιλίου in the same line.
Brothers: probably Γοργόνιος Ὀξυ(χολίου), l. 31, and Εὐσαββάθιος Ὀξυ(χολίου), l. 32.

Theosebeis: father/son pairs, Ἀπονήριος, l. 38, perhaps father of Ἀπονήριος Ἀπον(ηρίου), l. 41; Ἡδυχροῦς, l. 54, perhaps father of Εὐσαββάθιος Ἡδυ(χρόος), l. 48, and of Εὐτρόπιος Ἡδυχ(ρόος), l. 55; Ξάνθος, l. 40, presumably father of Ξάνθος Ξάν(θου) in the same line and perhaps of Πολυχρόνιος Ξάν(θου), l. 42.
Brothers: Γληγόριος Τυχι(κοῦ) and Τυχικὸς Τυχι(κοῦ) both in l. 44; Εὐσαββάθιος Ἡδυ(χρόος), l. 48, and perhaps Εὐτρόπιος Ἡδυχ(ρόος), l. 55; Καλλίμορφος Καλ(λιμόρφου?), l. 43, and perhaps Κλαυδιανὸς Καλ(λιμόρφου?), l. 50; Ξάνθος Ξάν(θου) and perhaps Πολυχρόνιος Ξάν(θου), l. 42.
14 Cf. for instance *Donateurs* 5, 7, 13, 30, etc.

III COMMENTARY: THE JEWISH INSTITUTIONS

For the forms of citation employed below, see pp. vii–viii.
For the nature of probable dates of rabbinic sources, classical scholars unfamiliar with the subject should consult Schürer–Vermes–Millar I, 68–99, and the comments added to the following list of abbreviations:
m   – the Mishnah (c. A.D. 200)
t   – the Tosephta (c. A.D. 230)
ARN – Aboth de-Rabbi Nathan (c. A.D. 230)
Mekh. – Mekhilta ⎫
Siphra   ⎬ Halakhic Midrashim (c. A.D. 200)
Siphrê   ⎭

The above Tanna'itic sources afford good evidence for the institutions and usages of the late second and early third centuries A.D., and often for earlier periods (all dates in this list are dates of completion).
    y   – Jerusalem (or 'Palestinian') Talmud (c. A.D. 400–425)
Pes.RK – Pesiqta de-Rab Kahana ⎫
Gen.R. – Genesis Rabba   ⎬ Early Haggadic Midrashim
Lam.R. – Lamentations Rabba ⎪ (c. A.D. 400)
Tanh. – Tanhuma   ⎭

The above early 'Amora'ic sources reflect conditions of the third and fourth centuries, but y and Pes.RK contain some quotations (*baraitoth*) of a date and purpose similar to those in the Mishnah and Tosephta: the Haggadic Midrashim contain narratives that are sometimes dateable to the first or second centuries A.D. (parallels with Ps.-Philo, *Lib. Antiq. Bibl.*, with *II Baruch*, etc.).
    b – Babylonian Talmud (compiled c. 500, revised in the course of the sixth, perhaps also the seventh century A.D.)
Exod.R. ⎫
Lev.R.   ⎬ Later Haggadic Midrashim (fifth to seventh centuries A.D.)
et sim. ⎭

The above are later 'Amora'ic sources; b also contains many *baraitoth* from Palestinian Rabbis of the first to early third centuries (Tanna'itic period) although it would seem (by comparison with parallel texts in y) that the tradition had by now become somewhat confused. This no doubt also applies to the late Haggadic Midrashim, but in both cases these texts do fill out details of what is merely implied or alluded to in the early sources, and can be valuable to the historian where they do so on the basis of preserved information rather than logical deduction or literary imagination (it is often impossible, to be sure, to sort out which is which). Note that *baraitoth* in b frequently embody more reliable traditions than those in the earlier y.

tg –*Targum*, generic term for Aramaic translations of parts of the OT, often paraphrastic and explanatory. Of varying dates, some before the second century A.D., some late (tg *Ps-Jon*. is seventh century) in their final redaction, but containing a large proportion of earlier material; the Dead Sea Scrolls and the New Testament, for example, show evidence of exegetical traditions that parallel those in the Targumim, as does Pseudo-Philo's *Lib. Antiq. Bibl.*, but other materials in the Targumim are clearly late.

Face a. For the date of face *a* and its relation to face *b* see pp. 19–22. On the names see pp. 93–115.

Line 1. Θεὸς βοηθός: probably an invocation of divine aid, as found at the head of a number of Greek Jewish inscriptions, and occurring also in Psalms,[1] or the abbreviated epistolary salutation of present-day orthodox Jews בעזרת השם (*be-azerat ha-Shem*), 'with the help of God'; but it could be the beginning of a statement, see below on δο[. 1 or 2.].

πατέλλᾳ: there are no word divisions in the text here, but we think it most probable that the words should be divided as printed, and that the noun is in the dative case. Πατελλᾶς (-άδος) is not attested and a suitable meaning here is not obvious. Πατελλάδαι (-άδων), again unattested, has been suggested to us as a name for a private Jewish group, perhaps a neighbourhood association or a trade-organisation, that could have owned the monument (presumably the πλῆθος of l. 7, since the decany of l. 3 is differently named in ll. 4–5). But this assumes an explanation of the decany as analogous to the governing-body of a *collegium* (on which see p. 28); in any case this would be inconsistent with the stress on religious status in the Jewish community which is evident throughout the list of decany-members, see further pp. 41–65. The decany seems, consequently, rather more likely to be an organ of the Jewish community as a whole than an organ of a private association not connected to the synagogue, such as a trade-organisation.

No words compounded with πάτελλα are attested. Moreover in any compound word, e.g. πάτελλα compounded with δοτήριον, the linking vowel should be *omicron* and not the *alpha* that stands on the stone (πατελλοδοτήριον). Πάτελλα, on the other hand, is an attested word, a Latin loan word fully integrated into the Greek inflectional system already in the first century A.D.[2] In Latin the first meaning is 'dish, plate, pan', as used in the kitchen or at table, but it also has the sense of 'offering-dish', particularly, although not exclusively, in the cult of the Lares; in the Republican period, but not later on present evidence, it is attested, once only, for an object presented as a military decoration.³ In the Greek papyri it occurs with the first, secular, sense of the Latin,⁴ and that also seems to have passed into Hebrew where it is found, transliterated, in use for a cooking-pot or a basket, commonly a basket for dates.⁵ We have only found four epigraphic usages; three in Latin, of which one in Italy, of 90 B.C., denotes a military decoration, and two in modern Rumania, probably of the fourth century A.D., refer to the plates on which they are scratched,⁶ with one in Greek, in Asia Minor, of the third century A.D., which appears to designate an item in a list of objects dedicated to Artemis, perhaps with the religious sense of the Latin, but possibly for a simple dish.⁷

Attractive though it would be to see here (as suggested to us by Professor Hengel) an extension of the military use – a tablet honouring the dedicators – the fact that a *patella* is never attested as an honour except in 90 B.C., when it did not in fact have the meaning of 'honorary tablet', seems to rule it out. We feel that there is no authority for any use unrelated to that of 'utensil' – whether for secular or for religious purposes; that is the only meaning for which there is evidence in the imperial period, and it appears in Greek and Hebrew, as well as in Latin. But if so what is this word doing in the present context? The Mishnaic Hebrew word for 'dish', תמחוי (*tamḥui*), is used in the Mishnah and Tosephta and in both Talmudim as the name of a charitable institution,⁸ organised in Jewish communities for the daily collection (in a dish, in fact) and distribution of cooked food *gratis* to the poor and vagrants (compare ἡ διακονία ἡ καθημερινή of the early Christian community of Jerusalem,⁹ a daily distribution of food to widows [? and others], which is likely to be copied from a Jewish community institution; this might indicate that such charities were extant in Palestine in the thirties of the first century A.D.). This interpretation of πάτελλα would fit the εἰς ἀπενθησίαν τῷ πλήθι of ll. 6–7. But why does it appear on this inscription? We are obviously dealing with a building inscription, see on l. 7; πάτελλα, we suggest, could stand for the distribution station for charity food – i.e. a community soup-kitchen. Such a place is also called *tamḥui* in the rabbinical sources just listed.¹⁰ The accepted dates of completion of the Mishnah and of the Tosephta (*c.* A.D. 200 and 230) guarantee that the institution was current at the earliest likely date of our inscription in Palestine Jewish communities. If this interpretation of πάτελλα is correct (and assuming an early date for our text), the *tamḥui* was current, or being introduced, early in the third century in diaspora communities as well. The historical significance of this will be discussed in chapter IV.

This leaves δο[..], possibly a complete, but possibly an abbreviated word, which might, on the face of it, be related to δέμω, 'build', or δίδωμι, 'give'. In either case, a convincing formula which uses the nominative case of πάτελλα seems to us to be difficult to conceive; neither πάτελλα δομηθεῖσα nor πάτελλα δοθεῖσα seem very likely. But with the dative πατέλλᾳ there are a number of possibilities: δῶμα (δόμα), δόμος, δόμημα, would mean 'a building for the *patella*', δόσις 'a giving' to it; δόται, δοτῆρες, δόντες, would announce 'the donors to the *patella*'; δότε would appeal to the readers to give to it: if θεὸς βοηθός were integrated into the sentence, there could be an appeal to God to help the building or the donors; or, with δός at the end, God who is our help would be asked to give to the *patella* – but that seems less probable since it is men who are required to give charity, while God gives crops. There may well be other possibilities; we are uncertain how to choose.

2–3. οἱ ὑποτεταγμένοι: 'the below-listed'. This is a list of contributors to a construction fund, paralleled most closely in Jewish Greek inscriptions by the list of contributors to the fabric of a synagogue at Berenice in Cyrenaica in A.D. 56 (although there amounts of money given are also inscribed).[11]

3. δεκαν(ίας): the word appears in one other Jewish inscription in a catacomb at Rome where Frey printed Δεκανίας on the assumption that it was a name, and Leon regarded the meaning as obscure.[12] Its second appearance in a Jewish context, in our inscription, leads us to suspect that we have the name of a Jewish institution otherwise unattested in Greek or Latin. Of what sort?

Δεκανία is rare in literary Greek: *LSJ* cite one instance only from Arrian, who used it as an equivalent of λόχος, 'troop'. In papyri and ostraca of the Ptolemaic period it represents a local group listed, or land unit defined, for administrative purposes (? tax, ? corvée).[13] The simple equation of δεκανία with Latin *decuria*[14] is speculative and based on no evidence. However, from Amblada in Pisidia there are inscriptions referring to groups of four *decani* who seem to be tribal officers.[15] From Philippopolis in Thrace there are inscriptions of the third century in which δεκανεύοντες or δεκανεύσαντες appear, apparently as the chief officers of tradesmen's *collegia*.[16] At Adraha in provincia Arabia, in what may be a paramilitary context, there are three third century inscriptions (one under Gallienus, one under Aurelian, another under the emperor whose name is lost) which refer to a δεκανία, in one case apparently meaning a building, and to an ἀρχιδέκανος (who is once described also as a quaestor, once as τῶν πρώτων, and is therefore presumably a civic official). H. G. Pflaum argued that the city was divided into wards, each under an ἀρχιδέκανος, responsible for the construction, maintenance and manning of a section of the city's defence works.[17] This variety of meanings indicates that δεκανία was used as a portmanteau word, as was Latin *decuria*, for a formal group or organisation, or its governing council, having no necessary connection with the number 'ten'.

Nevertheless, δεκανία in a Jewish context irresistibly brings to mind the *minyan*, a quorum of ten men who must be present to make possible congregational prayer, public readings from the scriptures, wedding and funeral services, etc.[18] And there is in fact an institution mentioned in the Mishnah, the עשרה בטלנים ('asarah batlanim), 'the ten men of leisure' who 'frequent the synagogue', and, in order to do so, 'abstain from work'.[19] The object of this constant attendance of ten is to ensure that a *minyan* will always be present, therefore that prayer will always be possible in the synagogue. Only a town that can supply ten such men can be considered a large city.[20] The ten are learned men,[21] as, presumably, are the φιλομαθεῖς of Aphrodisias, to whom the δεκανία appertains. The *batlanim*, however, abstain from work because they are supported, at least in the middle ages, by the community.[22] Nevertheless, it may be that they began, in antiquity, as those rich enough to afford leisure; Schürer–Vermes–Millar argue, indeed, that if ten suitable men can only be found in a large city, the *batlanim* cannot be the poor; they must be the rich.[23] S. Krauss argues that they are the governing body of a community,[24] but his evidence is all drawn from late sources; also, as Schürer points out, congregations in small towns do not have *batlanim*, but must necessarily have governing bodies. Rich men, then, would be free to attend, but not necessarily compelled to attend, weekday services. Our δεκανία consists of those rich enough to initiate the building of the μνῆμα of l. 8 out of their own resources (see on ll. 6–8). ll 9–26 show that it may have had as many as eighteen or nineteen members; but then ten could be a minimal number for such a group, within which synagogue duties might be fulfilled in rotation. Of course, if the hand of the cutter changes so that ll. 21–7, as well as the entry at the side of ll. 9–17, were later additions (see p. 4), and supposing also that the two sons named in ll. 10, 12, were not decany members, but appear because they contributed along with fathers who were, then the list of decany-members as originally inscribed did contain ten names only. But there are too many hypotheses here for the point to convince.

Δεκανία could also indicate a burial society. From the fourth century A.D. onwards societies for the burial of the poor attached to Christian churches are attested, their members being called *decani* or δεκανοί.[25] It may well be in this sense that an ἀρχιδέκανος appears in the Christian period at Aphrodisias, and *decani* in some other Asia Minor cities.[26] The term δεκανία, along with the institution, could have been borrowed by the Christian church from diaspora Jewry. Burial societies have been clearly attested in Jewish communities since the fourteenth century A.D.; such a society is called a חברא קדישא (*ḥebra' qadisha*'), a 'holy association'. Jewish Law forbids the acquisition of material benefit from the dead; there are, therefore, no commercial undertakers in Orthodox communities, and burial becomes a function of the communities themselves. The members of burial societies prepared bodies for burial (washing the corpse and so on), saw to their proper sepulture (particularly for the bodies of the poor and solitary), and comforted mourners; often they had charge of the cemetery. Membership was an honour, and persons of high social station were to be found in these societies.[27] Such was the case in the Middle Ages, and the early modern period; to what degree would it apply among the Jews of Roman times? Josephus says that Jews must not leave a corpse unburied.[28] The Tosephta mentions חבורות (ḥaburoth), i.e. associations, in Jerusalem before its destruction, one of which collected the bones of the dead, while another visited mourning families.[29] In 1940 Beth She'arim, in Israel, a favourite burial-site for Jews all over the East in the third and fourth centuries A.D., yielded a Greek inscription from a synagogue destroyed in 352: 'Ριβ Σουμωῆλος συστέλλον(τος) καὶ 'Ιούδα κοιμ(ῶντος).[30] Rabbi Samuel's title uses the verb συστέλλειν, which in this context would mean, as it does in Acts, 'cover' or 'wrap';[31] κοιμῶν, used of his associate Judah, indicates 'laying to rest'. Rabbi Samuel wraps (quite conceivably in a shroud), Judah lays to rest; these men are probably involved in the burial of the dead. If these are titles put up in the synagogue, then this implies, as Lifshitz and Robert noted, that their functions were formal. We therefore have here what seems to be firm evidence for a Jewish burial organisation in Palestine in the third or early fourth century. And we learn of a ḥaburah that occupied itself with funerals and burials in late third or early fourth century Babylonia from a statement attributed to Rabbi Hamnuna, who died c. 320.[32] Could the same have existed in the western diaspora as well, for instance at Rome and Aphrodisias? Quite possibly; and this interpretation would fit the ἀπενθησία of l. 6, if we take that word literally, and the μνῆμα of l. 8, in the commonest sense of the word (see below on both). But there is an obstacle to accepting this. We seem to read at ll. 26–7, in the erased text, Σαμουηλ πρεσβευτὴς ἱερεύς, 'Samuel *presbeutes*, priest', apparently (at least at one time) listed among the members of the decany. *Kohanim*, descendants of the priestly families that had served in the Temple of Jerusalem, are forbidden by biblical law to enter cemeteries (except for the burial of close relations), let alone to touch the bodies of the dead;[33] they may not even brush against a tomb (sepulchres were 'whited' to warn them away). It would be unthinkable for such a one to become a member of a burial society, to care for the bodies of the dead. The Beth She'arim synagogue inscription, just cited, makes it clear that even so exalted a member of such an association as Rabbi Samuel handles dead bodies himself. Samuel the priest, if we are right in our reading, cannot do that by law; if he is, or was at any time thought to be, a member of the δεκανία, the δεκανία is not a burial society. What, then, is it? A further examination of the context will help.

4. τῶν φιλομαθῶ[ν] κὲ παντευλογ(- - ων): φιλομαθής is a standard Greek word, see *LSJ s.v.*, common in κοινή: it means in Strabo 'lovers of learning', in Polybius 'serious students'.[34] It occurs in the Septuagint, and thirty times in the works of Philo of Alexandria.[35] In Philo, at *de posteritate Caini* 137–8, at

de gigantibus 60, and at *de somniis* 1 (i).11, it clearly means 'student' or 'learned person'; compare the patristic use of φιλομαθῶς, 'with zeal for knowledge', 'learnedly'.³⁶ Similarly, in an inscription at Rome a rabbi is qualified as διδάσκαλος νομομαθής;³⁷ compare the New Testament, where rabbis are called νομοδιδάσκαλοι.³⁸ In the Sardis synagogue a priest (name lost) is also called σοφοδιδάσκαλος.³⁹ A Greek funerary epigram at Lorium near Rome⁴⁰ is interesting in this context:

ἐνθάδε ἐν εἰρήνῃ κεῖτε Ῥουφεῖνος ἀμύμων
θεοσεβὴς ἁγίων τε νόμων σοφίης τε συνίστωρ
ἐτῶν κα΄ ἡμ(έρων) η΄ ὡρ[ῶ]ν ι΄.

Was Rufinus a Jew? As a student of the holy laws, he studied either the Roman *lex sacra* (in which case he was a *pontifex*, and we should expect his commemorative inscription to be in Latin), or (which is more likely) Jewish Law. What does it mean that he is called θεοσεβής, as are two of the members of our decany (Emmonios and Antoninos, *a*, ll. 19, 20)? Perhaps not much: the word (with an indulgent false quantity in the first syllable) makes a convenient metrical fit for the beginning of a hexameter and may have only adjectival significance ('God-fearing'). But Rufinus clearly does want to be remembered as an investigator of the laws and wisdom of his people. Other funerary inscriptions at Rome laud the deceased as νομομαθὴς ἀσάλ[ευτος?] and [ν]ομομαθής, or as μαθητὴς σοφῶν καὶ πατὴρ συναγωγῶν. Πατὴρ συναγωγῆς is an honorific title granted to a benefactor of the community; why would such a high personage nevertheless like to be thought of as a μαθητὴς σοφῶν? Because it translates the Mishnaic phrase חלמיד חכם (*talmid ḥakham*), meaning a student of the rabbinical law.⁴¹ The term refers to those learned in the Talmud, therefore often to rabbis; in antiquity some references seem to imply young students, but others apply to the sages themselves, the great expositors of the Law.⁴² Rabbi Yohanan, in the third century, gave a series of definitions (for tax-exemption purposes) that seems to include both students and sages;⁴³ similarly, until recently, the English word 'scholar' was applied equally to schoolboys and *savants*. The picture is further clouded by the clear requirement, laid down in Mishnaic times, that *every* Jew become, as far as he was able, a scholar of the Law; R. Joshua ben Levi, for example, taught that 'he who occupies himself not in the study of the Law is called "reprobate"'.⁴⁴ To what degree this demand was actually fulfilled in Palestine *c.* A.D. 200 we are not sure, let alone to what degree, if any, the ideal of universal study would have been realised in the diaspora at this time. It is, however, conceivable that the Jews of Aphrodisias could, in response to the teachings of the Palestinian rabbinate, regard study of the Law as the ideal occupation for all members of the community. In that case οἱ φιλομαθεῖς οἵ καὶ παντευλογ(?) could be the pious name of the Aphrodias synagogue; if so, the δεκανία could be its governing body, just as we have seen above that δεκανεύοντες might be the chief officials of third-century trade associations.

Two objections may be raised to this. Of the ancient synagogues of which we know the names, none bears pious names. We know, for example, of eleven to fifteen synagogues in Rome;[45] four are named after important individuals (e.g. Agrippa), two after quarters of the city, one or two after the trade of the members (the Calcarenses are perhaps lime-kiln workers?), the rest after their nationality or place of origin (e.g. the Tripolitans). In Jerusalem, we know seven synagogues, mainly named by nationality (e.g. 'of the Alexandrians').[46] In Tiberias we find a synagogue 'of the Boule' and one 'of the textile-workers';[47] in Sepphoris one 'of the Babylonians' and one 'of the Rebellion'.[48] Elsewhere in Palestine, several others are named by place.[49] All those mentioned in the book of Acts in Asia Minor and Greece are named by place,[50] but the author may simply be omitting their proper names, as the authors of the Gospels do. In Arsinoe, we find a προσευχὴ Θηβαίων, in Corinth a συναγωγὴ τῶν Ἑβραίων, in Rhegium probably a [συναγωγὴ τ]ῶν Ἰουδαίων.[51] In Babylonia most synagogues are named by place,[52] but a 'Synagogue of Daniel' and another 'of the Romans' are known.[53] This would seem sufficient to make it unlikely that the synagogue of Aphrodisias was named τῶν φιλομαθῶν τῶν καὶ παντευλογ(-?-ων).

The second stumbling-block is that, if the δεκανία were the governing body of the synagogue, one would expect more than one possible archon (l. 10) in the list of the eighteen or nineteen of its members, and at least some πρεσβύτεροι, Elders (Samuel Περγεούς and Samuel the priest are probably not Elders, see on ll. 9–12, 26–7), or *gerontes*. The Jewish γερουσίαι of which we know seem to be composed of archons at the upper level, presbyters or *gerontes* at the lower level of membership.[54] Πρεσβύτερος is frequent in the Jewish inscriptions of Asia, including Caria.[55] Compare the list of donors to the construction fund for the synagogue at Berenice in Cyrenaica in A.D. 56, which begins with ten archons.[56] So, by analogy, our list should also begin with a group of archons if δεκανία does mean 'council of the synagogue'. It is, therefore, improbable that this is the case.

What then? On the face of it the word φιλομαθεῖς would seem to indicate some sort of educational group, perhaps what is nowadays called a *Beth ha-Midrash*, a house of exegetical learning. The normal Babylonian term is *Beth Midrash*; in Palestine the name is *Beth Wa'ad* or *Beth Talmud*, 'House of Assembly (of the wise)' or 'House of Study'. All these terms refer to a secondary school for youths and study-hall/lecture-hall for adults engaged in the study of rabbinical Law. By the Middle Ages synagogue and *Beth ha-Midrash* are indistinguishable, but the two were considered separate institutions in antiquity.[57]

We know that *Battei Midrash* existed in the eastern diaspora; in Babylonia we are told that not only youths, but married men, fathers, returned home late from studying there.[58] On the Sabbath, public study sessions were held there;[59] this may well be identical with the use of the school hall, on Sabbath afternoons, for popular instruction in scripture and exegesis (*midrash*),[60] and also with the instruction in the house of study in Palestine mentioned in the Mishnah.[61] The *Beth Midrash* is therefore a centre of adult education by the end of the second century A.D., at least in Palestine. After the Hadrianic persecution, a *Beth Sepher* (elementary school) and a *Beth Midrash* were normal in each community in the Holy Land.[62] But does any of this apply to the western diaspora? There is no unambiguous evidence for it.[63] It is possible, but only possible, that the φιλομαθεῖς of Aphrodisias are those who attend weekly public lectures at the *Beth Midrash*, or who study there in the evenings, and that the δεκανία is their association or governing body (both otherwise unattested). The difficulty with this is that the Septuagint provides a perfectly good Greek translation for the *Beth Midrash* of the Hebrew original of Ben Sira', namely οἶκος παιδείας,[64] and it is hard to see why the Jews of Aphrodisias would refer to such an institution without using this term. On balance, the hypothesis is not a convincing one.[65]

The *yeshibah*, an academy of secondary and higher education in rabbinical subjects, must also be considered (usually called *Beth Midrash* in Palestine before A.D. 70).[66] The *yeshibah* did exist in the ancient diaspora; we hear of one established at Rome by Rabbi Matya ben Heresh in the second century A.D., as well as of four *yeshiboth* established in Babylonia in the same century.[67] We know also of a *yeshibah* functioning in Sidon, again in the second century A.D.[68] It is, however, rather unlikely that Aphrodisias, never hitherto known as a major centre of Jewish life in the west, would support a *yeshibah* at so early a date. More conclusively, perhaps, we know that the Palestinian and Babylonian *yeshiboth* of the Mishnaic and Talmudic periods were each organised around some great sage (in Babylonia the *Rosh Yeshibah*, 'Head of the Academy'). R. Matya b. Heresh at Rome was such a sage (*tanna*') who had emigrated from Palestine. At Dubbura, in the Golan Heights (ancient Gaulanitis), Israeli archaeologists have found a Hebrew lintel inscription reading: 'This is the *Beth Midrash* of the rabbi Eleazar ha-Kappar', whom we know, from Mishnaic references, to have been a *tanna*' of the fifth generation, i.e. active in the second century A.D.[69] *Beth Midrash*, in Palestine, in connection with the name of a *tanna*', must refer to an academy (Babylonian *yeshibah*); this inscription shows that, in the second century, a *yeshibah* would be named after its head (perhaps, in time, after its founder). Since the φιλομαθεῖς at Aphrodisias mention no sage's name, they are not likely to have been the students or graduates of a *yeshibah*.[70]

We do know, however, of private associations for the study of rabbinical Law in Palestine in Mishnaic times, and ἡ δεκανία τῶν φιλομαθῶν might well describe such a private study group. The Mishnah mentions groups of ten formed for the joint study of the Law,[71] and Geza Vermes reminds us that the Qumran sect, too, studied the Law in groups of ten.[72] Biblical עדה ('edah 'assembly, congregation') in Mishnaic Hebrew refers also to courts or prayer meetings of ten.[73] Private study groups are frequently found in the Jewish communities of late medieval and early modern times, where they are often called *Ḥebra' Shas* (חברא ש"ס), 'Talmud association'; they study assigned portions of the Talmud together, and celebrate the completion of a whole tractate with a solemn feast.[74] Δεκανία, therefore, might well be the translation of Hebrew *'edah*, 'assembly', or *'agudah*, 'band', or simply *ḥaburah* (Aramaic *ḥebra'*), 'association', and the δεκανία τῶν φιλομαθῶν could represent a private adult education society, perhaps developed from an original group of ten, rather than a public institution. This would account for the paucity of community officials in its membership, and the ability of its members to make donations to the μνῆμα, which one would not ordinarily associate with students, φιλομαθεῖς. Whether, however, this could also account for the δεκανία, without qualification apparently, mentioned in Rome (see n. 12) we cannot say.

5. τῶν κέ (καί): see also face *b*, ll. 20, 28; for the formula ὁ καί see briefly I. Kajanto, *Onomastic studies* (1963), p. 48; it came into use in the Hellenistic world, very particularly to link native and Greek personal names, see Lambertz, *Glotta* 5 (1912) 99–170, J. P. Rey-Coquais, *Bulletin du Musée de Beyrouth* 29 (1977) 148.

παντευλογ(--ων): The only attested word which could be involved here is παντευλόγητος, a rare one which is not found in Jewish Greek sources and corresponds to nothing in Jewish sources in Hebrew or Aramaic. It is used of the Virgin Mary by Ephraem Syrus who died in A.D. 373.[75] Εὐλογητός in the Septuagint is usually used of God, occasionally of man.[76] Once, at Deut. 7:14, εὐλογητός is applied to the people of Israel ('Thou shalt be blessed above all peoples'), but εὐλογημένος is more frequently used in that connection (Num. 22:12, Deut. 28:3, Isa. 65:23). In the New Testament, however, perhaps reflecting later Jewish usage, the word εὐλογητός always refers to God,[77] and μακάριος is used of men:[78] εὐλογητός is used of God in Jewish inscriptions.[79] How, then, could παντευλόγητοι be used of men in our inscription? We may compare an inscription from Syrian Apamea: the Antiochene *archisynagogus*, Ilasios, in A.D. 391, donates a floor mosaic at the entrance of the Apamean synagogue, wishing εἰρήνη καὶ ἔλεος ἐπὶ πᾶν τὸ ἡγιασμένον ὑμῶν πλῆθος where ὑμῶν πλῆθος clearly means the community at Apamea.[80] It is, then, possible for Jewish communities in the Greek world to be called 'sanctified'. The use of ἁγιωτάτη συναγωγή to designate communities in the Greek diaspora may also be a parallel; it is attested at Deliler, near Lydian Philadelphia, at Side in

Pamphylia, at Hyllarima in Caria, at Gerasa in Jordan, at Beroea in Macedonia and, probably, at Larissa in Thessaly.[81] Use of this common epithet may well have developed under the influence of the nomenclature of Hellenistic Greek associations, which frequently call themselves ἱερώτατος, e.g. the ἱερώτατον νέον Βάκχιον at Thasos, and the ἱε]ρώτατον συνέδριον τῶν [γ]ναφέων at Cyzicus.[82] Note also that a small 'holy community' עדה קדושה (*'edah qadoshah*) of scholars was set up in Jerusalem in the late second or early third century:[83] and that a community at Jericho calls itself a קהלה קד(י)שה (*qehillah qadishah*), also meaning 'holy community,' in the fifth century:[84] similarly early modern communities, both Sephardic and Ashkenazic, were called 'the holy community of (place-name)'.

So then, if ancient Jewish communities may be called 'most holy' and 'sanctified', and if the people of Israel may be called 'blessed' in the Greek (and in the Hebrew) Bible, what would be wrong with 'wholly blessed' here? But the former are epithets for an entire people or community, and we have already seen that the φιλομαθεῖς οἳ καὶ παντευλόγ(?) cannot be the community as a whole. It would seem rather contrary to the spirit of Judaism for a private group to assume that they could be, by nature or by the nature of their activities, wholly blessed. It has therefore seemed to us proper to explore two other, though unattested, possibilities – παντεύλογοι, παντευλογοῦντες. Παντεύλογοι, which should mean 'wholly reasonable', would be possible, but seems a little lacking in religious connotation. For παντευλογοῦντες, however, 'those who praise unreservedly', there is a near parallel in Mishnaic Hebrew, since εὐλογέω, like Hebrew ברך (*barakh*) can mean either 'bless' or 'praise'. The *Mekhilta de-Rabbi Ishmael*, a Halakhic Midrash of the second century A.D., commenting on Exod. 13:3, cites R. Hanina, the nephew of R. Joshua, as saying that the Biblical passage refers to המברך (*ha-mebharēkh*); this, preceded by the article, *ha*, is the *Pi'el* participle of ברך (*barakh*). *Barakh*, in the *Pi'el* verbal form, means, in rabbinical Hebrew, 'bless, praise, speak a benediction';[85] J. Z. Lauterbach translates this word as 'one who recites the benediction'.[86] (Compare שליח ציבור [*sheliaḥ tzibbur*], the usual designation in the rabbinical literature for the reader/leader *pro tempore* in the synagogue service.[87]) 'Benedictions' (*berakhoth*) or 'doxologies' are set forms for the praise of God on various occasions of daily life, but also set prayers of praise in the synagogue liturgy, especially the 'eighteen benedictions'; here probably the benedictions in the synagogue are meant, since this citation continues 'and what do they respond after the *mebharēkh*?'. A Greek translation of *ha-mebharēkh* could be ὁ εὐλογῶν. The παντ- in παντευλογῶν could be an equivalent of διὰ παντός, in which case the word need not be derived from Hebrew; it could be a Greek neologism for those who pray full-time, as members of a permanent synagogue quorum might be thought to do. In any case, παντευλογ(οῦντες) would make sense in a Jewish context –

'those who wholly praise (the Lord)', or 'those who constantly recite benedictions'. Is this compatible, however, with our reading of φιλομαθεῖς, as 'scholars (of the Law)'? Are we to think of the δεκανία as a society both for the study of the Law and for prayer (in a private group or in attendance at synagogue services)? This is in fact possible.

In the Tosephta,[88] and in Semahoth (which is a late, extra-canonical tractate of the Babylonian Talmud that does, however, contain some early material,[89] and in this case attributes its information to one of two homonymous rabbis of the second and third centuries respectively), we find a description of the ḥaburoth (associations, religious confraternities) of Jerusalem before its fall, to which we have already alluded. The members of some visited the houses of those in mourning, the members of others went to banquets, of others to circumcisions, of still others to the cemeteries to gather scattered bones.[90] This may tell us little or nothing of the situation in Jerusalem before A.D. 70, but it does at the least give some idea of the variety of Jewish associations known to Palestinian and Babylonian compilers by the third and sixth centuries A.D. What of the associations in the western diaspora in antiquity? We have no evidence, or none recognised as such. If we turn, however, to Europe in the late Middle Ages and the early modern period, we find plentiful evidence of Jewish associations, which, again, tells us nothing about conditions in antiquity, but might help us to understand what οἱ φιλομαθεῖς οἳ καὶ παντευλογ(οῦντες?) *could* originally have meant. For the European associations bear, for the most part, pious names, that have little or nothing to do with their actual activities or purpose. In Rome, in the seventeenth century, for example, an association meeting for daily devotion and study on the Sabbath (not unlike our students and reciters of prayers?) is called the מנוחת אמת ואמונה (*menuhath 'emeth wa-'emunah*), 'Resting Place of Truth and Faith'. One society for educational purposes was called חברת עץ חיים (*ḥebrath 'etz hayyim*), 'Society of the Tree of Life'. 'In finding titles for such societies there was no limit to the fancy. Every Bible phrase that was apt (or not apt) for the purpose was chosen at one time or another.'[91] If this were true of the diaspora in antiquity, then οἱ φιλομαθεῖς οἳ καὶ παντευλογοῦντες could be the title of a Jewish association for any benevolent purpose; the title of the society would not necessarily reveal its activity. We recall, however, that ancient synagogues did not bear pious names as they do today, so why assume that ancient Jewish associations did? One piece of evidence suggests that they might have done. A floor inscription of the third century synagogue at Sardis, cut after A.D. 212, names the donors as the φυλὴ Λεοντίων. Robert derives Λεόντιοι from the lion of Judah[92] – a case of pious nomenclature then? The interpretation has aroused controversy, since it is not clear what a φυλή is here – Lifshitz argued that it was not a tribe but a family;[93] it might also be an association: we cannot tell.

JEWISH INSTITUTIONS 37

The δεκανία of Aphrodisias could, in fact, be any beneficent association, with a pious name, or, for that matter, with a descriptive name, since, in all Jewish societies of the late medieval–early modern age, 'members met together at regular intervals to dine or to pray, *they prayed and studied together*'.[94] Since prayer and study are the principal, almost the only, religious exercises of Judaism after A.D. 70, and since all Hellenistic-Roman associations engage in religious exercises, it is logical to assume that ancient Jewish associations did indeed study and pray together. In that case, ἡ δεκανία τῶν φιλομαθῶν τῶν καὶ παντευλογ(ούντων?) might be a descriptive and not a pious name for an association denominated by its religious activities, without any reference to its social purpose. It could be a guild, it could be a charitable society, it could be a general-purpose benevolent society, it could even be the *baṭlanim* who guarantee a quorum at synagogue services. Without further evidence, we cannot know which. We should note, however, that the חבר עיר (*ḥeber'ir*), mentioned in the Mishnah, the Tosephta, and later sources, which can be translated 'town association', appears to fulfil (for small communities?) several of these functions at once: apparently that of a prayer quorum;[95] also some of the duties of a funeral (but not necessarily a burial) society;[96] also the supervision and collection of communal charity.[97] Members are assumed to be well known to all the community, i.e. they are social leaders.[98] All of which would explain why a group involved in charity might be called the δεκανία, in the sense of 'the Ten'; they are also involved in guaranteeing the presence of a quorum in the synagogue. This might, therefore, be the most economical interpretation of the function of the δεκανία; that, unfortunately, does not guarantee that it is the correct one.[99]

Why, however, does our δεκανία have a name, whether pious or descriptive, when that mentioned in the Roman funerary inscription (p. 28) appears to be ἡ δεκανία *tout court*? Possibly the Roman synagogue to which the deceased belonged was one of the smaller ones, its community unable to support more than one (all-purpose) benevolent society, while Aphrodisias could perhaps support several specialised societies each of which needed a distinguishing name. Possibly, although there was only one δεκανία to a community, the members in Aphrodisias desired the added *cachet* of an association name, whereas those in Rome did not. Or perhaps in the Roman case, the heirs could not afford to have the full name of the deceased's association carved on his tombstone. One hypothesis, however, seems eliminated by this text; the Roman δεκανία could not be a craft guild, since 'of the guild' is insufficient information to identify a deceased craftsman in so developed a city as Rome, with dozens of crafts represented. If the Roman δεκανία was not a craft guild, the Aphrodisian was probably not one either.

The above interpretations of δεκανία, φιλομαθεῖς and παντευλογ(οῦντες?)

are, of course, speculative. But they have at least the merit of bringing the terminology of this inscription more or less into the mainstream of Jewish life in Roman antiquity. The alternative, by contrast, is to imagine a hitherto unexampled and quite inexplicable Jewish institution, with incomprehensible names, appearing uniquely in a smallish Jewish community in the hills of Caria, for reasons impossible to construe. It may be hoped that further discoveries will cast some light on this puzzle.

6. ἀπενθησίαν: not otherwise attested, seems more likely to be a neologism than a spelling error for ἀπενθείαν; the adjective ἀπένθητος is in fact known, and occurs in the Septuagint at LXX 2 Mac. 5:10. Πένθος seems to be used mainly of the suffering of mourning (and in the Septuagint passage cited ἀπένθητος is for 'unlamented'), so that εἰς ἀπενθησίαν might mean 'to alleviate grief' (which would accord with the interpretation of μνῆμα as 'tomb', see on l. 8). But πένθος can also be used of 'a grievous misfortune' (as in Hdt. 3.14, Pi. *I.* 7 (6).37), and ἀπένθητος is glossed by Chantraine as 'sans souffrance, sans inquiétude',[100] which would give here 'for the relief of misfortune' or 'suffering' (fitting with our interpretation of πάτελλα as 'soup kitchen').

7. πλῆθος here means 'community', cf. a donation of A.D. 391 to the synagogue of Apamea in Syria, with good wishes ἐπὶ πᾶν τὸ ἡγιασμένον ὑμῶν πλῆθος,[101] and, from the end of the second century B.C., an inscription which seems to refer to the Jews living at Onias' temple at Leontopolis as [τοῦ πλή]θους τῶν ἐν τῷ τεμέ[νει κατοικούντων Ἰουδαίων].[102] Πλῆθος as a synonym for κοινόν occurs several times with reference to Greek associations, for example the Dionysiac artists;[103] it is therefore reasonable to make the same equation here.[104]

κτίζω means 'to found' (an institution) or 'to build' (a building).[105] It occurs in a number of Jewish Greek texts, cf. Σαμουηλ Εἰδδέου πρεσβύτερος τῶν Ἰουδέων ἔκτισεν.[106]

8. ἐξ ἰδίων is, of course, normal in Greek building inscriptions and well attested also in Jewish ones.[107]

μνῆμα: the normal meaning in Greek and Jewish Greek, wherever it is readily identifiable, is 'tomb.'[108] Now one of the charitable activities of Jewish antiquity was to arrange burial for the poor;[109] this activity might include construction of a public tomb for those who could not afford private ones. So although δεκανία in l. 3 ought not to mean 'burial society' (see p. 30), a suitable charitable act for any Jewish society would be to initiate and support construction of a public tomb: the suitability is illustrated by an inscription from Tlos, in Lycia, recording that one Ptolemaios, son of Leukios, gave his own tomb to the community, for all Jews.[110] In classical antiquity, of course, Jews had to be laid to rest in caves or catacombs or rock-cut tombs, not buried in the ground (although the latter was the custom in Babylonia). No rock-cut tombs have been observed as yet in the immediate neighbourhood of Aphrodisias. There is, however, another possibility, in the custom of erecting solid structures, with their own entrances, as monuments (called *nephashoth*) over the tomb, of which several examples survive, from Herodian times, in Jerusalem (e.g. 'Absalom's Monument' in the Vale of Kidron); we have a mid-second century A.D. reference to such memorials.[111] It is perfectly conceivable that such a monument was erected as a public tomb in Aphrodisias, that this inscription is its dedication, cut on a stele at its entrance, and that μνῆμα here means 'memorial' or 'tomb'. This would give us a simple and straightforward interpretation of our inscription; except that πάτελλα in l. 1 would then become incomprehensible. If πάτελλα does not stand for the building erected by the listed donors it does not seem to make much sense; if it does stand for that building, we have been unable to find any way in which it can also stand for 'tomb'. But can the word μνῆμα stand for anything *other than* tomb?

It could mean, in poetic Greek, 'memorial, remembrance, record',[112] also 'monument'[113] and 'memorial'.[114] In prose it usually means *sepulcrum*, but can mean *monimentum*.[115] Possibilities for a specifically Jewish usage, however, appear in Aramaic and Greek building-inscriptions found in synagogues of Syria–Palestine. On the mosaic of the synagogue of Noarah (Na'arah) near Jericho[116] we read לטב (ד)(דכירין) (*dekhirin le-ṭaḇ*), 'may they be remembered for good'; the continuation is 'all those who collaborated or gave or will give to the holy place'. Other inscriptions contain the same formula – 'may they be remembered for good' – with or without the names of individual contributors;[117] cf. a fragment of this phrase on the mosaic pavement of the synagogue of Beth Alpha (sixth century).[118] Similarly the fourth-century synagogue inscriptions of Hammath-Gader (Arabic El-Hammeh) all begin 'may they be remembered for good', and continue with a donors' list.[119] To these add the same formula from the mosaic floor at Beth She'an, and on marble fragments from the synagogue at Susiya.[120] The prevalence of this phrase is no doubt to be attributed to the presence of a parallel in the Bible, in the book of Nehemiah, where it is addressed to God – in Hebrew, זכרה-לי אלהי לטובה – literally '(May it be) a memorial to me, my God, for good', followed by 'all that I have done for this people'.[121] It is clear that the pious Jew, from Nehemiah's day onward, hoped that his benefactions to his people or community might stand as a memorial for him before his God. We have an example of this in Greek in the New Testament: the centurion Cornelius, who is described as φοβούμενος τὸν θεόν (Acts 10:2), and is, therefore, in some sense a judaizer, is visited by an angel who tells him in a vision that (Acts 10:4) Αἱ προσευχαί σου καὶ αἱ ἐλεημοσύναι σου ἀνέβησαν εἰς μνημοσύνην ἐνώπιον τοῦ θεοῦ (cf. Acts 10: 31). It is clear from the synagogue inscriptions that this hope specifically applies to donations to building funds. The same idea, that for a Jew a building donation is a memorial, is also to be found in Greek inscriptions: on a building inscription at Ed-Dumer, near Damascus, μνησθῇ Θανόμου καὶ Σεμουέλου υἱεῖ Ἔσθρη καλῶς ἐπήισεν ἀνήλωμα;[122] in a synagogue donor's inscription from Hammath Tiberias, probably of the fourth century A.D. or later, μνησθῇ εἰς ἀγαθὸν καὶ εἰς εὐλογίαν Προφοτοῦρος ὁ μιζότερος ἐποίησεν τὴν στοὰν ταύτην τοῦ ἁγίου τόπου;[123] compare the chancel screen of the synagogue at Azotus (Ashdod), [εἴη ..?.. τὸ ἀγ]αθὸν κὲ [ἡ] εὐλογία⟨ν⟩.[124] This sentiment, and its connection with construction for the benefit of the community, is made even clearer on a painted Aramaic inscription found on a fragment of plastered wall a hundred metres north of the synagogue of Dura-Europus,[125] which reads 'May (...) Ahijah, son of (...)h, of the Benei Levi, be remembered for good before the God of Heaven. Amen', followed by זאת דכרה לטב (*zata' dekharah le-ṭab*) 'this is a memorial for good'. Μνῆμα would, of course, be a perfectly adequate translation of *dekharah* ('memorial'). We have what may be an example of this in a Greek inscription from Shabha in Syria (Philippopolis), of the fourth century A.D., on a lintel above the window of a house: Ἰουδέων μνῆμα.[126] The lintel, in its original architectural context, could have stood over the doorway of a building, but could equally well have stood over the entrance to a common tomb. The building in Dura called *dekharah*, however, can *not* have been a tomb; its location, 100 metres north of the synagogue, which was built against the south-west wall of the city, brings it well within the city walls.[127] Now, according to the Mishnah, graves must be located far from town, fifty cubits at least from the nearest house;[128] even if we cannot be sure that the Mishnah was in force at Dura at the time of this inscription, the laws of both Rome and Athens require burial outside the city, and we may presume that the same would be true of the civic laws of the Seleucid colony of Dura-Europus. If the *dekharah* is not a tomb, what is it? The word could, of course, apply to the inscription itself, but on what wall was it painted if not that of Ahijah the Levite's tomb? Necessarily on the wall of something that Ahijah had donated in the hope of being remembered for good, therefore probably a construction for community use. We cannot be sure whether the μνῆμα of the Aphrodisias inscription was originally located within or outside the city; it was found within the circuit of the city wall, but could have been brought from outside to a point within the limits of the town for re-use (see p. 2). It seems clear, however, from the Dura painted inscription that a construction that is not a tomb can be called a memorial (to its donor) in Jewish Aramaic, therefore why not in Jewish Greek? The translation of μνῆμα in our inscription could therefore be 'memorial (building)'; this is compatible with πάτελλα meaning 'soup-kitchen' in l. 1. If, however, another meaning could be found for πάτελλα, μνῆμα would then be freed to stand for 'public tomb'.

Lines **1–8**, we may therefore tentatively translate the heading of our inscription as follows:

God our help. $\begin{Bmatrix} \text{Givers to} \\ \text{Give to} \\ \text{Gift to} \\ \text{Building for} \end{Bmatrix}$ the soup kitchen. Below (are) listed the (members) of the decany of the $\begin{Bmatrix} \text{students} \\ \text{disciples} \\ \text{sages} \end{Bmatrix}$ of the law, also known as those who $\begin{Bmatrix} \text{fervently} \\ \text{continually} \end{Bmatrix}$ praise God, (who) erected, for the relief of suffering in the community, at their personal expense, (this) memorial (building).

In l. 1 an alternative would be:

God help the $\begin{Bmatrix} \text{givers to} \\ \text{gift to} \\ \text{building for} \end{Bmatrix}$ the soup-kitchen

In ll. 6–8 an alternative would be:
for the alleviation of grief in the community...(this public) tomb.

9. Ἰαηλ προστάτης: Jael may be a woman's name:[129] the title is no obstacle to its being so here, since women are often given titles of high synagogue or community office in the diaspora;[130] but it is more probably a man's, see p. 101, list A, no. 34.

Philo usually employs προστάτης and προστασία in the sense of the title or office of the 'president' of a community,[131] which it could have here. But the word can also apply to the patron of a pagan Hellenistic religious society,[132] i.e. one who represents and defends its interests; that a woman can fulfil such a function is suggested by St Paul's reference to Phoebe as προστάτις,[133] presumably because she has looked after the interests of the Christians and of the apostle at Rome. The position of προστάτης, if it refers to patronage of the community, would be similar to that more usually designated by πατήρ (or μήτηρ) συναγωγῆς:[134] if, as here, to the protection of a particular Jewish confraternity, the position would be similar to that of the patrons/patronesses of Hellenistic cult societies.

9–17 (left margin). Σα/μου/ηλ/πρεσ/βευ/τῆς/Περ/γε/ούς: apparently added in the margin as an afterthought.[135] It seems very possible that this entry is a version of the one erased from ll. 26–7, either with a correction of the second designation (which we think we can probably read as ἱερεύς in l. 27, see p. 10), or with a perversion of it by the later mason. Samuel might have been thought too elevated a personage to remain at the bottom of the list, or, as has been suggested to us, if he was not normally resident in Aphrodisias (see below), it may have seemed unsuitable to list him in column with the regular members of the decany – in either case we should have an explanation both for the marginal entry and for the erasure.

11–13 (left margin). πρεσβευτής (cf. also ll. 26–7): this is not a standard community title – for members of the *gerousia* the standard word is πρεσβύτερος,[136] and there is a little evidence to suggest that, in the Byzantine period at least, it might sometimes be παλαιός (for this term at Aphrodisias and Chalcedon see App. no. 1*a*). Where πρεσβευτής is attested elsewhere (at Joppa for a man and at Rome for a woman[137]) it may mean no more than 'old'; here, since Samuel is a comparatively common name (cf. also found at *a*, ll. 13, 21, *b*, l. 30), a simple distinguisher for individuals would be necessary – and for the use of 'old' and 'younger' in such circumstances cf. *b*. ll. 11, 17. Another proposal has been put to us by Professor Martin Hengel, that the word here denotes an envoy of the patriarch in Palestine[138] (see also pp. 80–4), who would naturally be placed at the side of the list since he would not be a member of the Aphrodisian community; but when the Greek word for a patriarchal envoy is attested (not at present before the fourth century) it is always ἀπόστολος, and all known ἀπόστολοι are Palestinian in origin and members of the Rabbinical High Court. It could perhaps be that, if Samuel really came from Perge (see below), he came as an envoy from the Jews in that city to the Jews at Aphrodisias; but this is highly speculative.

15–17 (left margin). Περγεούς: the only explanation we can suggest is that this is a form of the ethnic for the city of Perge in Pamphylia, for which the attested norm is Περγαῖος; since St Paul visited and preached in Perge it is apparent that there was a Jewish community there in the first century A.D.,[139] cf. the Jewish community, well-attested epigraphically, at the neighbouring city of Side.[140]

10. ἄρχ(οντι?): ἄρχων is frequent in Jewish inscriptions, and represents a community magistrate or other member of the executive board of the community council (the latter usually called γερουσία).[141]

11. Παλατῖν(ος?): for our rejection of a patronymic here, see p. 9. In the fourth century A.D. and after, *palatinus*/παλατῖνος is the title of a subordinate financial officer in the department of the *comes sacrarum largitionum*, or that of the *comes rerum priuatarum*, as well as the designation for troops of the central field army, and of one type of the imperial guards. Earlier, however, and already in the first century A.D., it refers to one who is in the emperor's service at the palace;[142] פלטיני (*PLṬINI*), in rabbinical Hebrew, means 'officials of the palace', obviously a loan-word;[143] a funerary inscription from Beth She'arim

JEWISH INSTITUTIONS 43

in Israel reads μημόριον Λεοντίου πατρὸς τοῦ ῥιββι Παρηγορίου καὶ Ἰουλιανοῦ παλατίνου ἀπὸ χρυσοχῶν;[144] since Julianus is a παλατῖνος ἀπὸ χρυσοχῶν ('ex-goldsmith'), he seems more likely to have exercised the goldsmith's craft at or for an emperor's court, than to have worked as a financial official in a provincial governor's service as proposed by Lifshitz.[145] Theodotus, in the present inscription, would also seem likely to be a former employee of the court. A history of such employment could, of course, give a resident of a small provincial town tremendous social prestige, which would account for his position near the top of this list, and his ability to include his son's name (l. 12) in the list of donors, as only the *prostates* Jael otherwise does (l. 10).

13. Σαμουηλ ἀρχιδ(έκανος?): for our rejection of a patronymic here, see p. 9. Of the two possible titles, ἀρχιδιάκονος is unknown in Jewish Greek sources, so that ἀρχιδέκανος seems the better choice, in which case Jael the *prostates*, with his son the archon, along with Theodotus the former court employee and *his* son, precede Samuel on this list because of their social standing, as perhaps does Samuel *presbeutes*, for whatever reason his name was added here in the margin: we need not, therefore, be astonished to see a club's president appearing third or fourth on, rather than at the head of, a list of its donating members. He is, however, a proselyte: is it possible that a Jewish society for study and prayer (and we know not what else) would have had a mere proselyte for its president? But there are three proselytes on this list, all members of the δεκανία, exhibiting the well-known zeal of converts; and the Aphrodisian Jews would no doubt agree with the Palestinian rabbis who ruled that a proselyte was, at law, the complete and unquestioned equal of the Son of Israel, the Jew by birth (see following note).

13. προσήλ(υτος): three men are so designated (ll. 13, 17, 22) and since they are clearly distinguished from those described as θεοσεβεῖς (*a*, ll. 19, 20, *b*, ll. 34ff.), proselytes and *theosebeis* cannot be identical as is sometimes suggested. It is instructive, indeed startling, to find three proselytes publicly so called on this list (see also Joses at l. 17, Joseph the son of Eusebius at l. 22); in the first place because there are only three of them, compared with a total of fifty-four *theosebeis* on both faces of this inscription (for comment on the number and nature of *theosebeis* see on *b*, l. 34); in the second place because there are any at all, since conversion of a gentile (involving circumcision) is a capital crime throughout the Roman empire for most of the period to which this text is likely to belong. It must be observed at the outset that this need not necessarily have applied in Aphrodisias which was a free city, with a right to use its own laws, from 39 B.C.,[146] so that Roman laws were not automatically in force there, although the city might adopt any of them as its own by civic legislation.

The anti-conversion laws are actually anti-circumcision laws. They begin in the reign of Hadrian, who made the act of circumcision a crime, assimilating it to castration,[147] which, by the *Lex Cornelia de sicariis et ueneficiis*, was punishable, for Roman citizens by deportation (*relegatio*) and confiscation of goods – later, for *humiliores* by death, doubtless already the fate of *peregrini* found guilty under this law.[148] Antoninus Pius, by a rescript, relaxed Hadrian's decree, exempting the children of Jews from its application;[149] we know from papyri that Egyptian priests could also be exempted, on receiving individual permission from Alexandria;[150] but the law still forbade circumcision of a gentile. A reiteration of this prohibition by Septimius Severus is mentioned:[151] *Iudaeos fieri sub graui poena uetuit*, which Mommsen interpreted as referring to circumcision (cf. Origen, *c. Cels.* 2.13; in his time Samaritans were persecuted for circumcising, which was allowed to Jews only). This Severan reiteration demonstrates that the Antonine law was insufficiently enforced, i.e., that circumcision of gentiles had occurred, that circumcision was a known step by which a gentile became a Jew, and that around A.D. 200 the Roman government was increasing the pressure against such conversions.[152] Heliogabalus abrogated the law against circumcisions, and circumcised himself, after the manner of his Canaanite ancestors.[153] Clearly, then, under Caracalla Severus' ruling had still been in force, as is also demonstrated by the papyrus evidence of exemptions from it granted to some Egyptian priests during Caracalla's reign. Therefore, at the most likely time for our inscription, circumcision of a gentile would be illegal in the empire as a whole.

And yet, as we have seen, the Antonine law must have been broken if Severus felt it necessary to renew it. And we do know of individual proselytes in the period between Hadrian and Heliogabalus. Aquila, for example, the translator of the Bible into Greek, became a Jew and was circumcised after the Bar Kokhba war:[154] the rabbinical sources mention proselytes in connection with rabbis of the generation of the persecution;[155] in the early 'Amoraic period (third century) we hear of proselytes in Palestine and Syria.[156] The law, then, was often broken with impunity, and was obviously difficult to enforce under ancient conditions.

Nevertheless the law was felt to make conversion to some degree dangerous. This, at any rate, is the explanation for the discussion, among Palestinian rabbis, as to whether a gentile could become a proselyte by immersion in the ritual bath alone, or whether circumcision was also required. Rabbi Joshua (early second century A.D.) was ready to accept mere immersion, as was Rabbi Yehudah ben Ila'i (*c.* A.D. 130–160),[157] but most rabbis insisted on both. In the diatribes of Epictetus (early second century), however, we find what may be evidence for conversion by baptism alone in the diaspora: discussing a favourite theme, those who give merely lip-service to stoicism, but do not practise it, the philosopher says that of such waverers it can be said (*Diss.* 2.9.20): 'οὐκ ἔστιν Ἰουδαῖος, ἀλλ' ὑποκρίνεται. ὅταν δ' ἀναλάβῃ τὸ πάθος τὸ τοῦ βεβαμμένου καὶ ᾑρημένου, τότε καὶ ἔστι τῷ ὄντι καὶ καλεῖται 'Ιουδαῖος' ('he is no Jew, he is but acting. When, however, he adopts the determination of one who has been immersed and has made his choice, then he both is in fact and is called a Jew').[158] In short to be immersed is to become a real Jew, not just one who plays the Jew, a judaizer: since the analogy is with Stoicism, the implication is that becoming a real Jew can force you to change your life in a way that play-acting does not, as becoming a real Stoic would force you to live the βίος στωϊκός, and not just chat about it. In that case circumcision would come in very well here; it would reinforce Epictetus' analogy with the disadvantages of taking philosophy seriously. That he nevertheless only mentions baptism *may* imply that this was sufficient for conversion in the Jewish communities he knew, that circumcision was not required. In a Sibylline Oracle (*Orac. Sib.* 4.164) from about A.D. 80 prayer to God and bathing in 'living waters' is recommended to gentiles as a way to avoid the terrors of the Last Judgment; conversion seems to be meant, but circumcision is not mentioned.[159] Whether this opinion was held in Aphrodisias we have no idea. Therefore the three proselytes of our Aphrodisias inscription may or may not have been converts circumcised in conscious violation of the law, *if* the Roman law against circumcision had been adopted in Aphrodisias: that there are only three full proselytes, as opposed to fifty-four *theosebeis*, men interested in Judaism (see p. 48–66), might seem to indicate that to become one was in fact an unusual, therefore probably a risky, step to take in Aphrodisias.

What, finally, is a proselyte? A gentile who, by purificatory immersion in the ritual bath, and (say the rabbis) by circumcision, has become a Jew, with all the legal and religious rights, privileges, duties and disabilities of a Jew, on exactly the same basis as one born a Son of Israel. According to Talmudic law he has cut off his ties with his gentile family, takes a new, Jewish, name (our three proselytes have Jewish names), and is supposed to call himself the son of Abraham rather than the son of his gentile father (Joseph, at l. 22, retains his gentile patronymic, as Samuel at l. 13 may – but probably does not – do, see p. 9, 94). All of which explains why the three proselytes are members of the δεκανία; they are required to obey the 613 commandments in the Pentateuch, and as much of their rabbinical elaborations as are known or accepted in Caria, to the same degree as any born Jew, but they do not have the born Jew's knowledge of the Law, acquired in childhood and youth; therefore they must study to learn the laws they are required to obey.

What, incidentally, was the rabbinical attitude towards conversion and converts in antiquity? By and large, it was favourable, all through the Talmudic period, although there were those who disagreed. Then when did the Jews adopt an anti-conversion policy? Not until forced to do so by the hostility of the Christian and Muslim state.[160]

15. ψαλμο(λόγος?): for the word proposed see p. 9. For the meaning, cf. a ψαλμῳδός in an inscription recently found at Rome, probably also of the third century, although the archaeological evidence is not, perhaps, quite conclusive. The most likely occasion for a specialised Jewish psalm-singer to exercise his art would be the synagogue service, in imitation of the Temple-singers of Jerusalem; but it has been held that there was no singing in the synagogue services of diaspora communities before the Byzantine period. There is, however, some evidence to suggest otherwise. In Alexandria we hear of Jews gathered in the hippodrome to be massacred, singing psalms and hymns on their miraculous deliverance (III Mac. 6:32, 35; 7:13, 16). The event is almost certainly fictional, but the author, in the first century B.C. or first century A.D., presumes general familiarity among Egyptian Jews not just with texts but with standard melodies of liturgical song (how else can they be thought to sing together?), and this is more likely to stem from a common experience of congregational worship than from any other cause. Moreover psalm-singing is attested in the Christian liturgy of the west already in the third century and the Christians are very likely to have taken it from the Jews.[161] It may then be accepted that there is no valid reason why the Aphrodisian Jews should not have included a psalm-singer as early as the early third century. An alternative, but we think, less attractive possibility might be that Benjamin was a Levite, claiming descent from the Temple-singers (there is no other evidence of such a genealogical claim). On balance, it looks as though ψαλμο(λόγος) here makes it even more probable that psalm-singing (in Greek, no doubt) was common in synagogue services in the western diaspora by the third century, and that it involved a choir, or at least individual designated singers, rather than general congregational singing alone.

16. εὔκολος: given the number of homonyms (cf. l. 23 and b, ll. 6, 7, 10, 22, 27, 28), Judas needed a distinguishing tag – for the description 'good-tempered' cf. 'sweet' in l. 25; but it may be used as a name, see p. 99, list A, no. 21.

17. προσήλυτος, see on l. 13.
19. θεοσεβής, see pp. 48–66.
20. θεοσεβής, see pp. 48–66.

22. προσήλυτος, see on l. 13. It is to be noted that this man retains a patronymic, perhaps because, with his new name, he needed distinguishing from homonyms, possibly even from a homonymous proselyte. Since the pietistic father's name does, of course, occur for Jews (see p. 100, list A, no. 24 and b, l. 6), as well as among Christians, and, indeed, pagans, it suggests the possibility of a family interest in religion, which could have brought the father into the category of *theosebeis*, with results for the son such as are delineated by Juvenal.[162]

23–5. The three names introduced by καί and in a different hand may well have been later contributors; but we can only guess at the reason for the change of formula.

25. νεκτάρις: Σαβάθιος probably required a distinguishing tag, cf. a homonym in l. 18; for the description 'sweet', cf. 'good-tempered', l. 16, but it may be used as a name,[163] see p. 103, list A, no. 50.

27. For the possible identity of the erased name with that of the Samuel entered beside ll. 9–17, see pp. 41–2; on πρεσβευτής see p. 42, on ἱερεύς see p. 30.

Face *b*. For the date and the relation to face *a* see pp. 19–23. On the names and the trade-designations see pp. 93–123, chapters V, VI.

St Paul at Athens is recorded as addressing, in the synagogue, two classes of men listed in succession:[164] διελέγετο μὲν οὖν ἐν τῇ συναγωγῇ τοῖς Ἰουδαίοις καὶ τοῖς σεβομένοις, and cf. the reference in the inscription at Panticapaeum cited p. 54, recently reinterpreted independently by H. C. Bellen and B. Lifshitz as τῆς συναγωγῆς τῶν Ἰουδαίων καὶ θεο⟨ν⟩σεβῶν.[165] We may, then, take it as possible that it was a widespread custom to distinguish those who attended synagogues into Jews and 'God-fearers', whoever the latter were. Here in l. 34 is one category heading – ὅσοι θεοσεβῖς – above a list containing only a very few immediately-recognisable Jewish names, see pp. 55–6, which should correspond with the second category. The upper list, which contains a considerable number of recognisably Jewish names, should then correspond with the first category, the full Jews (principally, if not entirely, born Jews). How they were described is uncertain – perhaps as Ἰουδαῖοι, possibly as, Ἰσραηλῖται; Ἑβραῖοι (cf. the inscriptions given under App. no. 1) is now thought to be a Byzantine development.

If, as we think probable, there was such a heading, it differentiated the names that follow on face *b* from those listed on face *a*. Therefore those on face *b* are no longer being named as members of the decany. In which case they are, presumably, ordinary members of the Aphrodisias community, here probably named as additional donors to the project initiated by the decany.

11. γέρων: This is unlikely to be a title for an elder, for which the normal word is πρεσβύτερος, see p. 42; the contrast with a homonym who is νεώτερος, in l. 17, strongly suggests that the meaning is simply 'old'.

16. ξένος: Eusabbathios needed a tag to distinguish him from homonyms (ll. 15, 17, 24, 32, 48). Ξένος is once used in the Septuagint for a proselyte;[166] if it were so used here it would be presumptive evidence against the contemporaneity of the two faces (although not conclusive, since Eusabbathios could have begun to use the term at a time when the more outspoken word seemed dangerous,

but retained it as a matter of custom, when other men became more adventurous); but this sense is so rare that it is probably better to suppose him an immigrant from a Jewish community elsewhere, cf. also, perhaps, a Pergaian, face *a*, ll. 15–17.

17. νεώτερος, see on l. 11.

20. See also ll. 28, 30, ὁ κέ, ὁ καί; see on *a*, l. 5.

34. Θεοσεβῖς: what is a Θεοσεβής? This has been one of the most disputed questions of Jewish-Greek epigraphy. Θεοσεβεῖς have been variously characterized as half-paganized Jews, judaizing pagans, very pious Jews or very benevolent and high-minded pagans, having no religious attachment to, but a certain financial generosity towards, the synagogues. There are those who would like to identify them with a group of gentile sympathizers with Judaism, mentioned, but not very well delineated, in the Talmudic literature. The present inscription seems to go some way towards solving this question. We may begin by trying to clear the ground of some terminological confusion.

In the rabbinical sources from about A.D. 300 onwards we hear of the יראי שמים (*yirei shamayim*), 'those who fear Heaven', where Heaven is a well-known metonymy for 'God'.[167] The *Mekhilta* (*loc. cit.*) distinguishes *yirei shamayim* from גרי צדק (*gerei tzedeq*), i.e. proselytes. God-fearers are, therefore, not proselytes, although they are gentiles. They are also often referred to as *Gerei sha'ar*, 'strangers/proselytes of the gates', but never in Talmudic literature. Also as *Gerei toshab*, 'sojourners', but this term is only occasionally equivalent to 'God-fearers'.[168] Otherwise it refers to pagans dwelling in Palestine, also called בני נח (*benei Noah*), 'sons of Noah'. About the latter there is elaborate legal discussion in the Mishnah and the Talmudim: they are required to promise not to worship idols; they are required to obey the seven commandments to the sons of Noah, a code of universalist ethics of which the details vary, or they are expected to obey almost the entire Torah.[169] This is all utopian fantasy, since the Jewish authorities in Palestine did not have power to enforce such rules (punishment for a violation of one of the seven laws is decapitation),[170] and the Babylonian Talmud admits as much, saying that the law of the *ger toshab* is in force only when the Jubilee law is observed, i.e. when there is Jewish sovereignty.[171] In any case the Sons of Noah are not the same as the God-fearers. Therefore it is an error to say, on the basis of these passages (as is often done), that the God-fearers are required to obey the seven commandments to the Sons of Noah; we do not know what they are required to obey (see further pp. 58–64). The rabbis' attitude to them is varied: some say that if they do not convert fully within a year they are to be regarded as pagan in all respects,[172] which does imply that they are gentiles inclined towards Judaism, who are thought of as not quite pagan, indeed as prospects for conversion. Other rabbis are not only less suspicious but encouraging in the extreme: for them the *yirei shamayim* are more welcome in Paradise than even the Jews. There will be a share in 'the world to come', i.e. in the resurrection, even for the pagan good; the 'Righteous of the Nations of the World' will certainly have that reward.[173] R. Eleazar (c. A.D. 280–320) says that God-fearers can be expected to rise from the dead at the resurrection, when they will become full proselytes.[174] Note that *yirei shamayim* is usually, but not exclusively, a technical term; it is also used to denote 'God-fearing' men, gentiles or Jews.[175]

Jakob Bernays[176] first identified the *yirei shamayim* of the Talmud with the *metuentes* of Juvenal and the φοβούμενοι/σεβόμενοι τὸν θεόν of the book of Acts. The problem is twofold: are all these equivalent to the θεοσεβεῖς who appear in the epigraphic evidence (as σεβόμενοι do not and *metuentes* only rarely), and if so, what do these words mean? Kirsopp Lake thought that there was insufficient evidence that the various ancient words for God-fearers had any technical sense.[177] Others have shared his scepticism.[178] Many now maintain that θεοσεβής in particular can mean only *pious*, as in all non-Jewish Greek occurrences since Herodotus.[179] Professor Louis Robert believed that while φοβούμενοι and σεβόμενοι can mean those who sympathise with the Jewish religion, θεοσεβεῖς cannot.[180] A review of the evidence is unavoidable, given this degree of disagreement.

In the first place φοβούμενοι/σεβόμενοι τὸν κύριον/τὸν θεόν is the Septuagint's version of Hebrew יראי יהוה or יראי אל (*Yirei Adonai, Yirei'El*), those who fear the Lord (or) God, in a number of passages in the Psalms.[181] θεοσεβής is the Septuagint's version of Hebrew ירא אלהים (*yere' 'Elohim*), one who fears God, in several other passages of the OT.[182] Therefore it seems reasonable to suggest that all the Greek words used for God-fearers in the early Christian era were intended to mean the same as the (almost interchangeable) Hebrew biblical terms, which are also the direct source for the Talmudic *yirei shamayim* (where 'God' has become 'Heaven' according to the usual metonymy). This would suggest, but not prove, that all these terms are synonymous.

Josephus says, with obvious exaggeration, that there was not a single city, neither of Greeks nor of barbarians, to which the customs of Sabbath rest, fasting, lighting of lamps, 'and many' of the dietary laws had not spread.[183] These are Greeks and barbarians, therefore probably non-Jews who imitate selected Jewish observances. He also speaks of a great multitude of Greeks drawn to the religious services (ταῖς θρησκείαις) of the Jews at Antioch 'and these (the Greeks) in some measure they (the Jews) had made a part of themselves'.[184] Siegert[185] points out that τρόπῳ τινί indicates that such Greeks do not have a clearly defined status in the Jewish communities. Again Josephus tells us that nearly all (another obvious exaggeration) the wives of the pagans of Damascus had been brought over to the Jewish religion (τῇ Ἰουδαϊκῇ θρησκείᾳ)[186] perhaps in the same ill-delimited way. What such people might be called we read elsewhere; it is: Ἰουδαΐζοντες, 'those who imitate Jews'.[187] In Babylonia, at Charax, a Jewish merchant, Ananias, persuaded the wives of the king of Characene τὸν θεὸν σέβειν ὡς Ἰουδαίοις πάτριον ἦν. Through them, he persuaded Prince Izates of Adiabene, then in fosterage at the court of Characene, to do the same; and when Izates returned home, he found that his mother had already been instructed (by another Jewish merchant) εἰς τοὺς ἐκείνων (sc. Ἰουδαίων) μετακεκομίσθαι νόμους.[188] So it is clear that τὸν θεὸν σέβειν, to respect/fear God after the manner of the Jews (as Izates did), was not the same as to adopt the Jewish Law (as Izates' mother did), but some lesser commitment; and, indeed, when, on his accession, Izates proposed to undergo circumcision, Ananias, regarding this as impolitic, objected: δύνασθαι δ' αὐτὸν ἔφη καὶ χωρὶς τῆς περιτομῆς τὸ θεῖον σέβειν[189] i.e. he advised him that he could 'fear/respect the divine' without circumcision. To be a God-fearer is something short of becoming a full Jew, but it does involve some kind of commitment to some aspects of Judaism: Ananias continues εἴ γε πάντως κέκρικε ζηλοῦν τὰ πάτρια τῶν Ἰουδαίων, 'if indeed he has genuinely decided to pursue wholeheartedly the ancestral ways (?practices, ?teaching) of the Jews'.

Was Poppaea, wife of the Roman emperor Nero, a θεοσεβής? Josephus called her that,[190] but we have already seen that Josephus was eager to exaggerate the impact of the Jewish religion on pagans; here he is probably engaging in the attractive pastime of discovering Jews or converts, real or imagined, in high places: it is, however, impossible to envisage the empress attending a synagogue service. She could have been (or have been thought to be) sympathetic to, but could not have been seen to be an open adherent of, the Jewish religion. Therefore θεοσεβής is necessarily used loosely of her – but we have already seen that its cognate, τὸν θεὸν σέβειν, is a loosely-defined term (see above on Izates). We should, however, note that θεοσεβής is here used by a Jewish Greek author of a gentile favourable to Judaism (whether he is correct as to the fact or not), and not of a pious Jew. Josephus intends to assimilate Poppaea's case to that of Izates.[191]

Philo uses none of these terms, but does seem to know the category. In describing the Jewish festival held annually on the island of Pharos at Alexandria, in commemoration of the completion of the Septuagint translation of the Pentateuch, he notes that, as well as Jews, παμπληθεῖς ἕτεροι always attend,[192] i.e. quite a crowd of 'others', who must be gentiles, presumably those with some sort of interest in Judaism (although not necessarily: simple curiosity-seekers are possible, as those who, in present-day New York, attend Chinese New Year or Ḥasidic *Simkhath Torah* celebrations to watch the dancing in the streets).

In Luke's Gospel the centurion of Capernaum (? in the Roman army, ? in that of Antipas) adheres to Judaism with great zeal,[193] but none of the terms

JEWISH INSTITUTIONS 51

we have been considering is used. Another centurion, Cornelius (quite possibly a Roman, see p. 58), is described in Acts as φοβούμενος τὸν θεόν and very zealous; he is a gentile, but not a proselyte (Luke has Peter, the Jew, admit that for him to be in Cornelius' close company could be thought to violate the Law).[194] Paul usually preaches in the synagogues of the cities he proselytizes[195] and finds in them both Ἰουδαῖοι and Ἕλληνες.[196] These Ἕλληνες are likely, on the face of it, to be the same as the σεβόμενοι Ἕλληνες[197] mentioned elsewhere in Acts, therefore the equivalent of the σεβόμενοι τὸν θεόν of other passages,[198] who (since both terms, as we have seen, are Septuagint Greek for closely similar Hebrew terms meaning God-fearers) are doubtless the same as the φοβούμενοι τὸν θεόν of Acts 13:16, 26. At one point Luke has Paul address his synagogue audience as ἄνδρες Ἰσραηλῖται καὶ οἱ φοβούμενοι τὸν θεόν;[199] the use of the article is against the possibility that there is hendiadys here. Similarly, in Athens, Paul διελέγετο μὲν οὖν ἐν τῇ συναγωγῇ τοῖς Ἰουδαίοις καὶ τοῖς σεβομένοις.[200] He tells the Jews of Corinth that 'from henceforth I will go unto the gentiles',[201] and, having departed, goes to the house of Justus, σεβομένου τὸν θεόν;[202] Justus, like Cornelius, is therefore a gentile; gentile and *theosebes* are interchangeable terms. It is with the God-fearers that Paul has many of his best results, in terms of conversion;[203] this is why it is so important to the history of Christianity to understand who they are.

That is indicated not only by the later account in Acts, but also in Paul's own letters. He writes these letters to converts who are gentiles and exerts himself to demonstrate, against what Judaeo-Christian preachers have said, that the merely believing gentile convert is as good as the law-fulfilling Jew or circumcised proselyte (e.g. Gal. 4:2–5). However, he is obviously not writing to gentiles who are strangers to Judaism, as is shown by the ubiquitous Old Testament references and metaphors that are the point of departure for so many of his arguments. Luke, when he describes Paul addressing a purely pagan audience, as at Lystra or Athens, attributes to him a non-biblical, stoicizing rhetoric, which is much more like what one would expect to see in the letters if Paul were writing to an audience freshly rescued from polytheism. It is the God-fearers who fit the model of gentiles familiar with the Septuagint, and it is therefore they, converted to Christianity by Paul, who are the likeliest addressees of his letters.[204]

So far, then, we have a loosely-defined category of gentiles, both men and women, who imitate some Jewish customs and laws, but do not become full proselytes, yet who (since Paul finds them in the synagogues) attend synagogue services.

Do the *metuentes* of Latin literature and epigraphy fit this picture? In Juvenal's account, a father who is *metuentem sabbata* and abstains from eating swine's flesh is succeeded by sons who *nil praeter nubes et caeli numen adorant*, who undergo circumcision, and later *Iudaicum ediscunt et seruant ac metuunt ius*.²⁰⁵ The circumcised sons, who study and keep the Law, are obviously proselytes: the father, who is content to 'fear' the Sabbath and abstain from pork, is clearly not, by implied contrast. Is *metuens* used of the father as a technical term? *metuo* is not so used of the sons who *metuunt ius*; and there is nothing to distinguish the two uses. It is possible that Juvenal had a known Jewish technical term in mind, and makes not reference but ironic allusion to it here; but we cannot be sure of it. However, note the father's habits: he observes the Sabbath, and at least one dietary taboo: one is reminded that Josephus speaks of gentiles who imitate the Sabbath rest and 'many' dietary laws. Here we have a Roman version of the same thing. Horace refers to similar men, stigmatizing *unus multorum* who observes the Jewish Sabbath.²⁰⁶ Probably also similar are those in the reign of Domitian *qui uelut inprofessi Iudaicam uiuerent uitam*, but who failed to pay the Jewish tax and might be asked by the collectors to demonstrate that they were uncircumcised:²⁰⁷ these men are God-fearers and not proselytes;²⁰⁸ indeed they perhaps cannot be proselytes if they are not circumcised; and yet, in some way, they lead a Jewish life. It is clear enough that there were such people in Rome: what were they called?

The *metuentes* of the inscriptions for the most part present the same ambiguity. Latin *metuens* can mean (with the genitive case) paying respect to a pagan god.²⁰⁹ By itself it may be thought to have a Jewish reference because it so neatly translates φοβούμενος/σεβόμενος (τὸν θεόν). Examples of *metuens caeli*, or *Dei*, or *Domini*, with no specific divine name would be welcome, but are not attested.²¹⁰ We do, however, have a funerary inscription from Pola in Istria (therefore probably from the late Empire when Jews first settled in northern Italy)²¹¹ which describes the mother of the dedicators as *religionis Iudaeicae metuenti*.²¹² This means that the remaining inscriptions in which *metuens* appears without predicate could be either Jewish or pagan: their epitaphs at Rome are all found outside Jewish catacombs,²¹³ as one would expect of those who are not full Jews (they would be buried in their family tombs).

We should note, however, that in a late Hebrew literary source, one of the Haggadic Midrashim completed between A.D. *c*. 700 and *c*. 900, there is a legend of the (apparently historical) visit of four Palestinian rabbis to Rome very late in the first century A.D.; there they encountered a member of 'the king's Senate' (סנקליטו, *sunklito*), who was a ירא שמים (*yere' shamayim*, 'God-fearer').²¹⁴ This might have been Flavius Clemens, who was killed by his cousin the emperor Domitian for 'atheism';²¹⁵ he is sometimes thought, whether correctly or in what degree we do not know, to have been converted to Judaism (the God-fearer in Deut.R. speaks of 'the God of the Jews' and is, therefore, not himself envisaged as a full proselyte). The actual identification is speculative, but it is interesting that the rabbis are pictured as finding, *in Rome*, a member of a class of gentiles which they can recognise as *yirei shamayim*, 'those who fear Heaven'. By the date of the redaction of the Midrash, *yirei shamayim* had ceased to be discussed in rabbinic circles for several centuries, consequently the information, or fictional detail, must go back before that. Therefore, whatever the God-fearers of the west were called in Latin, they belonged to the same class as the rabbinic fearers of Heaven.

In Greek were they called θεοσεβεῖς? The term is employed in inscriptions, both in the west and in the east, but of φοβούμενοι and σεβόμενοι τὸν θεόν inscriptions say nothing, and of θεοσεβεῖς as a class literary and religious texts after the Septuagint[216] say nothing. *Theosebeis* appear in funerary inscriptions in Rome (Agrippa of Phaina in Trachonitis;[217] Eparchia θεοσεβής;[218] and perhaps, in the Jewish catacomb on the Via Appia, [-'Ιο]υδέα προσή[λυτος – ? – ?θ]εοσεβ(ή)ς.[219] The word θεοσεβής recurs in a Greek verse epitaph at Lorium, but there it may have been chosen for metrical convenience and have merely adjectival significance (see p. 31 and n. 40): if not, it records the θεοσεβής Rufinus, who would like to be thought an ἁγίων τε νόμων σοφίης τε συνίστωρ, i.e. a serious student of the Jewish laws and wisdom; this might be a highly interesting parallel to the two *theosebeis* who are members of the decany of the φιλομαθεῖς, but, although we can be fairly sure that Rufinus is talking about Judaism, we cannot be sure that he is not a Jew, pure and simple, who just wishes to be remembered as 'God-fearing'. The word is also found in Venusia (now Venosa) in southern Italy in a Latin transliteration of the sixth century A.D.; *Marcus, theuseues*, who was buried in a Jewish hypogeum.[220] The certain Roman θεοσεβεῖς are buried in non-Jewish cemeteries, but at the date of the Venusia inscription Italy was very heavily christianized and there may have been no other cemetery where Marcus could rest in peace. Does the fact that he is described by this transliterated designation rule out the possibility that *metuens* is the Latin technical term for the same status? Not really; this could have arisen in virtue of variation either of place or of time.

From elsewhere we have Euphrosyne θεοσεβής in Rhodes; Eirene θεοσεβής in Cos; Capitolina θεοσεβής at Tralles, a great lady locally who gives marble revetments to the synagogue; Eustathios ὁ θεοσεβής, at modern Deliler near Lydian Philadelphia, who provides a water-basin for the synagogue; Aurelius Eulogius and Aurelius Polyhippus, each a θεοσεβής, revealed by the excavation of the great synagogue of Sardis as donors of sections of the mosaic floor (to be dated, it is now thought, in the middle of the fourth century).[221]

These inscriptions so far tell us nothing that will help us define the status of θεοσεβής, except that some of them were rich enough to make donations and that they made them to synagogues, sometimes in fulfilment of vows,[222] which indicates that they took part in Jewish worship in some way. There is nothing here to prevent the θεοσεβεῖς from being Jews, born and bred, who regard themselves, or are regarded by the community, as distinguished for piety.

In the theatre at Miletus a notoriously difficult inscription reserves a section of the seating as τόπος Εἰουδέων τῶν καὶ θεοσεβῶν.[223] Some have followed Schürer[224] in thinking that there is an error here for Εἰουδέων καὶ τῶν θεοσεβῶν. Others prefer to keep the text as it stands, taking θεοσεβῶν as an assertion of the piety of the Jews,[225] while H. Hommel[226] regards the group as one of God-fearers who, because of their close association with Jews, are called such. There is an impasse here, but we do not find it altogether natural that, whoever drafted the text in this position (whether Jews themselves or theatre administrators), the whole Jewish group should be described in it as 'those who are also called pious'. At Panticapaeum, in a manumission inscription of the second century A.D., a recent reinterpretation, made independently by H. C. Bellen and B. Lifshitz, gives τῆς συναγωγῆς τῶν Ἰουδαίων καὶ θεο⟨ν⟩σεβῶν,[227] suggesting the opposite of the Miletus text (taken at its face value): Jews and θεοσεβεῖς are considered part of the same community, but must be named separately: does this imply separate categories? This could well be so, but is not necessarily so; in the two words linked by καί there could be a hendiadys. But the τῶν καί of Miletus could equally be an error. Bellen[228] and Lifshitz,[229] like Schürer, think it an error for καὶ τῶν, Lifshitz arging that it was a mistake of a pagan employee of the city, ignorant of the distinction between Jews and *theosebeis*. Other interpretations are possible, none are conclusive.[230] The two inscriptions in question here cancel each other out; they can be made to agree absolutely, and that in either direction, or to disagree entirely. The Panticapaeum inscription, however, does make one thing certain: θεοσεβεῖς cannot be generous but uninvolved gentiles; whether Jew or gentile, they are considered part of the synagogue community *by* that community.[231]

The Aphrodisias inscription may throw some light on the problem of the *theosebeis*. Face *b*, ll. 34–60 lists fifty-two of them in some connection with the Aphrodisian synagogue, and two others are named as members of the decany on face *a*. Altogether there are fifty-four of them, whereas there are only three proselytes (all in the decany). There are fourteen Jews *simpliciter* on face *a*, and there were over fifty-five on face *b* (some names being lost at the top) – in all something over sixty-nine Jews, of whom sixteen are in the decany. This would mean at least about one hundred and twenty-five families attending the synagogue (for the most part those giving donations are likely to be heads of families – although some of the God-fearers – if that is what *theosebeis* are – may not have brought their families over to their beliefs). We cannot, unfortunately, know, or even legitimately guess, what proportion of the community would be too poor to contribute to a charitable foundation for the benefit of the poor; our lists do include a number of craftsmen, so at least we are not dealing exclusively with landowners (see further on p. 116). Whatever the absolute number of Jews in Aphrodisias (perhaps a thousand or so at the most), slightly less than half of those able or willing to contribute to the construction here are *theosebeis*. But *theosebeis* are not drawn from a restricted social group: nine are city-councillors (*bouleutae*), eleven to thirteen are craftsmen, tradesmen or workmen (see below); we must also consider the possibility that some in this category may have been too poor to contribute to the building fund, having been attracted to the synagogue in the first place, perhaps, by its charitable institutions and thereafter developing an interest in the religion. In that case the proportion of *theosebeis* on the donors' list could be about the same as that in the non-donor membership of the synagogue. Whether or not this was so, they were still a significant component of this diaspora community, which we suddenly know better than any other in antiquity. This component is, however, in some way not the same as, and, indeed, somehow inferior to, the majority of those in the synagogue, the Jews *stricto sensu*. We can tell because the two *theosebeis* in the decany list (*a*, ll. 19, 20) are placed low on it, at the end of what may have been the original list (see p. 4), while the fifty-four *theosebeis* on face *b* are listed *after* the first category on that list. The heading of the first category is lost, but we assume, by analogy with the texts cited on p. 51, from Acts and from the inscription at Panticapaeum, that it included the word 'Ιουδαῖοι or 'Ισραηλῖται; and in those texts φοβούμενοι or θεοσεβεῖς come second, as θεοσεβεῖς do here. There is something not quite kosher about them. It cannot be their social standing, since there are nine *bouleutai* on the list (*b*, ll. 34–8); these cannot be members of the governing body of the Jewish community – whatever the *theosebeis* are they could not monopolise all the places on the synagogue council, and, in any case, tenure of such office would hardly match their inferior position on these lists. Therefore they must surely be members of the city council (see further p. 58, 66–7). Therefore they are inferior by virtue of their status in the synagogue, not of their status in society.

It would appear likely then that the *theosebeis* are other than, and somehow less than, born Jews. And the onomastic data on our list are compelling (see also pp. 94–5). On the list of theosebeis there are perhaps sixty-three persons named. Of these names, two have Jewish connections, or probably so – Εὐσαββάθιος (l. 47), Ὁρτάσιος (l. 49); one may or may not be Semitic (ΙΟΥΝΒΑΛΟΣ, l. 43, see p. 108); two are Greco-Roman names popular among Jews, but also, of course, much used by pagans (Ἀλέξανδρος, l. 50, Ζωτικός, l. 52). The rest are ordinary gentile names. On the upper list, as on that of the decany on face *a*, the proportion is different. In the decany list on face *a*, if we deduct the names of the three proselytes and two *theosebeis*, there are eighteen persons certainly named, of whom nine have biblical names and four names strongly favoured by Jews (more than two-thirds). In the upper list on face *b*, there are seventy-four persons apparently named (eighty-one names) – twenty with biblical names, twenty-three with names favoured by Jews (well over one-half). The conclusion that those named in the first two lists are born Jews, and that those in the third are not, seems hard to escape.

What then are the *theosebeis* of Aphrodisias? Gentiles surely, since nearly all have gentile names. What of the handful who do have Jewish names? They could be sons of fathers who were *theosebeis* and quite naturally gave their children pious names; the influence of such fathers on their sons was, as we have seen, denounced by Juvenal (pp. 51–2). It is significant that these men with Jewish names have fathers with gentile names – there are no Jewish names among the patronymics here. There is then nothing in favour of regarding them as Jews by birth.

The *theosebeis*, however, are attached to the synagogue. In Panticapaeum we have seen that the synagogue is described as 'of the Jews and the *theosebeis*': in Aphrodisias, fifty-four *theosebeis* contribute to a charitable enterprise of the Jewish community and two are members of a decany which defines itself as a group given to study and prayer. Gentiles who attend the synagogue are described by St Luke in the book of Acts and called φοβούμενοι or σεβόμενοι τὸν θεόν. Presumably while there they join in prayer and in alms-giving indeed Cornelius the centurion, a φοβούμενος τὸν θεόν, is praised by an angel for his charity and his prayers (see also p. 58).[232] The Θεοσεβεῖς of Aphrodisias answer to the same description (they contribute to charity; some join Jews in study and prayer). Θεοσεβεῖς and φοβούμενοι/σεβόμενοι τὸν θεόν are all Septuagint terms translating biblical Hebrew phrases meaning 'those who fear God', the differences arising simply from an attempt to indicate, without copying, the Bible's use of three different Hebrew names of God in these passages (see p. 48). The Greek terminology is therefore almost certainly derived from the Greek bible, where these terms all mean the same thing; those designated by them certainly appear to do the same thing, in the synagogues visited by Paul and that in Aphrodisias alike. Consequently, it seems not only economical but reasonable to suppose that these designations are interchangeable. Why is it that Luke employs one set of terms and the inscriptions another? Perhaps because the inscriptional evidence begins in the second century A.D. and there has been a change of fashion since the first; or, Luke may regard the longer terms as more literary, or more self-explanatory. But, judging by the epigraphic evidence, *theosebeis* is the designation in common use by the second century A.D. at least. We should translate, simply, 'God-fearers,' exactly as we do Luke's phrases.

But what do God-fearers *do*? They attend the synagogue and pray and give alms. And is that all? Some do more: they join study-groups to read and discuss the Law and take part in directing the community's charitable activities (the two members of the decany). But if some do more, others do less. If we examine the trade designations by which a number of the God-fearers in this inscription identify themselves, we find some odd possibilities. Paramonos (b, 1. 57) is either an ἰκονο(ποιός) or an ἰκονο(γράφος), that is, either a sculptor or a painter of pictures with images (see under Trade Designations, list B, no. 5). We have rabbinic rulings in Palestine from the later third and from the fourth century (possibly from the mid-second) that permit Jewish artisans to work on objects decorated with representations of living beings for the gentile trade, even on idols, so long as they (the Jews) do not worship them.[233] There are, of course, opinions to the contrary.[234] The Tosephta records a ruling that permits an image that is placed inside a house, so long as it is for decoration only:[235] this legitimizes wall-painting by the early third century,[236] and explains the frescoes of the synagogue at Dura-Europus; but a contrary opinion is also preserved.[237] Whether this Palestinian controversy was known at Aphrodisias, which side of the argument Aphrodisian Jewish opinion would have preferred, whether the Jews of the Greek-speaking diaspora thought of painting at all in terms of the prohibition against *graven* images (note the as yet unpublished figurative wall-paintings in the recently-cleared Jewish catacombs of the Via Appia Pignatelli in Rome),[238] we do not know. The same is also true of the λατύ(πος), stone-cutter/carver, of b. 1. 49, if he worked on relief-carving: again we cannot be sure. Compare the God-fearer Elpidianus of b, 1. 54: he appears to be an ἀθλη(τής) – at least that is the only way we have been able to fill out his designation. The Jews may be thought to have remembered that they had once had to fight a war against the Greeks, in part over Greek athletics (the books of Maccabees are part of the Septuagint). On the other hand we know of several Jews enrolled in the ἐφηβεία here and there in the diaspora,[239] which requires athletic training; Elpidianus' employment (if he *was* an athlete) may or may not have been repugnant to the Aphrodisian community's idea of Judaism: we cannot tell. The same applies to the God-fearer Alexander at b, 1. 50, who may have been a πύ(κτης): could one be a Jewish boxer? We do not know. The ἰσικιάριος of b, 1. 51 is a seller (and presumably a producer) of mincemeat; but what sort of meats does he use? The Emperor Diocletian tells us of *isicia porcina*, but also of *isicia bubula* (beef);[240] would a mince-maker necessarily switch to using ritually-slaughtered beef once he began attending the synagogue? If not, all his products are non-Kosher. Here again we cannot tell whether or not a God-fearer's trade causes him to break Jewish Law. We can in all five cases simply observe that it is possible, and that no such problem arises in connection with the trade-designations of the list of Jews. This suggests that God-fearers may be in some way free of laws that bind Jews, but it hardly proves it.

Proof that God-fearers can in fact break even so basic a law as the commandment to rest on the seventh day, and still be considered not only God-fearers, but pious, is to be found in the Book of Acts. The by now familiar centurion Cornelius was εὐσεβὴς καὶ φοβούμενος τὸν θεόν (Acts 10:2) and he sent a στρατιώτην εὐσεβῆ to find Peter (Acts 10:7); in this context perhaps the soldier is also meant to be a God-fearer, since the same adjective is attributed to him as to his superior. Cornelius is envisaged by Luke as serving in one of the auxiliary cohorts garrisoned at Caesarea.[241] His name suggests that he may be, or is imagined to be, a Roman citizen, but he could be of peregrine origin.[242] If so, he is necessarily a gentile, as are his soldiers, since a decree of Julius Caesar forbade the exaction of military service from Jews in Judaea;[243] the auxiliaries we hear of in Judaea thereafter are, until A.D. 70, drawn from the gentile *poleis* founded by Herod at Sebaste and Caesarea[244] (there are no legionaries in this equestrian province). Cornelius then is a gentile God-fearer and a senior non-commissioned officer in the imperial army. His case may well be non-historical, but it does show us what Luke believes about God-fearers: they can be gentile soldiers. Soldiers have to be prepared to drill or fight on the seventh day. Therefore God-fearers can break the sabbath laws and still be called, as Cornelius and his subordinate were, εὐσεβεῖς. This is peculiar, but seems to be the case.

No less intriguing are the nine *bouleutai* who appear at the head of the list of God-fearers (ll. 34–8): being a city councillor in antiquity involves one's presence at public pagan sacrifices (e.g. at the opening of all council meetings); it seems that this is not possible for religious Jews, until some sort of special arrangement is made for them by a decree of Severus, which allows them to serve as *bouleutai* if their city chooses them (see *ad* l. 35, *infra*). (It is possible that we are missing a Jewish councillor or two on the list of full Jews – we are missing the first few names on face *b* – or that our explanations for their absence may be incorrect; it is however probable that there were no Jewish councillors on these lists: see commentary on *b*, l. 35.) But the question is, can even God-fearers sacrifice to the pagan gods and retain their status in the synagogue? The God-fearers who are members of the decany are studying the Torah, we suppose: at the other end of the spectrum, could those who are members of the *boule* be sacrificing to false gods? G. F. Moore suggested that in such cases 'men who occupied a place of prominence in the community, or held office in the city or state, must have made a compromise like Naaman between their belief and the duties of their station, and performed their part in the festivals and other ceremonies of the public religions – if you did not *believe* in the gods it was an empty form'.[245] We have seen that there is an air of vagueness about Josephus' description of God-fearers, and in the rabbinical definitions of *yirei shamayim*. And if they are not sure, how can we be sure, what God-fearers were supposed to do?

We have said that in rabbinical sources the term *gerei toshab* refers largely to pagans living in a future Jewish state, but sometimes to God-fearers in the present (those normally called *yirei shamayim*). When we hear of *gerei toshab* who accept all but the dietary laws, or only monotheism and the seven commandments to the sons of Noah,[246] it is clear that the rabbis are thinking in terms of their experience of judaizing pagans in the real world. When they are thinking of pagans in the future Jewish polity, they require of them monotheism, or obedience to the seven commandments, sometimes even obedience to almost the entire Torah (see p. 48): of this group obedience is required to this or that. But other pagans are said to 'accept' this or that prescription. Does this imply that God-fearers decide for themselves how much of Judaism they will accept?

What were the seven commandments? On the one hand, we find commandments[247] against (1) idolatry; (2) incest; (3) murder; (4) profanation of the name of God; (5) robbery; (6) a positive commandment on the duty to form instruments of justice; (7) a ban on eating parts cut out of living animals. On the other hand we are told that the tanna'itic school of Manasseh omitted from the Noachide commandments those on the courts and on blasphemy (6 and 4 above), and substituted prohibitions of emasculation and 'forbidden mixture' (of plants, in ploughing, etc.). Other rabbis added different prohibitions.[248] The redactors of the Babylonian Talmud[249] seem to think of this short code as a minimum requirement, but the existence of variant versions implies that there was no fixed rule.[250]

We have also to bear in mind that often what the rabbis enunciated as a rule was only a *desideratum*, or an exercise of the legal imagination dealing with some subject not under their control: some rules are enforceable laws, but some are moral exhortations, and others are utopian fantasies, pious hopes.[251] Therefore even in the case of the seven commandments our extra-Talmudic evidence seems to indicate that God-fearers are not forcibly required to obey these precepts, but rather an ideal situation is imagined in which they could be expected to obey them. We shall see that this is probably the case.

We have no Greek texts specifically addressed to God-fearers. There are, however, passages in those Old Testament Pseudepigrapha that were originally written in Greek, or that seem to be Greek adaptations rather than straight translations of Hebrew or Aramaic texts, which make sense only if we assume that they are addressed to existing God-fearers, or are intended to recruit new God-fearers, or otherwise to spread an attractive image of Judaism among the pagan public: such passages seem likely to be protreptic. The third *Sibylline Oracle*, for example, of the second or first century B.C., transmits advice to gentiles on how to avoid the dreadful consequences of the Last Judgment, which it has just described: they must worship 'the living One, eschew adultery, homosexuality and infant exposure, for the immortal is angry at whoever commits these sins'.[252] This is good advice, but one notes that it involves a rather short list of commandments: the pagan may be saved from the wrath to come by the avoidance of far fewer sins than the Jew; one notes also that it is not the same list as the rabbinical Noachide commandments. What would a pagan who worshipped 'the living One' and eschewed the worst sins of his kind be called? We are not told.

Further short lists of rather general ethical precepts appear in other Jewish Greek works; unlike the third *Sibylline Oracle*, they are not specifically addressed to gentiles, but they cannot be addressed to Jews, for in some of the same works (*Letter of Aristeas*, IV Maccabees) Jews are held to the fulfilment of even the dietary rules in the Torah.[253] These general precepts are also to be found in the Essenizing *Testaments of the Twelve Patriarchs*, which emanate originally from a sect notorious for its extreme devotion to the minutiae of law.[254] They are also to be found in II Enoch (late first century A.D.), III Baruch (first to third century A.D.) and the *Testament of Abraham* (first century A.D.) promoting charity and hospitality, denouncing murder, adultery and theft. The *Testament of Abraham* does not even mention those specifically Jewish sins that one would have thought it impossible to omit, such as breaking the Sabbath laws, infringing dietary laws, worshipping idols. This is, to be sure, not universal in the literature of the Greek-speaking Jews; IV Maccabees emphasizes loyalty to the dietary laws as more important than the preservation of life, and *Joseph and Asenath* stresses the importance of those commandments that set the Jews apart from gentiles.[255] Even Philo, the arch-allegorizer, insists on fulfilment of the whole Law, despite the fact that it is, for him, only allegory for the truths of philosophy; he condemns those allegorists and secularists who deny the need for its practical application.[256] The existence of tracts stressing the ritual Law alongside those that ignore it in favour of general ethical rules, the coexistence in the same pseudepigraphic works of sections that stress the ritual Law and sections that ignore it, promoting instead general ethical rules, lead us to suspect that this 'Jewish ethical universalism' (Sanders' phrase) is in fact addressed not to a Jewish but to a pagan audience, identifying Judaism as the equivalent of philosophical ethics (particularly Stoic ethics), and advising pagans on what they ought to do to please God. But might it not be addressed to some brand of Reform Jews? Probably not; the available evidence suggests that while the Greek-speaking diaspora is perfectly capable of entertaining hellenist, stoicizing ideas in theology and ethics, in legal matters it could not advocate the abrogation of any part of the Torah.[257] We may suggest that the presumably anti-Mosaic hellenizers of Jerusalem in the second century B.C. had put paid to any serious anti-legalist Judaism, by becoming involved in persecution by the gentile state. Tarred with that brush, opposition to the Law could hardly raise its head among the Jews of the Greco-Roman period.[258]

That is the context for passages like the following from Pseudo-Phocylides: 'Do not cheat in measuring, but weigh evenly. Do not commit perjury, either in ignorance or willingly'; 'Bridle anger; it can lead to murder'; 'Do not eat blood. Abstain from what is sacrificed to idols'.[259] The last is a highly-abbreviated dietary code; it cannot be meant for Jews. It is interesting in the light of the following.

The 'Apostolic decree',[260] a rule agreed upon at the Apostolic Council where Paul, Peter and others met to discuss the extent to which the gentile converts to Christianity had to follow Jewish Law, is currently agreed by many to be a kind of Christian God-fearers' rule:[261] it prohibits idolatry, unchastity and 'blood' (? shedding of, ? eating of – the latter is the likelier in the light of Pseudo-Phocylides 25, just cited). These are cognate to, but not the same as, three of the Noachide commandments (against idolatry, incest and eating parts cut from a living beast), suggesting again that there was no fixed rule, although there were leading ideas, about what God-fearers should not do. An earlier version of a rule for pagan converts, which the Jerusalem church had tried to impose on the Pauline communities, forbids consumption of meats sacrificed to idols, of blood, of (meat of) strangled (animals), and condemns unchastity.[262] These are all taken from the rules for *gerim*, resident aliens, in Leviticus,[263] with whom Paul's converts are equated: the actual Apostolic decree is a compromise with Paul's near-antinomianism for gentiles, and may well correspond to some known model of guidelines for God-fearers. Whether he ever enforced these rules on his congregations is not clear (cf. Gal. 2:7–10). The stricter version preserved in Acts nevertheless became the Christian rule for *kashruth* until the fourth century.[264] But Paul gives another list in I Corinthians,[265] this time his own. He bars meat sacrificed to idols, incest, idolatry, homosexuality, fornication; also thieving, covetousness, drunkenness, reviling, extortion. Paul knows God-fearers well – as we have seen, many, if not most, of his conversions were made among them – and he has preached to them that they need not follow the Law in order to be saved; their status will be equal to that of Jews who carry out the whole Law; Christ's sacrifice has removed that distinction. If he nevertheless imposes specific rules, they must be of a kind that God-fearers will not find too burdensome, so that they will not fear that their adherence to Christianity has worsened their condition. Therefore, Paul's laws are probably a fair indication of what, roughly, was expected of God-fearers in some synagogues.

So, a limited restriction of diet, a prohibition of unchastity and/or incest, of homosexuality sometimes, of theft or murder or infanticide according to taste, and then any general ethical advice that an individual author thought appropriate: such seem to be the laws of the God-fearers, and they are not universally agreed upon; therefore one must assume that they were not universally applied. Was the individual free to choose his own rules? That seems entirely possible. Did standards vary from community to community? That also seems possible, but we do not know; the evidence suggests variation, but not what kind of variation.

A prohibition of idolatry does appear fairly often in the various rules for God-fearers: are they, then, forbidden to take part in pagan worship? This proves difficult to decide. For Juvenal, as we have seen, a father who was content to observe the Sabbath and avoid the pig was succeeded by sons who worshipped *nil praeter nubes et caeli numen*.[266] As Siegert points out[267] this fourteenth satire follows a formal scheme in which the inclinations of the fathers turn into the unchecked vices of the sons, i.e. sons always greatly exceed the sins of their fathers; in which case, if the sons worship the God of Heaven exclusively, it would appear that the father did not. Epictetus does say, apparently of God-fearers, ὅταν τινὰ ἐπαμφοτερίζοντα ἴδωμεν, εἰώθαμεν λέγειν "οὔκ ἐστιν Ἰουδαῖος ἀλλ' ὑποκρίνεται".[268] This is the same passage we dealt with above (pp. 44–5) on conversion by baptism; the context is the same, the tendency of men to study, but not practise, stoicism; 'Why do you call yourself a stoic when you are not.... Why do you act the Jew when you are a Greek?' is the intention of the passage. Therefore, ἐπαμφοτερίζω here does not necessarily mean 'practise both religions', but something more like 'behave in an undecided manner'. Commodian, however, the third-century Latin Christian author of hexameter acrostics addressed to pagans, says (at 1.24.11–14):

> quid in synagoga decurris saepe bifarius?...
> ut tibi misericors fiat quem denegas ultro?
> exis inde foris, iterum tu fana requiris;
> uis inter utrumque uiuere, sed inde peribis.

Bifarius is a vulgarism meaning 'double one', 'two-faced':[269] the rest is clear enough; the subject rushes from synagogue to pagan shrine, and wishes to live between both, with a foot in both camps, as it were. Commodian's thirty-seventh poem is addressed to *qui Iudaeidiant fanatici* (where *di* in the verb is probably provincial Latin for *z*, and *fanatici* is popular Latin for *fanorum cultores*, judaizers who remain worshippers at pagan shrines):

> quid? medius Iudaeus, medius uis esse profanus?...
> exis pro forebas, inde et ad idola uadis (1.37.1, 8).

And what is the attitude of the Jews to this? Commodian complains that they do not warn judaizers that God's law forbids it, as they should:

> dicant illi tibi si iussum est deos adorare[270]...(1.37.10–11).

The biblical Law, he says, knows no such permissiveness, and the Jews are guilty in this regard (i.e. they permit it). Therefore pagans who attend the synagogue

JEWISH INSTITUTIONS 63

can also worship at the temples of the gods, with the (at least tacit) consent of the Jews.

This is clear, but perhaps not entirely trustworthy: Commodian is writing religious polemic; the Latin fathers are given to rhetorical exaggeration. The witness of Commodian is, however, confirmed in the fifth century by Cyril of Alexandria, probably the most ruthless of the church fathers in argument, but in this particular context (a work of ethical homiletics) writing without an axe to grind, about a nearby province. Jethro the Midianite, priest of the Lord, according to the Septuagint at Exod. 18:11–12, had said that now he knew that the Lord was great παρὰ πάντας τοὺς θεούς. Cyril explains that, although Jethro worshipped ὑψίστῳ θεῷ, he also recognized other gods (Earth, Sky and the Astral Bodies); this, Cyril said, had continued to his own day, when there were men in Phoenicia and Palestine who called themselves θεοσεβεῖς, whose way of worship was not purely according to the Jewish customs, nor yet wholly Greek, but as though darting about and distributing themselves εἰς ἄμφω.[271] Cyril's evidence seems unambiguous, and confirms Commodian's: therefore it seems likely that some God-fearers do not give up their association with pagan cult. But only *some*: it seems improbable that the Aphrodisian God-fearers who are members of the decany would have joined, or been allowed to join, a society for the study of the Law and prayer if they were still practising pagans; God-fearers can, but, surely, they do not necessarily, also worship the pagan gods.

A fourth-century rabbinical argument[272] as to whether *benei Noah* ought to be required to bless the name of God, sometimes cited on this subject, is, when read in its context, a discussion of whether such men should be required to give up their lives in martyrdom (*quiddush ha-Shem*, sanctification of the name) in a time of persecution, rather than offer pagan sacrifice, and is therefore not relevant here. What is, however, relevant, if inconclusive, is a reference to the case of Na'aman, to whom, says the Talmud, the Noachide laws applied, for he had permission to bow down to Ba'al-Rimmon, although not where Jews were present.[273] Would this apply to the God-fearers? We cannot know.

How early can we trace pagan worship by God-fearers? As early as St Luke's Cornelius the centurion, it seems. For Cornelius, whether real or imaginary, would have had to (would have been understood to) take part in *public* military cult when his unit sacrificed to the *signa* of the cohort, to the Roman gods, to former and for present emperors, as was the routine practice of auxiliary as well as legionary troops of the Roman army.[274] Such men, in the late first century A.D., could be thought to be God-fearers. The evidence for this religious latitude is therefore early as well as late imperial in date.

It is, then, probable that the spectrum of permissible behaviour for a

God-fearer included pagan worship (this would explain the position of the God-fearing city *bouleutai* at Aphrodisias, if their position needs explaining). But what is also probable is that there was no clear definition of what was required of God-fearers, simply various lists of *desiderata*. There is too much disagreement in our sources to be explained away, unless we come to this conclusion. 'Die Gottesfürchtigen waren Heiden, und es liegt in der Sache dass ihre Unterscheidung von der übrigen Heidenwelt, wie sie von den Quellen nahegelegt wird, in keiner Weise *scharf* zu ziehen ist';[275] the emphasis is Siegert's and well placed. Saul Lieberman expressed himself on this subject with his usual intellectual sanity. The

fearers of Heaven... were not entirely converted to Judaism; they sympathized with only some of the Jewish precepts. And, of course, it can never be expected that different individuals who have not embraced the Jewish faith as a whole should evince exactly the same interest in the same laws and precepts. It is natural and human for one to have liked the Jewish Sabbath, for another to have been attracted by the Jewish holidays, while still others were impressed by the Jewish Day of Atonement (and the ideas associated with it)...[276]

How are we to explain this lack of definition for the category of God-fearers, their freedom from rules in an otherwise legalistic religion? We have no evidence on which to base an explanation: what follows is speculation. The easiest way for such a situation to have come about is if the existence of God-fearers had never been intended, if there had simply been (*c.* 200 B.C.?) curious pagan visitors to the synagogues in the diaspora, who had stayed on, and slowly turned into permanent hangers-on. As their status had never been planned, it was never defined. The rabbis, as usual, eventually tried to reduce the phenomenon to rules, but, as often, could not agree. Perhaps this, or something similar, could explain the anomaly that the God-fearers represent in Judaism.

The God-fearers were, however, able to perform a Jewish religious rite that was forbidden to Jews: they could sacrifice to God. Jews could only do so, by biblical Law, at the Temple of Jerusalem, which was no more, after A.D. 70; but since God-fearers were not 'children of the covenant', i.e. were not subject to the whole Law, in theory they could sacrifice to the Jewish God anywhere. That they did so in practice is indicated by rabbinical discussion in the Mishnah and the Tosephta,[277] where such sacrifices are taken for granted. Of the gentiles it is said in the second or third century that '*goyim* are permitted to erect an altar everywhere and offer sacrifice to Heaven'.[278] There is a discussion of such altars in the colloquies between Yehudah Ha-Nasi' and the emperor 'Antoninus' (of which the contents are no doubt fictional but must represent rabbinical opinion of the third or fourth century).[279] How early were such sacrifices made? The *praetor peregrinus* at Rome for 139 B.C., P. Cornelius Scipio Hispanus, expelled certain Jews from Rome for trying to interest Romans in their *sacra* and also *arasque priuatas e publicis locis abiecit*, according to Valerius Maximus:²⁸⁰ Jewish private altars can only refer to those employed by gentiles to honour the God of Israel. Josephus²⁸¹ cites a decree of Sardis from the time of Julius Caesar, granting, among other things, a τόπος to the Jews, where they can gather for εὐχὰς καὶ θυσίας τῷ Θεῷ. Bickerman²⁸² suggests that these 'sacrifices' must be made by God-fearers. A small, flat-topped stone block from Pergamum,²⁸³ inscribed in letters dating to about the second century A.D.,²⁸⁴ names Θεὸς Κύριος ὁ ὢν εἰς ἀεί (as Nilsson points out, this must refer to the Septuagint's ἐγώ εἰμι ὁ ὤν [Exod. 3:18]);²⁸⁵ a second inscription on the same stone reads: Ζώπυρος τῷ Κυρίωι τὸν βωμὸν καὶ τὴν φωτόφορον μετὰ τοῦ φλογούχου ('to the Lord, the altar and the lamp-stand with the lantern'). The remains of altars dedicated Θεῷ Ὑψίστῳ, at various places in the East, are notoriously difficult to identify as Jewish (the title is common for many gods and godlings in the eastern Mediterranean), and so, in each case, may or may not be further archaeological evidence for the sacrifices of God-fearers;²⁸⁶ the same applies to the pillar altars dedicated Θεῷ Ὑψίστῳ in what may or may not be the pre-Christian-era synagogue at Delos.²⁸⁷ But it is obvious what Greek-speaking Jews would call gentiles interested enough in Jewish religion to sacrifice to the Lord of Hosts: they would have been thought to be, and so were, God-fearers.

What then is a God-fearer? He is someone who is attracted enough to what he has heard of Judaism to come to the synagogue to learn more; who is, after a time, willing, as a result, to imitate the Jewish way of life in whatever way and to whatever degree he wishes (up to and including membership in community associations, where that includes legal study and prayer); who may have had held out to him various short codes of moral behaviour to follow, but does not seem to have been required to follow any one; who may follow the exclusive monotheism of the Jews and give up his ancestral gods, but need not do so; who can, if he wishes, take the ultimate step and convert, but need not do so, and is, whether he does or not, promised a share in the resurrection for his pains. Such men make up a significant proportion of the population of the only synagogue community where we have quantitative evidence of their existence; whether this would commonly be true elsewhere is anyone's guess. Their earliest appearance seems to be in the Septuagint version of II Chronicles, which, following the Hebrew, reads πᾶσα συναγωγὴ Ἰσραὴλ καὶ οἱ ἐπισυνηγμένοι (meaning proselytes) and then adds, without the authority of the Hebrew, καὶ οἱ φοβούμενοι,²⁸⁸ as something different from, but related to, Israel and the proselytes. The date is *c*. 200 B.C.²⁸⁹ As we have seen, Cyril of Alexandria reports θεοσεβεῖς in Palestine in the fifth century A.D. (see p. 63), and an inscription records one in Venosa in Italy, probably in the sixth (see p. 53); the latter is our best approximation to a final date for them. (On God-fearers, see further at pp. 93–122, *infra*.)

34–8. βουλευτής; on the resolution of the abbreviations see p. 12; on the identification of the βουλή of which these men are members as the city-council, p. 55; on possible social implications of the inclusion of nine *theosebeis* in its membership, p. 127.

From the point of view of the city there is clearly no formal reason why anyone who had Aphrodisian citizenship, and could meet such property-qualifications as were prescribed for the office, should not be a member of the city's council at any time.[290] The nine *theosebeis* listed here as councillors must fall into this category of appropriately propertied citizens of Aphrodisias. Why, however, are there no Jewish councillors? It is, of course, just possible that a tiny number appeared at the top of face *b* in the area damaged or lost, rather more if face *b* continues an inscription begun on another stele (see p. 19). But we should not expect to find practising Jews in civic office before the edict of the emperors Severus and Caracalla (issued jointly, therefore, between 198 and 211),[291] which allowed cities to recruit them into their councils. And even after that the evidence from other cities suggests that we should not expect to find many anywhere. Eight Jews are attested as councillors at Sardis, where a Jewish councillor at Hypaepa is also recorded.[292] From elsewhere in Asia Minor one is known at Corycus in Cilicia Tracheia;[293] perhaps two in Phrygian Acmonia, where the Jew, Aurelius Frugianus Menocritus, was *agoranomos*, *sitones* and *paraphylax*, and the probable, but not quite certain, Jew, Tib. Flavius Alexander, was *boularch*, *strategos*, *eirenarch*, *sitones*, and *agoranomos*.[294] With every allowance made for the comparative rarity of references to specific councillors of any origin, it seems likely that the number of Jews in that office anywhere was low.

Ulpian adds to his record of the ruling of Severus and Caracalla that the emperors imposed *necessitates* on Jewish office-holders, but without infringing their *superstitio*.[295] This need not necessarily mean more than that the Jews had to pay the customary *summae honorariae* for office,[296] but could mean that additional burdens were laid on them to compensate for their freedom from providing the sums and the personal effort that pagans would expend on pagan rites associated with office. The *necessitates* may in fact have induced a disinclination in many Jews to serve after all. Moreover, although it is often stated dogmatically that the emperors exempted Jewish office-holders from participation in pagan rites – and something of the sort, we suppose, is implied by the formula relating to their *superstitio* – we have no precise information on the matter, and no idea how, in fact, it was managed. Many Jews may have felt that the arrangements in their cities were unsatisfactory.

For Aphrodisias it is unclear whether the imperial ruling preceded or

JEWISH INSTITUTIONS 67

succeeded our inscription; if it preceded, we do not know whether the city adopted it into her procedures; and if she did, we cannot tell (at present) whether she was willing to apply it in practice. It may also be that no Jew had the local citizenship (see p. 124–5), so that a preliminary enfranchisement would have been necessary for his advancement. And while we believe that there probably were Jews at Aphrodisias of sufficient wealth to qualify for office (see p. 127), they may not have been very anxious for its burdens; and they would have been very seriously concerned, as the *theosebeis* need not have been, about presence at pagan sacrifice.

NOTES

1 ΘΒ in *Donateurs* 70 (*CIJ* II.964), 89 (*CIJ* II.1427), perhaps 84 (but this is thought by some to be Christian), and, in variant formulae, e.g. with εἶς θεός, *Donateurs* 61 (*CIJ* II.848), *CIJ* II.864, with Κύριος or Κύριε, *Donateurs* 64, 77a, G. M. A. Hanfmann, *BASOR* 187 (1967) 18, n. 23a, LXX, Ps. 17:2.
2 See *BGU* 781.VI.21.
3 *OLD s.v.*; E. Pottier in Daremberg/Saglio, *Dictionnaire des antiquités classiques s.v.*; V. M. Maxfield, *The military decorations of the Roman army* (1981) 62, 96–7; N. Criniti, *L'epigrafe di Asculum di Gn. Pompeo Strabone* (1970) 234–5; the last two both equate it with the φιάλη of Polybius VI.39.
4 *LSJ* and Preisigke-Kiesseling, *Wörterbuch s.v.*
5 m Kel. 16.5; t Shab. 12 (13).15; y Shab. 7.2.10c, 39f., 15.1: 15a, 45; m M.Sh. 1.10; y M.Sh. 1.3, 52d 3; Gen.R. 74.4; Lam.R. ad 3:16 (6).
6 *CIL* VI.37045 (*ILS* 8888); E. Popescu, *Inscriptiones intra fines Daco-Rumaniae repertae Graecae et Latinae anno 284 recentiores* (1976) nos. 401a, 440 (owed to C. M. Roueché).
7 W. M. Ramsay, 'The Tekmoreian guest-friends', in *Studies in the history and art of the eastern Roman provinces* (1906) 319; there is useful discussion of the text by W. Ruge in *RE*² v.1, *s.v.* 'Tekmoreioi'.
8 m Pe'ah 8.7; Pes. 10.1, cf. t Pe'ah 4.8; y Pe'ah 21a; b B.B. 8b.
9 Acts of the Apostles 6:1.
10 For descriptions of the institution of *tamḥui* in the first few centuries A.D. see Schürer–Vermes–Millar II.437, Moore, *Judaism* II.176–7; S. Krauss, *Talmudische Archäologie* III (1912) 66–74, with earlier treatments listed there.
11 *Donateurs* 100; see Lüderitz, *Cyrenaika* 72 for a later text.
12 *CIJ* I.11; Leon, *Jews* 265.
13 Arrian, *Tactica* 6.1; H. U. Instinsky, *RAC* III.603–10, *s.v.* 'Decanus'; Preisigke, *Wörterbuch s.v.*, citing P.Oxy. 1512.2, P.Fay. 156, Mey. Ostr. 666, Ostr. Tait II.1923.
14 So *LSJ s.v.*, see also *TLG*; for comment see Instinsky, *cit.* n. 13.
15 So J. and L. Robert, *Bull. Ep.* 1969.576, commenting on A. S. Hall, *AS* 18 (1968) 79, no. 26.
16 See J. and L. Robert, *Bull. Ep.* 1961.399, commenting on *IGB* III.1.917, 1401 *bis*.
17 *Syria* 29 (1952) 317; the texts are *SEG* XVI.813–14.
18 m Meg. 4.3.
19 m Meg. 1.3; y Meg. 1.6.70b; b Meg. 5a.
20 b Meg. 17b, b BK 82a; cf. m Meg. 1.3.
21 y Meg. 1.6.70b.
22 Rashi *ad* b Sanh. 17b.
23 Schürer–Vermes–Millar II.438–9.
24 *Synagogale Altertümer* (1922) 103ff.
25 *CJ* 1.2.4, of 409, 1.2.9 = XI.17.1, of 439; K. R. Mentzou, Συμβολαὶ εἰς τὴν μελέτην τοῦ

οἰκονομικοῦ καὶ κοινωνικοῦ βίου τῆς Πρωίμου Βυζαντινῆς περιόδου (1975); L. Robert, *RPh* 48 (1974) 189–90, commenting on *IG* x.ii.1, no. 66; *id*. *REG* 79 (1966) 764–5, commenting on *Corinth* VIII.3, no. 556.

26 *IGCA* 269, undated (Aphrodisias); *ibid*. 108 of c. 538 (Ephesus); perhaps *MAMA* VIII.46, undated (Lystra).
27 Louis I. Rabinowitz, *Encycl. Jud*. VIII (1971) *s.v*. 'Hevra (Havurah) Kaddisha'; M. Grunewald, *Encycl. Jud*. (Berlin) V (1930) *s.v*. 'Chewra Kadischa'.
28 Josephus, *c. Apion*. 2.211; cf. Deut. 21:25, Tobit 1:17f.
29 t Meg. 4.15, cf. b Sem. 12.
30 *Beth She'arim* no. 202; see B. Lifshitz, *RBi* 67 (1961) 62 and J. and L. Robert, *Bull. Ep*. 1961.808.
31 So Blass-Debrunner, *Grammatik des neutest. Griechisch* (1949) *s.v*., cf. Acts 5:5f. where the meaning is clarified by comparison with the Syriac version.
32 b M.Kat. 24*b*.
33 Lev. 21:1–4.
34 For example Strabo 14.673; Polybius 1.2.8, 2.56.11, 12.
35 LXX proem. of Ecclus.; H. Leisegang, *Index verborum*, in Cohn and Wendland, *Philonis...Opera* VII.2, *s.v*.
36 Lampe, *A patristic Greek lexicon s.v*.; Origen, *c. Celsum* 2.53; Athenasius, *de decretis Nicaenae synodi* 2; Isidorus of Pelusium, *Epp*. 1.449.
37 *CIJ* I.333.
38 Lk. 5:17; Acts 5:34.
39 Hanfmann, *cit*. n. 1, 29, with fig. 48.
40 *CIL* XI.3758 (*CIG* 9852, Kaibel 729).
41 *CIJ* I 113, 193, 508; cf. φιλόνομος, *ibid*. 111 und in an unpublished catacomb in the Via Appia Pignatelli at Rome (*Time Magazine*, 23rd May, 1977), φιλέντολος, *CIJ* 132, 203, 509; in 203 the deceased is φιλόλαος, φιλ[έντολος?], φιλοπένης, all at once. For the meaning see Juster I.455, n. 3; Leon, *Jews* 193.
42 E.g. b Ket. 111b; b Pes. 49a, 'marry your daughter to a talmid ḥakham'; see L. Ginzburg, *Students, scholars and saints* (1928) 35–58.
43 b. Shab. 114a.
44 m Ab. 6.2.
45 Leon, *Jews* 135–66.
46 t Meg. 3 (2).6; y Meg. 3.1.73d; see W. Bacher in *Hastings' dictionary of the Bible* (1909–10) IV, *s.v*. 'Synagogue', 637a, and S. Krauss in *RE*² IV A.2 (1932) *s.v*. 'Synagoge', col. 1294.
47 y Ta'an. 64a.51; y Shek. 2.47a.
48 y Ber. 1.4a.27; y Bik. 65b.17.
49 y Meg. 74a.67; y Ta'an 68b.34; y Meg. 70a.49; b Shab. 139a *etc*.; see Bacher, *cit*. n. 46.
50 Acts 13:14; 14:1; 15:19; 16:13; 17:1; 10:17; 18:4, 7.
51 Wilcken, *Chrest*. 180, col. iii. l. 113, *CIJ* I.718; B. Lifshitz (ed.), *Prolegomenon* to *CJI*, 625b; see R. Flacelière, J. and L. Robert, *Bull. Ep*. 1939.583, A. Ferrua, *RAC* 26 (1950) 227, cf. *Bull. Ep*. 1955.303.
52 Bacher, *cit*. no. 46.
53 b 'Erub. 21a; b Meg. 26b.
54 Th. Reinach, *REJ* 26 (1893) 170–1; Juster I.440–2; Krauss, *Synagogale Altertümer* 139–46 and in *RE*² IV A.2, col. 1313; V. Tcherikover, *Hellenistic civilisation and the Jews* (1961) 302–3; S. Applebaum, 'The organisation of the Jewish communities in the diaspora', in Safrai/Stern I. 464–503.
55 Cf. at Hyllarima, *Donateurs* 32; for a list and discussion see L. Robert, 'Inscriptions grecques de Side', *RPh* 32 (1958) 42, n. 6.
56 See n. 11.
57 y Ber. 7b; b Meg. 26b, 27a; b Ber. 17a, 28b, 64a; cf. the later Deut.R. 7.1.
58 y Ber. 17a.
59 b Git. 38b.

JEWISH INSTITUTIONS 69

60 b Shab. 116b (citing R. Nehemiah of the second century A.D.), cf. b Suk. 53a.
61 m Shab. 16.1, cf. y Shab. 15c, t Sot. 7.9ff. On public lectures see Moore, *Judaism* I.214–16.
62 y Ḥag. 76c; Pes. RK 120b; b Ket. 103b; b BM 85b.
63 For ambiguous evidence see Josephus, *AJ* 16.164, Philo, *Hypoth.*, *ap.* Eusebius, *PE* 7.13, neither of them necessarily referring to a school; the same applies to the 'School of Tyrannus' at Ephesus in Acts 19:9, on which see Alfred Loisy, *Les actes des apôtres* (1920) 725 – probably a rhetor's lecture-hall.
64 LXX Ecclus. 51:23.
65 On *Beth Midrash* see Kaufman Köhler, *Jewish encycl.* III (1971) 116–18, *s.v.* 'Bet ha-Midrash'; Natan Efrati and R. Aaron Rotuhoff, *Encycl. Jud.* IV (1971) 751–2, *s.v.* Bet [ha-] *Midrash.*
66 E.g. b Shab. 17a, b; b 'Erub. 13b.
67 A *baraita*, i.e. pre-A.D. 200 citation, at b Sanh. 32b, cf. *Siphrê* 2.80, y Ned. 6.8, b Ber. 63a.
68 m AZ 3.7; Gitt. 4.7; t Nidd. 4.6 (cases heard); t AZ 1.8; Nidd. 6.6; Par. 4.9 (rabbis educated).
69 D. Urman, 'Jewish inscriptions from Daburra, Golan', *Qadmoniot* 4 (1971) 133 (in Hebrew).
70 On early *yeshiboth* see Moshe Beer, *Encycl. Jud.* II (1971) 199–205, *s.v.* 'Academies in Babylonia and Erez Israel'.
71 m Aḥ. 3.6, cf. b Ber. 63b, 'form yourself into אגודות (*'aggudoth*, bands) to study the Torah'; cf. also b Ta'an. 7a.
72 *CR*, col. 6.
73 t Sanh 13.3, b BK 90b, 91a, b Sanh. 1.6, b Meg 23b; cf. y Ber. 4.11c, *et al.*
74 On associations for adult education in the Talmudic period, see Israel M. Goldman, *Life-long learning among Jews* (1975) ch. V, and S. Safrai, 'Education and study of the Torah' in Safrai/Stern II.945ff.; for the same in late medieval and early modern Jewry, see Salo Baron, *The Jewish community* (1942) I.348–74, Jacob Katz, *Tradition and crisis* (1961) 156–67.
75 Asseman, *Opera omnia* 3.534E; the second example cited by Lampe, *A patristic Greek lexicon – Sermo de Symeone et Anna* 10 (*PG* 18.372C), attributed to Methodius of Olympus – probably dates from the ninth century. Lampe translates 'blessed by all', perhaps not quite precisely since by analogy with e.g. παντάγαθος, παντάρετος, cf. Jewish Greek παντοδύναμος (LXX Wisd. 7:23), the sense of the prefix is 'wholly'.
76 Gen. 26:29, 43:28; Deut. 28:6; Jdg. 17:12, *et al.*
77 Mk. 14:61; Lk. 1:68; Rom. 1:25, 9:5, *et al.*
78 E.g. Mk. 5:3–11, Lk 6:20–2.
79 Lifshitz, *Prolegomenon* to *CJI*, no. 681a, ll. 5–6, from Asenovgrad in Bulgaria; *CIJ* I.690, l. 2, from Gorgippia, Bosporus; similarly Lifshitz, *Prolegomenon* to *CJI*, 690a. J. and L. Robert have argued (*Bull. Ép.* 1968.478, p. 518) that it is inappropriate to restore εὐλόγειτο[ς ὁ λαός] in a painted text in the annex to the Sardis synagogue (G. M. A. Hanfmann, *cit.* n. 1, 10) and that the original proposal, εὐλόγητο[ς ὁ θεός], should be preferred (Hanfmann, *BASOR* 177 [1965] 26).
80 *Donateurs* 39 (*IGLS* 1320, *CIJ* II.804).
81 *Donateurs* 28 (*CIJ* II.754), 32, 36 (*CIJ* II.781), 78 (*CIJ* II.867 – ἁγιο[τάτῳ] τόπῳ); L. Robert, *Hellenica* III (1946) 105; *id.*, *cit.* n. 55, p. 73, n. 44, with comment on all these inscriptions.
82 See Poland, *Vereinswesens* 169.
83 y M.Sh. 2.53d, Eccl.R. *ad* 9.9, Yalk, 1b.989, *et al.*; see S. Safrai in *Scripta Hierosolymitana* 23 (1973) 62–78.
84 Hebrew synagogue inscription: *Sefer ha-Yishuv* I.88; J. Baer, *Tziyyon* 15 (1950) 9ff. (both in Hebrew), cf. at Hammam Lif, *CIL* VIII.12457a: *sancta sinagoga*; the source for this designation is biblical (Exod. 19:6; Lev. 19:1).
85 Dalman, *Aram.-neuhebräisches Handwörterbuch zu Targum, Talmud und Midrasch, s.v.*
86 In his edition (1933) I.138. Cf. b Ber. 33a *in fin.*
87 m Ber. 5.5, and often in later literature.
88 t Meg. 4(3), 15, b Sem. 12.
89 H. L. Strack, *Introduction to Talmud and Midrash* (1981 repr. of 1931 ed.) 73.
90 On these see A. Oppenheimer, 'Benevolent societies in Jerusalem' (in Hebrew), in *Pirkaim ba-Toledot Yerushalayim ba-Yomei Beit Sheni: Sefer Zikron le-Avraham Shalit* (1980) 178–90.

91 Israel Abrahams, *Jewish life in the Middle Ages* (1969 repr. of 1897 ed.) 327.
92 L. Robert, *NIS* 46, no. 6.
93 *Donateurs*, p. 27 on no. 19.
94 I. Abrahams, *cit.* n. 91, 328; the italics are ours.
95 m Ber. 4.7; can an individual recite the *Musaph* prayers on his own, or can they be said publicly by the *ḥeber 'ir*? Compare b R.haSh. 34b, the same contrast between private and public worship, with the *ḥeber 'ir* representing the latter.
96 b Sem. 11.2, 12.4; b. Ḥul. 94a, Sem. 14.13.
97 t Pe'ah 4.16, b Meg. 35a–b; in these cases the proper vocalization could be *ḥaber 'ir*, 'member of the town association'.
98 t Meg. 4 (3).29.
99 On *ḥeber 'ir* in rabbinical literature see Krauss, *Synagogale Altertümer* 125–42; S. Liebermann, *Tosefta ki-Feshuta* I (1955) 190 (in Hebrew).
100 For ἀπενθεσία see *LSJ Supplement* (1968) *s.v.*, following E. Fraenkel, *Hermes* 68 (1933) 242–4 (*Kleine Beiträge* I [1964] 371–4, a reference owed to Glen Bowersock); on πένθος and ἀπένθητος see *LSJ s.vv.* and P. Chantraine, *Dictionnaire étymologique de la langue grecque* (1968) *s.v.* πάσχω.
101 *Donateurs* 39 (*CIJ* II.804).
102 *CIJ* II.1450 (Lewis, *CPJ* III.144–5, is more cautious in restoration).
103 E.g. *Syll.*³ 604, ll. 16f.; see Poland, *Vereinswesens* 168.
104 Cf. πλῆθος at Acts 4:32, where the Authorised Version translates 'multitude', but 'community of the faithful' may perhaps be a better interpretation.
105 J. and L. Robert, *Bull. Ep.* 1951.236a, pp. 208–9; *id.* 1956.317.
106 *Donateurs* 58 (*CIJ* II.829).
107 E.g. *Donateurs* 13, 16 (*CIJ* II.738, 744).
108 To instances indexed in *CIJ* I add Lifshitz, *Prolegomenon* to *CIJ*, 696a–b, from Phthiotic Thebes.
109 Philo, *Hypothetica*, *ap.* Eusebius, *Praep. Evang.* 7.7; Josephus, *BJ* 4.317, *c. Apion* 2.211; see Juster I.480.
110 *CIJ* II.757.
111 m Shek. 2.5, citing R. Nathan ha-Babli; in general see Menaḥem Ebon, *Encycl. Jud.* IV (1971) 1515–23, *s.v.* 'Burial'; Meir Yolit, *ibid.* V (1971) 271–5, *s.v.* 'Cemetery'; S. Krauss, *Talmudische Archäologie* 71–82.
112 *LSJ s.v.*, citing e.g. Simonides, fr. 134, μνάματα ναυμαχίας.
113 *SIG* 213, at Sigeum, sixth century B.C.
114 Delphic epigram on the Persian invasion, on the temple of Athena Pronoia, early fifth century B.C., *ap.* Diod. Sic. 11.14.4.
115 *TLG, s.v.*
116 *CIJ* II.1203, fifth or sixth century A.D.
117 *CIJ* II.1204–5 (Noarah/Na'arah), 987 (Kefar Kana), 989 (Sepphoris), 1195 (Beth Guvrin), 885 (Isfiya), 981 (Chorazin); and (Ma'on), S. Yeivin, *Bull.... Rabinowitz Fund* 3 (1960) 36.
118 *CIJ* II.1165.
119 *CIJ* II.856–8.
120 S. Yeivin, 'Inscribed marble fragments from the Khirbet Susiya synagogue', *IEJ* 24 (1974) 201–9, esp. 20. On this formula in general see E. L. Sukenik, 'The ancient synagogues at El-Hammeh', *JPOS* 15 (1935) 122.
121 Neh. 5:19 (cf. 13:31).
122 *Donateurs* 61 (a poorer text in *CIJ* II.848).
123 M. Dothan, *Hammath Tiberias* (1983) no. 3, p. 61 and pl. 35.4.
124 M. Avi-Yonah, 'A new fragment of the Ashdod chancel screen', *Bull.... Rabinowitz Fund* 3 (1960) 69, supplementing *CIJ* II.961.
125 *CIJ* II.845.
126 *CIJ* II.863.

JEWISH INSTITUTIONS 71

127 Cte. du Mesnil du Buisson, 'Sur quelques inscriptions juives de Dura-Europus', *Biblica* (1937) 170f.; cf. the map in M. I. Rostovtzeff *et al.* (eds.), *Excavations at Dura-Europus: preliminary report, 7th and 8th seasons*, unnumbered final plate.
128 m BB 2.9.
129 As in Jdg. 4:18f.
130 Cf. women with the title 'archisynagogos' at Myndos, *CIJ* II.756, and Smyrna, *CIJ* II.741 (*I. Smyrna* I.295; see also L. Robert, *Hellenica* I [1940] 26, n. 4); 'presbyter', *CIJ* I, p. lxxxvi, n. 2; 'prostates', cf. also Joh. Chrys., *Adv. Iud.* 6.5. In general on women in the synagogue see now B. J. Brooten, *Women leaders in the ancient synagogue* (Brown Judaic Studies 36) (1982). In this connection it might be helpful to note that women also have the titles of high office in Greek cities – for example Phile in the first century A.D. held (presumably in an honorary capacity) the title of the highest office in Priene and built an aqueduct and reservoir – the title being, perhaps, the reward for her donation (*I. Priene* 208). There are also a number of women with the titles of office-holders at Aphrodisias (e.g. the four women recorded as *stephanephoroi* in *MAMA* VIII.492b, l. 12; 554, l. 16 with 555, l. 19; 560, l. 10; 571, l. 8); where anything else is known of them it appears that they are large-scale civic benefactors.
131 Leisegang, *cit.* n. 35, *s.v.*
132 Poland, *Vereinswesens* 346.
133 Rom. 16:2.
134 For examples see *CIJ* I.523 (Rome), 639 (Brescia); cf. *ibid.* 606, pateressa, (Venosa); see in general Frey, *CIJ* I, pp. xciv–xcv; Schürer III.89; Applebaum, *cit.* n. 54, 496–7.
135 For such an addition perhaps see *CIJ* II.972, from Kaysoun near the former Lake Huleh in Israel, a Jewish votive inscription ὑπὲρ σωτηρίας of the emperor Septimius Severus and his sons, M. Aurelius Antoninus and Septimius Geta, with, on the left margin, καὶ 'Ιουλίας Δόμνης Σεβ. – the καί, absent from the main text, together with the position of Julia's name, may suggest an erroneous omission remedied by insertion in the margin.
136 See L. Robert, *cit.* n. 55, 42, n. 6, and authors cited at 41, n. 4.
137 *CIJ* II.949 (Joppa); 1.400 (Rome).
138 A. H. M. Jones, *The later Roman empire* (1964), II.945 with III.321–2, n. 18.
139 Acts 13:13; 14:25.
140 L. Robert, *cit.* n. 55.
141 L. Robert, *cit.* n. 55, 40–1, and authors listed in notes thereon.
142 Martial, 4.45.2, *Parthenicus palatinus*, identified with Domitian's *cubiculo praepositus* (Suet., *Dom.* 17); see *PIR* P¹, no. 101.
143 S. Krauss, *Griech. u. lat. Lehnwörter in Talmud, Midrasch und Targum* (1899) *s.v.*, and sources cited there.
144 *CIJ* II.1006 (Beth She'arim 61).
145 'Fonctions et titres honorifiques dans les communautés juifs', *RBi* 67 (1960) 63; see J. and L. Robert, *Bull. Ep.* 1961.808; L. Robert, *cit.* n. 55, 42, n. 7. Another παλατῖνος, interpreted as a court official in Diocletian's court at Nicomedeia, is attested from the area of Izmit, *TAM* IV. 1. 255 (see most recently Öğüt-Polat/Şahin, *Epigraphica Anatolica* 5 (1985) 113, no. 27).
146 Cf. Reynolds, *Aphrodisias* 38, document 4, ll. 42f.
147 SHA, *Hadr.* 14.2; Modestinus, *Dig.* 48.8.11 *pr.*
148 Paul., *Sent.* 5.22.3; Ulp., *Dig.* 48.8.3.5; Bardesanes the Astrologer, *Le livre des lois des pays* (1899), a Romano-Syrian law-book, written *c.* A.D. 200.
149 Modestinus, *cit.* n. 147.
150 U. Wilcken, *Archiv f. Papyrusforschung* 2 (1902) 4–13; *id., Grundzüge und Chrestomathie der Papyruskunde*, I.128, II.102, nos. 74–7.
151 SHA, *Sev.* 17; Th. Mommsen, *RG* V (1885) 549 and nn. 1–2; Origen, *C. Cels.* 2.13. The passage in the SHA incorrectly parallels Severus' treatment of the Jews with his treatment of Christians and is therefore regarded as spurious on the latter (see e.g. T. D. Barnes, *JRS* 58 (1968) 32–50), although normally accepted on the former.
152 There is other evidence for this, e.g. Irenaeus, *Adv. haer.* 3.21.1, cf. Eusebius, *HE* 5.8.10,

Epiphanius, *De mens. et pond.* 14–15, Tertullian, *Adv. Iudaeos* I, Origen, *In Matth. Comm. Ser.* 16: Tertullian and Origen make it clear that there are conversions in the early third century.
153 SHA, *Heliog.* 7, Dio Cassius 79.11.1–2.
154 See n. 152, with the omission of Tertullian and Origen.
155 b Yeb. 47a; *Siphrê* 115 *ad* Num. 18:41.
156 b. Yeb. 46b (Palestine); y Yeb. 8.1.8d (Laodicea); y Kid. 3.14.64d (Tyre); y Bik. 1.4.64a (Emesa), cf. y Dem. 6.1.25b, y AZ 1.9.40b.
157 y Bikk. 1.4.64a; b Yeb. 46a.
158 See commentary by M. Stern, *Greek and Latin authors on Jews and Judaism* I (1974) 543, n. 20, with references there.
159 See M. Simon, *Verus Israel* (1964) 333. Consult also Strack-Billerbeck, *Kommentar zum N.T. aus Talmud und Midrasch* I (1926) 105, on this issue.
160 On proselytism and proselytes see I. Lévi, 'Le prosélytisme juif', *REJ* 50 (1905) 253–90; Strack-Billerbeck, *Kommentar, cit.* n. 159, II (1924) *ad* Mk. 3:6, 5:43, 23:15 and Acts 13:16; Moore, *Judaism* I.323–53, III.107–14; Bernard J. Bamberger, *Proselytism in the Talmudic Period*[2] (1968); W. G. Braude, *Jewish proselytising in the first five centuries* (1940); M. Simon, *cit.* n. 159, 334–51, 482–8; K. G. Kuhn, *RE Suppl.* IX (1962), *s.v.* 'Proselyten'; *id.*, *TWNT* VI (1959) 734ff., *s.v.*, Προσήλυτος; Menahem Elon, *Encycl. Jud.* XIII (1971) 1193ff., *s.v.* 'Proselytes'.
161 For a Jewish psalm-singer recorded in an inscription at Rome see *SEG* 26.1162 (*L'Ann. Ep.* 1976, no. 79), from U. M. Fasoli, 'Le due catacombe ebraiche di Villa Torlonia', *RAC* 52 (1976) 7–62, whose account of the tomb suggests that it is in an area probably in use in the third century A.D.; G. R. Horsley, *New documents illustrating early Christianity* (1981) no. 74, dates it in the third-fourth centuries, but with reservations due to uncertainty whether there was psalm-singing in the western diaspora at that date. For the rabbinical attitude to liturgical song (it belonged in the Temple, not the synagogue) consult I. Elbogen, *Der jüdische Gottesdienst in seiner geschichtlichen Entwicklung*[3] (1931) 502. On III Mac., in addition to the edition by R. Hanhart, *Maccabaeorum Liber III* (1960), see O. Eissfeldt, *The Old Testament: an introduction* (ET 1965) 581–2, and J. H. Charlesworth, *The Pseudepigrapha and modern research with a supplement* (1981) 149–51. Philo, *De vita contempl.* 80, often cited on this topic, describes singing of hymns (and metrical psalms?) by the Therapeutae at their great nocturnal festival (Pentecost?); this, however, as a record of sectarian monastic festal practice, is not necessarily relevant to what went on in the synagogues of ordinary men on an average Saturday afternoon (see on this passage appendix to F. H. Colson's LCL Philo, vol. IX, p. 524). For an early reference to Christian psalm-singing see Hippolytus, *Apostolic tradition* 26.29–31 (reference owed to Dr Mary Berry).
162 Juvenal, *Sat.* 14.96–101.
163 Kajanto, *LC* 284; see also p. 103, list A, no. 50.
164 Acts 17:17.
165 *CIRB* 71.11.9, 10; H. Bellen, *JbAC* 8/9 (1965/6) 171–6, and B. Lifshitz, *R. Bi* 79 (1969) 96; see J. and L. Robert, *Bull. Ep.* 1969.52 and 405.
166 K. G. Kuhn, H. Stegemann, *RE Supp.* XI, col. 1249, citing LXX Job 31:32.
167 Mekh. Nezikin 18*ad* Exod. 22:20; y Meg. 3.74a, Lev. R. 32, Gen. R. 53.9, Pss. R. 43.180a, 42.176b, Gen. R. 28.5, Deut. R. 224.
168 y Yeb. 81.8a; b Gitt. 57b, Sanh. 96b, AZ 65a.
169 b AZ 64b, 65a and Ger. 3.1, cf. y Yeb. 8.1.8d: on the commandments to the sons of Noah, t AZ 8 (9).4, b Sanh. 56a–60a. See also S. Krauss, *REJ* 47 (1963) 34ff.
170 b Sanh. 57a.
171 b Arak. 29a.
172 R. Yoḥanan (third century A.D.), quoted at b AZ 65a, cf. y Yeb. 81.8d (R. Ḥaninah).
173 b Sanh. 13.2.
174 y Yeb. 24b.
175 On these Talmudic terms the clearest account is in Bamberger, *cit.* n. 160; see also Moore,

JEWISH INSTITUTIONS 73

Judaism I.338–9, III.112, n. 104, S. Lieberman, *Greek in Jewish Palestine* (1942) 77, I. Lévi, *REJ* 50 (1905) 1–59, *ibid.* 51 (1906) 29, M. Guttmann, *Das Judentum und seine Umwelt* I (1927), Strack-Billerbeck, *Kommentar, cit.* n. 159, II.715–99, Leon, *Jews*, 253, n. 1.

176 'Über die Gottesfürchtigen bei Juvenal', in his *Gesammelte Abhandlungen* II (1885) 71–80.
177 'Proselytes and God-fearers', in Kirsopp Lake and H. Cadbury, *The beginnings of Christianity* I.v (1932) 74–96.
178 E. M. Smallwood, *JThS*, n.s. 10 (1959) 330ff.; N. J. McEleney, *NTS* 20 (1974) 325; L. H. Feldman, 'Jewish sympathisers in classical literature and inscriptions', *TAPhA* 81 (1950) 200ff.; most recently A. T. Kraabel, 'The disappearance of the God-fearers', *Numen* 28 (1981) 113ff.
179 Smallwood, *cit.* n. 178, 331; L. Robert, *NIS* 45; Kraabel, *cit.* n. 178.
180 *Cit.* n. 179, 41–5.
181 Pss. 115:11, 13; 118:2–4; 135:20; cf. Dan. 3.90 and III Macc. 3:4.
182 Exod. 18:21; Job 1.1, cf. Gen. 20:11; see Folker Siegert, 'Gottesfürchtige und Sympathisanten', *JSJ* 4 (1973) 109–164, at 109–112.
183 *c. Apion.* 2.282.
184 *BJ* 7.45.
185 *Cit.* n. 182, 139.
186 *BJ* 2.560.
187 *BJ* 2.463.
188 *AJ* 20.34–5.
189 *AJ* 20.41.
190 *AJ* 20.195.
191 On Poppaea's interest in Judaism see, in general, E. M. Smallwood, 'The alleged Jewish tendencies of Poppaea Sabina', *JThS* 10 (1959) 329–55 and *ead., The Jews under Roman rule* (1976) 278, n. 79; also E. Groag, *RE* x, cols. 946–8, *s.v.* 'Julia Severa', an aristocrat of Phrygian Acmonia, who is attested both as a priestess of the city's imperial cult at the time of Nero and as a builder of an οἶκος which became a synagogue (*Donateurs* 33, see also *MAMA* VI.264, *CIJ* II.766, L. Robert, *cit.* n. 55, 41, n. 1, J. and L. Robert, *Bull. Ep.* (1983) 31). Groag conjectured that Severa had been generous to the Jews in imitation of her patron goddess Poppaea; but it is not certain that Poppaea was empress at the time when Severa was priestess.
192 Philo, *De vita Mos.* 2.41.
193 Lk. 7:1–10.
194 Acts 10:22, 28. This is perhaps fictional, probably inaccurate (it is the gentile's house, not his company, that threatens impurity here), but it fits Luke's intention of showing Peter's new tolerance towards gentiles in action, and the point is lost unless Cornelius is a gentile.
195 Acts 13:5, 14; 14:1; 17:1–2, 10, 17; 18:4; cf. 18: 24–6 (Apollos does the same at Ephesus).
196 Ἕλληνες at Acts 14:1; 18:4; 19:10.
197 Acts 17:4.
198 Acts 16:14; 17:17; 18:7; cf. 13:43, σεβομένων προσηλύτων, where proselytes may or may not be meant literally.
199 Acts 13:16.
200 Acts 17:7.
201 Acts 18:6.
202 Acts 18:7.
203 Acts 13:43, cf. 48 (Pisidian Antioch); 14:1–2 (Iconium); 17:4 (Thessalonica); 17:12 (Beroea); 18:4 (Corinth).
204 Charlotte Roueché, of King's College, London, has kindly allowed us to appropriate her suggestions on these points.
205 *Sat.* 14.96–101.
206 *Sat.* 1.9.68–72.
207 Suet., *Dom.* 12.2.
208 H. Hommel, 'Juden und Christen im Kaiserzeitlichen Milet', *MDAI(I)* 25 (1975) 186–7 and n. 100.
209 Cf. *CIL* VI.390a: *Domini metuens/I(oui) O(ptimo) M(aximo) l(ibens) m(erito)/sacr(um).*

210 *CIJ* I.529 at Rome: *de]um metuens hic sita [est]* is on the base of a bust and more likely to be pagan than Jewish.
211 So Schürer, III.62.
212 *CIJ* I.642.
213 *CIJ* I.5, 285, 524, 529; see Lifshitz, 'Les Juifs de Venosa', *RPh* 90 (1962) 367–71, especially 368.
214 Deut. R. 2.24.
215 *PIR*² F. 240.
216 Where Job, for example, is θεοσεβής (Job 1:1).
217 *CIJ* I.500 (original provenance unknown), definitely Jewish, despite Leon, *Jews*, 247, n. 2, see L. H. Feldman, *cit.* n. 178, 204, n. 23.
218 *CIJ* I.228.
219 *CIJ* I.202; see L. Robert, *NIS* 43, n. 2; Feldman, *cit.* n. 178, 204, n. 24, suggesting that there may be two individuals here, one a proselyte and one a God-fearer; Leon, *Jews* 292, offers a restoration which eliminates the word – . . .]εος ἐβ[ίωσεν. . . .
220 Lifshitz, *Prolegomenon* to *CJI*, no. 619a, (*id.*, *RFIC* 90 [1962] 368).
221 *IG* XII.1.593, see L. Robert, *Ét. Anat.* 411, n. 5, *NIS* 44 (Rhodes); R. Paton and E. L. Hicks, *Inscriptions of Cos* (1891) 278, cf. J. and L. Robert, *Bull. Ep.* 1952.31, *NIS* 44 (Cos); *Donateurs* 30 (*CIG* 2924), cf. L. Robert, *Ét. Anat.* 109–12, citing E. Groag, *Jahreshefte* 10 (1907) 282–90, *NIS* 44 (Tralles); *Donateurs* 28, see also L. Robert, *Ét. Anat.* 411, no. 6, *NIS* 45 (Deliler near Philadelphia); L. Robert, *NIS* 39–40, nos. 4, 5 (*Donateurs* 17, 18) (Sardis; for the most recent discussion of the date of the mosaics see A. R. Seager in G. M. A. Hanfmann, *Sardis from prehistoric to Roman times* [1983] 173).
222 L. Robert, *NIS* 39f.
223 *CIJ* 748 (*SEG* 4.441); originally published by A. Deissman, *Licht von Osten* (1923) 391; see also nn. 224–230 below.
224 III⁴.174. M. Simon, for example, believes that the *theosebeis* of this inscription cannot be Jews ('Sur les débuts du prosélytisme juif' in *Hommages à A. Dupont-Sommer* [1971] 509ff., esp. 518).
225 Frey *ad loc.*; L. Robert, *NIS* 39; B. Schwank, *BZ* 13 (1969) 262ff.
226 *MDAI(I)* 25 (1975) 167–95.
227 See n. 165.
228 *Cit.* n. 165.
229 *JSJ* 1 (1970) 77–84, 4 (1973) 109–64.
230 See also J. and L. Robert, *Bull. Ep.* 1969.52; 1970.404, 405; M. Hengel, 'Proseuche und Synagoge', in G. Jeremias *et al.* (eds.), *Tradition und Glaube..., Festgabe...Karl Georg Kuhn* (1971) 174ff.
231 On God-fearers in general the best introduction is to be found in Folker Siegert, *JSJ* 4 (1973) 109–64; also valuable are L. H. Feldman, *TAPhA* 81 (1950) 200–8; K. G. Kuhn, *s.v.* προσήλυτος, *TWNT* VI.727–45; *id.* and H. Stegemann, *s.v.* 'Proselyten', in *RE Supp.* IX (1962) cols. 1248–83; G. F. Moore, *Judaism* I.323–53; see also Dom Leclerq, *Dict. d'archéol. Chrét.* 8.1 (1928) cols. 110–19, *s.v.* 'Judaisme' section X,, 'Paiens-judaïsants'; Strack-Billerbeck, *Kommentar*, *cit.* n. 159, II.215–23 (*ad* Acts 13:16) and 715–16 (Billerbeck coined the term 'Halbproselyten', which seems to overstate the case); E. Schürer, *SDAW* (1897) 200ff.; *id.*, *Geschichte* III⁴.174ff.; Juster I.274ff.; F. M. Derwacter, *Preparing the way for Paul* (1930); Kirsopp Lake, *cit.* n. 177, 74–96; H. Hommel, *cit.* n. 208; A. T. Kraabel, *cit.* n. 178. On individual sources: K. Romaniuk, 'Die Gottesfürchtigen in neuen Testament', *Aegyptus* 44 (1964) 66–91; G. Theissen, *ZNTW* 65 (1974) 214ff.; E. Haenchen, *Die Apostelgeschichte* (1956) 291; R. Marcus, 'The sebomenoi in Josephus', *Jewish Social Studies* 14 (1952) 247–50; L. Robert, *NIS* 43–45. On *metuentes*: J. Bernays, *cit.* n. 176; Schürer–Vermes–Millar II.314–15; G. La Piana, *HThR* 20 (1927) 391ff.; M. Simon, *cit.* n. 159, 326ff.; Leon, *Jews* 253; L. H. Feldman, cited above in this note; H. Bellen, *cit.* n. 165, 171. On *theosebeis*, in addition to the epigraphic articles cited above, see Georg Bertram, *TWNT* III.124–8; K. G. Kuhn, *TWNT* VI.732–4, 741–3.

JEWISH INSTITUTIONS   75

232 Acts 10:2, cf. 10:31.
233 b AZ 51b (citing R. 'Aqiba', cf. m AZ 4.4); b AZ 52a, and 19b. See, on the whole question of the rabbinical attitude to Jewish art in the Roman period, E. E. Urbach, 'The rabbinical law of idolatry', *IEJ* 9 (1959) 149–65, 229–45, esp. 158–65; M. Avi-Yonah, 'L'hellénisme juif', in *VIIIe Congrès Internationale d'Archéologie Classique, le rayonnement des civilisations grecque et romaine sur les cultures périphériques* (1965) 611–15; *id.*, 'Jewish art', in *Encyclopaedia of World Art* VIII (1963) 898–920; J. Gutmann, 'The "second commandment" and the image of Judaism', *HUCA* 32 (1961) 161–74; cf. G. Foerster, 'Art and architecture in Palestine', in Safrai/Stern II.971–1006; J. Gutmann (ed.), *No graven image* (1977), *prolegomenon* xi–lxiii; H. Shanks, *Judaism in stone* (1979) 143–50.
234 b AZ 52a.
235 t Kel. BM 4.8.
236 y AZ 3.3 (MS version 3.2) dates the origin of wall-painting to the time of R. Yoḥanan (*c.* 250–80) and says the rabbis 'did not forbid it'.
237 *Mekh. de Rashbi* (ed. Epstein-Melammed), 222.
238 See n. 41; note also a ζωγράφος from the Jewish catacombs of the Via Appia in Rome (*CIJ* I.109), a reference to ζωγραφία in the synagogue at Sardis (L. Robert, *NIS* 49, 51), and the verb ζωγράφειν applied to a donor's decoration of the walls of the 'amphitheatre' (probably a meeting-hall) of the Jewish community of Berenice, perhaps of 8–6 B.C. (*CIG* III.5362; G. and J. Roux, 'Un décret des Juifs de Bérénike', *REG* 62 [1949] 285ff.; the most recent of subsequent publications is Lüderitz, *Cyrenaika* no. 70).
239 Alexandria, *PSI* 1160 (*SB* 7448, *CPJ* 150), cf. the letter of Claudius, *P. Lond.* 1912 (*SP* 212, *CPJ* 153, E. M. Smallwood, *Documents illustrating the principates of Gaius, Claudius and Nero* (1979) no. 376); H. Musurillo, *Acts of the pagan martyrs* (1954) 1ff., 83ff.; Ptolemais, *SB* 8671; Iasos, L. Robert, *REJ* 101 (n.s. 1) (1937) 73ff. and *Hellenica* III (1946) 106; Hypaepa, *CIJ* II.755; Cyrene, *SEG* 20.740, 741. Philo, *De spec. leg.* 2.229ff., 246, *De opif.* 78, *De Joseph.* 81, approves of athletics for Jews, and sees no harm in them; see H. A. Harris, *Ancient athletics and the Jews* (1976); also M. Poliakoff, 'Jacob, Job and other wrestlers: reception of Greek athletics by Jews and Christians in antiquity', *Journal of Sport History* 11 (1984) 48–65.
240 S. J. Lauffer, *Diokletians Preisedikt* (1971) ch. 4.
241 There is some doubt as to the likelihood of the presence of a *cohors Itala* in Judaea before A.D. 70: we hear of one in Syria in 69, but that is another matter, see Schürer–Vermes–Millar I.365; on the other hand M. P. Speidel, *Ancient Society* 13/14 (1982–3) 233–40 argues strongly for its presence in Judaea.
242 A. N. Sherwin-White, *Roman society and Roman law in the New Testament* (1963) 156, 160–1.
243 Josephus, *AJ* 14.209.
244 Schürer–Vermes–Millar I.363–5, Josephus, *AJ* 14.356–66; 17.266; 20.176; *id.*, *BJ* 2.52.58, 63 *et al.*
245 G. F. Moore, *Judaism* I.326.
246 b AZ 64b, Ger. 3.1.
247 b Sanh. 56a (cf. Gen.R., Noah 24.8).
248 b Sanh. 56b.
249 b AZ 64b, cf. Ger. 3.1.
250 On the Noachide Laws see S. Krauss, *cit.* n. 169.
251 Jacob Neusner, *Invitation to the Talmud* (1984) 37–8.
252 *Orac. Sib.* III.762–6, in J. H. Charlesworth (ed.), *O.T. Pseud.* I (1983).
253 Aristeas 6.27–30 (second century B.C.), IV Maccabees 1:33, 2:50f., 5:26 *et al.* (second century A.D.).
254 *XII Test.*, Levi 14.4, Napht. 3.4 (*et al.*).
255 Cf. E. P. Sanders, introduction to *Testament of Abraham*, in J. H. Charlesworth (ed.), *O.T. Pseud.* I.876–9.
256 *Conf.* 2.2, *Migr.* 89–93.
257 See Simon, *cit.* n. 159, 56–79.

258 Philo (citations in n. 256) refers occasionally to such people, implying that they are rare as well as repellent.
259 Pseudo-Phocylides 15–16, 51–2, 25, in P. van der Horst, *The sentences of Pseudo-Phocylides* = *Stud. in Vet. Test. Pseud.* 4 (1978).
260 Acts 15.
261 W. D. Davies, *Paul and Rabbinic Judaism*[2] (1955) 117–18; Kirsopp Lake and H. C. Cadbury, *cit.* n. 177, I.iv, *ad* Acts 15; F. Siegert, *cit.* n. 182, 133–4; Martin Dibelius, 'Das Apostelkonzil', *ThLZ* 72 (1947) cols. 193–8; B. Reicke, in *Studia Paulina, Festschrift J. d. Zwaan* (1953) 172–87. *Contra*: T. W. Manson, *Rylands Library Bulletin* 24 (1940) 21f.
262 Acts 15:29 (par. 21:55).
263 Leviticus 17:8; 16:13; 18:26.
264 Gunther Strothotte, *Das Apostelkonzil im Lichte der jüdischen Rechtsgeschichte* (1955).
265 I Cor. 5 and 8; see also I Cor. 6:6 and cf. I Cor. 5:10.
266 Juvenal, *Sat.* 14.96–101.
267 F. Siegert, *cit.* n. 182, 154.
268 Epictetus, *Diss.* 2.9.20.
269 So Joachim Durel, *Les instructions de Commodien* (1912) *ad loc.* (162 nn.).
270 Cf. Commod., *Carm. Apol.* 685–8:
   Immo cum recipiunt tales, docere deberent
   Seruire non aliis, nisi tantum summo placere.
On Commodian see K. Thraede, 'Beiträge zur Datierung Commodians', *Jb für Ant. u. Christent.* 2 (1959) 90–144; cf. Josef Martin, *Traditio* 13 (1957) 17, and *id., Commodiani Carmina* (*CCSL* LXXVIII) (1960) *praef.*: our quotations are from this edition.
271 *De ador.* 3.92.3 (= PG LXVIII, 281).
272 b Sanh. 74b–75a.
273 II Kgs. 5.17–18; b Sanh. 74b.
274 A. von Domaszewski, *Die Religion des römischen Heeres* (1895) 27–9; Graham Webster, *The Roman imperial army* (1969) 189–90, 268. The *Feriale Duranum* is the ritual calendar of an auxiliary unit (Cohors XXA Palmyrenorum) from the third century, naming purely Roman deities and festivals (R. O. Fink, A. S. Hoey and W. F. Snyder, 'The Feriale Duranum', *Yale Class. Stud.* 7 (1940) 1–222); many altars at the edge of parade-grounds have been found in Britain (Webster, 268), indicating that attendance of entire units at sacrifice is normal; auxiliary *cohortes* have, and worship, *signa* (von Domaszewski, fig. 86: cf. Daremberg-Saglio, s.v. *Signum*). The centurion at Capernaum mentioned, but not named, at Mt. 8:5 and Lk. 7:2 might be another example (he built a synagogue for the Jews), but might equally not be: he could be (or be thought to be) seconded to service with the forces of the Tetrarch Antipas, on whose territory Capernaum stood, where Roman military cult presumably would not be in vogue (cf. the Roman officers Rufus and Gratus, in the service of Herod and Archelaus [Jos. *BJ* 2.52, 17.266]).
275 F. Siegert, *cit.* n. 231, 163.
276 S. Lieberman, *Greek in Jewish Palestine* (1942) 87.
277 m Zeb. 4.5, t Zeb. 5.6; cf. t Zeb. 13.1, y Meg. 1.B.72b, b.Zeb. 116b, citing later authorities.
278 Siphra *ad* Lev. 22:18 (Weiss, p. 83b).
279 y Meg. 1.13.72b.
280 1.3.3, *Epit. Nepotiani*: 'Hispanus' is Broughton's correction for the 'Hispalus' of the text (*MRR* I.482).
281 *AJ* 14.260.
282 'The altars of the Gentiles', *RIDA* 3e sér. 5 (1958) = *id., Studies in Jewish and Christian History* II (1980) 335–6.
283 M. P. Nilsson, *Eranos* 54 (1956) 167ff.
284 So Bickerman (*cit.* n. 281) 341.
285 *Cit.* n. 282.
286 F. Cumont, *RE* IX.444–50; A. B. Cook, *Zeus* II.2, 876–90; III.2, 1162–3; G. Bertram, *TWNT* VIII.613f., 616f.; C. Roberts, T. C. Skeat and A. D. Nock, *HThR* 29 (1936) 39–88; A. T. Kraabel, *GRBS* 10 (1969) 81ff., and references cited there.

JEWISH INSTITUTIONS

287 E. L. Sukenik, *Ancient synagogues in Palestine and Greece* (1934) 38, Belle D. Mazur, *Studies on Jewry in Greece* I (1935) 15–24; Sukenik, *Bull.... Rabinowitz Fund* I (1949) 8–23.
288 LXX, II Chron. 5:6.
289 H. R. Balz, *TWNT* 9 (1973) 203.
290 On these questions see A. H. M. Jones, *The Greek city* (1940) 171, 176.
291 *Dig.* 50.2.3.3 quotes from the text.
292 L. Robert, *NIS* 54–7, now supplemented by A. R. Seager, *cit.* n. 221, 171; it seems clear that at least some of the inscriptions which were originally attributed to the third century are more probably of the fourth.
293 *CIJ* II.788; not dated.
294 L. Robert, *Hellenica* 10 (1955) 149–50 and 253 (*CIJ* II.770); probably third century A.D.
295 *Dig.*, *cit.* n. 290.
296 See F. F. Abbott and A. C. Johnson, *Municipal administration in the Roman empire* (1926) 62, 76, 79, 87.

IV HISTORICAL SIGNIFICANCE

What does this inscription tell us that is of importance to the history of Judaism? In studying this text, we have found that reasonable interpretations of terms that seemed impenetrably obscure in the Greek would emerge on confronting them with the terminology of the standard rabbinical sources. We have therefore felt encouraged to make a more extensive use of such sources to interpret a diaspora document than is usual in Jewish-Greek epigraphy. The case for doing so is that it works: a consistent and, we hope, reasonable interpretation has come out of it. We point this out not by way of methodological advice: the problems posed by this particular stone turned out to require this particular method; for other stones this may not be so. But there are historical deductions to be drawn from the fact that this method works for this stone.

It would appear that, by the early third century at least, there is greater institutional parallelism between the Greco-Roman diaspora and Palestine than has hitherto been thought: the diaspora does not go its own independent way. As the Pseudepigrapha indicate, some at least of the Jews of the western diaspora are free to invent their own stoicizing/Platonizing *interpretatio Graeca* of Biblical theology. The authors of the *Constitutiones Apostolicae*, a fourth-century Christian work, appear to have borrowed several chapters (7.33–7)[1] from a lost Jewish-Greek prayer-book of (apparently) the second century A.D., which took a stoicizing view of God's nature and functions. A prayer-book may reasonably be thought to have been intended for liturgical use: ch. 39 reproduces the scheme of the *Qedusha* preserved in the present synagogue liturgy, which is believed to go back to the second century A.D.[2] This raises the possibility that a stoicizing version of Jewish theology appeared in at least some synagogue prayer-books in the Greek-speaking diaspora. In that case, the philosophical Judaism we know from the Pseudepigrapha could represent the creed of an unknown proportion of the communities in the western diaspora, and not just the opinions of hellenizing intellectuals.

Our new epigraphic evidence from Aphrodisias suggests that the western diaspora is, however, more or less at one with Palestine, by the late second to early third centuries, as to the requirements of the Law. To what degree? In some details the conformation is exact: for others we do not know, and will try

HISTORICAL SIGNIFICANCE   79

to guess. The parallelism between πάτελλα and תמחוי (tamḥui), for one, seems precise. The other possible parallels are less compelling. There are too many possible Hebrew translations of δεκανία for us to be sure what the word means: it might be a translation of a specifically rabbinical term, but it might also be a common Greek word for a society. As an association the decany could be an old diaspora institution and not a rabbinical novelty. On the other hand, φιλομαθεῖς, like other such words in Jewish Greek inscriptions, may translate the rabbinic *talmidei ḥakhamim* ('disciples of the sages'), but need not necessarily do so (Philo, who shows relatively little Pharisaic influence, uses it extensively).[3] Παντευλογ(οῦντες) might translate a liturgical term of rabbinical literature (*mebarekhim*), but, again, could be a Greek neologism for those who continually pray. None of these possibilities is therefore a clear demonstration of rabbinic influence: if there is Palestinian influence in them it could be much older, or we could be dealing with parallel evolution. The resemblances, however, demonstrate something else: whether by recent contact or by long association, by at least the third century Jews in Asia Minor think in the same institutional and educational terms, and organise associations for the pursuit of the same goals, along the same lines, as their co-religionists in Palestine. The Jews of Aphrodisias do not appear to be semi-pagan syncretists,[4] nor astrolators nor angel-worshippers nor proto-Gnostics: they are not sectarians at all, if we are to judge them by what they actually do.

The Mishnaic requirement that every community must have a soup-kitchen is met in Caria – if our interpretation of *a*, l. 1 is correct, and our dating of face *a* as contemporary with face *b* is accepted – early in the third century. The soup-kitchen is given its Mishnaic name and not some special and more comprehensible Jewish–Greek name: a hospice for travellers in a Greek-speaking synagogue at Jerusalem was called ξενών, for example;[5] this makes sense in Greek, as πάτελλα does not. In the latter case, for some reason, fidelity to the original is important. No one in the diaspora, however, can be confidently expected to read Hebrew: the Bible translations of Aquila, Theodotion and Symmachus, all made in the previous century, were more literal versions of the Hebrew than the Septuagint, whose errors had been used to support Christian theological claims in polemic (e.g. the Virgin birth). The official backing for new translations (Aquila's was encouraged by the Palestinian rabbis) seems to imply that large numbers of the Greek-speaking synagogues would be unable to check the accuracy of the Septuagint against the original Hebrew themselves. But the ignorance of Hebrew at Aphrodisias seems to have been thought to be such that no attempt was made to transliterate *tamḥui* (e.g. ?ταμεχωι), in the way in which Eustathius the *theosebes* transliterated the Aramaic word for wash basin (producing τὸν μασκαυλήν) when he gave one to a synagogue near Lydian Philadelphia.[6] *Tamḥui* is, in Aphrodisias, translated literally, with the kind of awkward literalness we often find in Aquila, from the Mishnaic Hebrew: Now Mishnaic Hebrew is almost certainly not the spoken language of Palestine by the third century: it was probably spoken in the south of Palestine as late as the time of the Bar Kokhba revolt alongside Aramaic (in what relationship we cannot define).[7] There were, however, as the aftermath of that revolt, very few Jews left in Judaea proper; the great majority were in Galilee, where they spoke Aramaic and/or Greek. Mishnaic Hebrew was, nevertheless, the spoken and written language of one class of Palestinians, i.e. Tanna'itic rabbis and their disciples. Now we know that the decany initiated the erection (not rebuilding or refurbishing) of the 'soup-kitchen', since they use the word ἔκτισαν, not ἐπεσκεύασαν or κατεσκεύασαν or the like. Therefore the 'soup-kitchen' now appears in the Aphrodisias community for the first time. A soup-kitchen is required of every community by Mishnaic law. Who has apprised the community of their (apparently previously unknown, perhaps previously ignored or insufficiently actualized) responsibility under this law? Presumably the same person who told them what the institution was called, translating literally from Mishnaic Hebrew. It is not a necessary conclusion (other explanations for this odd translation could be found), but it is clearly possible, that the person with the necessary knowledge to do this was a Palestinian, or Palestinian-trained, rabbi (or one trained in one of the, still very few, rabbinical academies elsewhere).

According to other evidence this is entirely possible. After the collapse of the Bar Kokhba revolt, and after the withdrawal of the subsequent persecution, in the reign either of Antoninus Pius or of Marcus Aurelius, the imperial government recognised either Rabban Simon II ben Gamaliel II, head of the principal rabbinical academy in Galilee, or his successor Rabbi Yehudah I, as hereditary *Nasi'* (נשיא), 'prince' (in the gentile world, ethnarch or patriarch). This title was granted in token of his position as a kind of native religious and legal authority, roughly analogous to the pre-A.D. 70 high priest, *vis-à-vis* the Jews of Palestine. That his authority may have been thought to extend to (or at least that his prestige was recognised in) the diaspora in the time of Simon II *might* be attested by the inscription of Stobi, in which anyone contravening the terms of the donation would be liable to pay a fine to the patriarch; but, just as Hengel has shown that it is *the* patriarch, not some regional authority, who is involved, he has also shown that the date of this inscription is probably the late third century.[8]

Simon II's son, however, Yehudah ha-Nasi', greatly expanded the powers of the Hillelite (patriarchal) dynasty, claiming the right to appoint or depose any communal official in Palestine or in the diaspora.[9] We learn from a Church father that the patriarch sent out his ranking associates on the rabbinical High Court (*Beth Din ha-Gadol*, much later called *Sanhedrin*) as ἀπόστολοι, emissaries, to collect taxes and to inspect, and if necessary depose, communal officers, whom they could remove for inadequacy.[10] Eusebius says that such men carry encyclical letters.[11] The Theodosian Code records the activity of these *apostoli*;[12] it is clear that they are a feature of fourth-century diaspora life.[13] We have reason to believe that much of this was the case by the time of Yehudah ha-Nasi' (*c*. 170 to *c*. 225). We know from the rabbinical sources that he sent out emissaries to the diaspora, with what title we are never told, but the usual Mishnaic Hebrew word for a deputy, commissioner, representative or agent sent out with full powers, in the rabbinic literature, is שליח, *shaliah* (in the Aramaic texts *sheliah*).[14] These emissaries were men of high rank from his *Beth-Din*.[15] R. Hiyya' bar 'Abba' went to Syria, Babylonia and Rome;[16] he laid down any needed regulations (*takkanoth*), collected money, and appointed heads of communities.[17] R. Me'ir, who was the patriarch Yehudah's teacher, had served as *Hakham* (i.e. chairman) of the great *Beth-Din*; his version of the rules of the oral law (Me'ir's Mishnah) became the basis of Yehudah's definitive version of the Mishnah. He seems, at the end of his career, to have been sent, either by Simon II or (just possibly) by Yehudah, to Asia, where he announced the intercalary month.[18] It has been suggested that עסיא, '*Asiya*', in the text need not mean Asia, but could mean a southern port, Etzion Geber, on the Gulf of Akaba;[19] however, it is said that R. Me'ir died in '*Asiya*', and asked for his coffin to be put on the shore, to be washed by the sea that touches the Land of Israel, until his body could be transported there.[20] It does not matter that the anecdote could be fictional; what matters is that the fourth-century 'amora' who wrote it down thought that '*Asiya*' is washed by a sea that touches the soil of the Land of Israel: Etzion-Geber is itself on the only corner of modern Israel that is touched by the waters of the Gulf of Akaba; that in the third century it could have been thought to be part of Israel, rather than of Edom, is practically impossible.[21] The redactor is therefore thinking of the Mediterranean and of the area of the Roman province of Asia. Rabbi Me'ir's presence there, to announce an intercalary month (carrying an encyclical letter, presumably, from the patriarch, who alone had the power to proclaim one), is confirmed by the Tosephta, at most a generation or so after the event.[22] Me'ir could, apparently, speak Greek, since he is said to have been friendly with the Greek philosopher *Avnimos ha-Gardi*, usually taken to be Oenomaus of Gadara, a Cynic philosopher of the reign of Hadrian.[23]

The chances are therefore good that Me'ir was a patriarch's apostle in Asia. What are the chances that he visited Caria in general and Aphrodisias specifically? Fair: a *shaliah*, as it was his duty to inspect the communities and collect their money, would have looked in on as many as possible in his area: Epiphanius, early in the fourth century, says the ἀπόστολος collects from every city in Cilicia.[24] What are the chances that Me'ir came to Aphrodisias early in the third century? Not, from an actuarial point of view, very good, but just barely possible: being a pupil of R. 'Aqiba"'s, Me'ir must have been a grown man at the time of the Bar Kokhba War: he might have seen out the second century and lived into the early third: he came to Asia at the end of his life. But the fact that Me'ir came to Asia, even if he did so in the generation before our inscription, proves that the patriarchs sent emissaries of the first importance to western Anatolia. One of them could have, and by the nature of this office should have, visited Aphrodisias towards the beginning of the third century.

What would he have done there? He would have accepted the *aurum coronarium* and the ἀποστολή, the two patriarchal levies on Jews of which we hear from patristic and Roman law sources; but he would also have advised on intractable legal problems brought to him by the community's judges (presumably the archons or the full community council), or brought to him by individuals; he would have made new regulations for the community where needed; he would have checked the competence and suitability of the synagogue officials and removed the unworthy; he would have attended and observed the synagogue service (our sources do not say so because it goes without saying); he ought to have checked the ritual institutions (ritual bath, slaughterers, etc.), to see that they were sound, the educational and charitable institutions (school, hospice, soup-kitchen), to see that they were up to the mark. He ought to have done these things because he was the representative of the man who was in the process of drawing up the definitive Mishnah where all these things are required of a Jewish community. It is in this context that the introduction of a soup-kitchen, labelled with an over-literal translation of a Mishnaic name, might best be imagined.

What then do we observe in Aphrodisias in the early third century? The beginning of the imposition of rabbinical orthodoxy on occidental Jewry, perhaps. For of course what *shaluhim* would be doing all over the Roman world would be the same, since they would all emanate, thanks to the blessing of the Roman state, from the same source, and the patriarch claimed authority over western Jewry as well. The patriarch seems to seek, and we must assume that he gets, uniformity of institutions, at least, from Gades to Charax. Why not uniformity of liturgy and of law? That would be more difficult. Outside Palestine and Babylonia-Iran (and, no doubt, some parts of Syria) nearly all Jews speak Greek; their Bible is in Greek,[25] their services are held in Greek,[26] according to Greek prayer-books, some (how many?) philosophically oriented as we have seen. Uniformity of liturgy and law would have been achieved by the imposition of compulsory Hebrew education for all, but that seems not to have been accomplished until the fourth, fifth and sixth centuries A.D., the beginning of our papyrological and epigraphical evidence of the widespread employment of Hebrew west of the land of Israel. Without a knowledge of Hebrew, there would be no uniformity of law: *shaluḥim* can try to prevent the worst deviations from orthodoxy, but how often can they visit, for example, Aphrodisias? Whatever the answer, they could not stay for long on each occasion, for there were too many communities to visit. They cannot have left books behind, for no one could read the Hebrew in which they were written. It seems possible that the Mishnah was not written down, or at least not publicly circulated outside the rabbinic academies, until the completion of the Talmudim (*c*. A.D. 400–600).[27] St Augustine still says that the *deuterosis* of the Jews is passed on by word of mouth, not written down.[28] Then how can the people follow the Law? Only if there is a rabbi among them who knows the Law by heart. But in order to have rabbis one must have *yeshiboth* to train them. We know that there were rabbis in Egypt in the second century A.D.; they put twelve questions to R. Joshua b. Ḥananiah, a Palestinian sage of early second century date.[29] But Egypt, like Sidon, where we also find rabbis in the second century,[30] is close enough to Palestine to be supplied initially with rabbis from there, and may soon have had *yeshiboth* of its own, as Sidon did:[31] our information concerns Alexandria; it does not assure us that rabbis control all communities in the city; it does not tell us what happened in the rest of Egypt, or when. But we do have papyrological evidence of a knowledge of Hebrew in the communities of upper Egypt *c*. A.D. 400: fragments of official letters to or from the heads of communities, in Hebrew,[32] found in Oxyrhynchus, which was not an important Jewish centre; this would authorise us to believe that a knowledge of Hebrew is widespread among Jews throughout Egypt by this date. Another fragment provides a text that parallels, but does not reproduce, part of the text of the Mishnah:[33] this might be from a rabbi's or a student's private notes,[34] and if so would be evidence of the study of the Mishnah. Dated in the fourth century are fragments (still from Oxyrhynchus) of *piyyutim*, liturgical and devotional poems in Hebrew.[35] The Jerusalem Talmud shows Palestinian '*Amora'im* of the early fourth century active in Alexandria, either in person or in written responses to legal consultation by Alexandrian rabbis.[36]

But what of the world further away from Palestine? It must have taken several centuries to fill the Roman world with rabbis. There are a R. Theudas and a R. Matya b. Ḥeresh in Rome in the second century A.D., the latter known to have emigrated from Palestine after the Bar Kokhba War, and to have founded a *yeshibah* in the imperial city.[37] In Venosa, in a catacomb which is thought to date to the fifth or sixth century, a Latin inscription refers to two *rebbites*;[38] if two rabbis are to be found in, or are visiting, a community as unimportant as that, rabbinism has taken over in Italy. There are Hebrew epitaphs at Tortosa, in Spain, and at Venosa, in the sixth century.[39] It appears to be in the early Byzantine period that Jews begin to call themselves Ἑβραῖοι rather than Ἰουδαῖοι.[40] The process of bringing orthodoxy to the Roman world must have been greatly facilitated by the written Mishnah (by c. A.D. 400, the publication date of the Jerusalem Talmud), which, in turn, may have lent additional urgency to the drive for universal Hebrew education.

By the sixth century the written Mishnah was sufficiently well-known in Constantinople for Justinian to forbid the teaching of the *deuterosis*,[41] so it is clear that Jews had been trained to read Hebrew from their youth in order to study it (the emperor was settling a dispute between those who wanted the scripture to be read in the synagogue in Hebrew and those who wished to retain Greek; the former appear to predominate, since the latter have to appeal to the crown). From that point on we may clearly speak of rabbinical orthodoxy in the west. The beginning of the process, the first reception of the Mishnah, we are now perhaps able to observe in Aphrodisias. If so, if what we see there is the hand of the Roman-appointed patriarch at work through his ἀπόστολος, then Judaism imposed unitary religious belief and practice on its adherents in the same way as Christianity did a century later – by the power of the Roman imperial state.

What, however, if this inscription (at least face *a*) hails from the fifth or sixth century A.D., rather than the early third? The earlier date seems to us markedly more probable, but probability is not proof; the possibility of a later date cannot be ruled out. The consequences would, in that case, be as follows:

Where, at *a*, l. 7, we have taken the use of κτίζω to indicate the introduction of the πάτελλα, with a later dating this becomes problematic: Aphrodisian inscriptions of the later Empire show a tendency to use κτίζω of buildings that seem, archaeologically, to be re-erections of earlier constructions,[42] or perhaps 'new' buildings cannibalized from older buildings of the same kind, e.g. baths.[43] The πάτελλα could be a reconstructed building of this kind, and ἔκτισαν could mean 're-built'. In that case we would have no idea when the institution was first introduced at Aphrodisias. By the fifth or sixth century we should imagine that the Jews there might know enough Hebrew to use the Hebrew word *tamḥui* on the stone, either in Hebrew letters or Greek transliteration, but they might equally well want to keep a by now traditional Greek version of the term for the 'new' building. The appearance of πάτελλα here would, therefore, tell us nothing about the date or circumstances of the imposition of rabbinical orthodoxy in Caria. On the other hand, the consonance of the terminology of Jewish associations between face *a* (the decany) and the Jerusalem and Babylonian Talmuds (the *ḥaburoth*), as well as with later Jewish associations, would be more significant, since the Jerusalem Talmud was completed by *c.* A.D. 400, the Babylonian by *c.* 500–600. The terminology and purposes of the decany could, in that case, be the result of direct Talmudic influence: we can imagine the presence of a rabbi permanently in Aphrodisias by this date, laying down the Law in detail; his absence from the membership-list of the decany need not weigh against his existence; medieval rabbis did not belong to the charitable associations of their synagogues either. Why, however, if there is a rabbi armed with a Talmud, or at least a Mishnah (Justinian's δευτέρωσις?), in the community, he should permit the decany to bear a purely Greek title, is difficult to understand, although not impossible to imagine (the hebraization of this community's institutions is just getting under way?). A late date is also not untenable for the God-fearers and proselytes on face *a*. It was illegal, under various laws of the Christian emperors,[44] to become a Jewish proselyte, the punishment being death for convert and convertor alike. Soon, however, this only applied to converts from Christianity:[45] pagan converts were still forbidden to circumcise by the laws of the Principate, never abrogated, but as there is no mention of the subject in the Theodosian Code, we may assume it was not regarded as a problem in the Christian Empire: these laws may have been a dead letter; the government might not have cared whether pagans became Jews. If so, it is entirely possible that some pagans, barred by the decrees of Theodosius I[46] from engaging in public or private cult of the old gods, would have preferred to join in the synagogue service rather than in the rites of the Church, since the Jewish worship was at least ancient and traditional, and was not identified with the persecuting state. If this were so, some pagans might go so far as to convert to Judaism, but not many; by the fifth or sixth centuries the rabbis would be enforcing circumcision for proselytes on whatever communities (if any) had been willing to accept mere baptism. Therefore the great majority of new adherents would be God-fearers. There are no late Roman laws forbidding this: so much is clear not just from their absence from the Theodosian Code (which is, of course, an incomplete record of imperial constitutions), but also from St John Chrysostom's sermons[47] against Christians who frequented the synagogues of Antioch on holy days in the late fourth century, which make no mention of the illegality, at that date, of such a practice. Chrysostom says that the Jews welcome them to the synagogue and encourage them to return; they must, in Jewish eyes, be the equivalent of God-fearers;[48] that they also go to church would be equated to the behaviour of the pagans, who also worshipped at the shrines of the gods. The canons of the Council of Laodicea, in the second half of the fourth century, include strictures against judaizing Christians;[49] the 38th canon forbids participation in Jewish rites. Consequently it is possible that some or many of the God-fearers on our list are (if the inscription is late) Christians (although in that case we would expect more Christian names), and, in any case, if Christians can attend Jewish services with impunity, *a fortiori* pagans can. The supply of pagans, however, would soon dry up: John of Ephesus reported his success in a Christian missionary tour of Asia, Caria, Lydia and Phrygia in 542, where he baptised eighty thousand pagans and Jews;[50] perhaps some of the latter (perhaps some of both) were God-fearers.

But if (as we think probable) the stone, on *both* faces, is early third century, how are we to interpret the list of God-fearers? After we have got over the surprise of finding so many of them, how shall we explain it? It may be that Judaism, in the watered-down form available to a God-fearer, was in this period much more attractive to pagans than we had thought up to now, and was, consequently, a more formidable rival to Christianity. We have already noted that ordinary craftsmen, tradesmen or workmen appear on our list of *theosebeis*; three fullers, a plasterer(?), a carpenter, one, perhaps two, smiths, and so on.[51] On this list, there may be as many as nineteen names to which trade-designations are attached, of which as many as eleven may be workmen, and two are artist-craftsmen, while one man may give his occupation as ἀρκά(ριος) (b. l. 56), another as πυ(λωρός) (b. l. 50), both possibly performing slave's jobs in a large household.[52] Therefore not only the philosophically-inclined are attracted to Judaism, by its monotheism and its appeal (in its Greek form) to abstract reason and the laws of nature; simple working men, too, indeed perhaps slaves, are drawn to the synagogue, by what? We can only speculate. Presumably it was the same things that drew such men and women to the oriental Mystery cults, or to Christianity, in that guilt-ridden age: a promise of immortality, of divine forgiveness for the contrite, of eventual salvation for the righteous. Also in the case of Judaism perhaps men were drawn by the very element of its teaching that we had always thought would most repel the curious pagan, the Law, a detailed guide to life that would leave one in no doubt as to what was to be done and what was to be avoided on all occasions, thereby relieving ethical anxiety to no small degree. In fact, however, the God-fearer could be guided by the Law to whatever degree he chose and no more (so our evidence seems to indicate), so that the Law could be a refuge, but never a burden. In this sense the Torah could have seemed a light to the gentiles.

We ought not to overlook, in this connection, what at first glance seems a material consideration, that Jewish obsession with charity of which the present inscription is one example. It is possible that some of the pagan poor attended the synagogue simply to be fed: Greek cities had no permanent arrangements for feeding the indigent (Rhodes, perhaps also Samos, seem to have been exceptions; in other cities there were distributions of money, but only at festivals, of food, but only at festivals and in famines).[53] Julian the Apostate wrote of the rôle of charity in favouring the reputation of Christians at the expense of pagans:[54] organised Christian charity appears to have been inspired by the existing charitable institutions of Jewish communities. But there is more to this than the need for food and shelter. The extraordinary proliferation of associations in the Greek cities, in the Hellenistic and Greco-Roman periods, has long been taken as a sign of the sentiment of individual isolation that seems endemic in complex urban societies. Men feel the need to belong to something larger than the nuclear family, less impersonal than the city; they feel the need to be part of a community. The Jewish communities looked after the physical needs of the unfortunate, but also, by the same token, they would have fulfilled the social needs of the prosperous, in a more all-embracing way than the trade-clubs and cult-associations of the pagan world: Jewish communities were proverbially tight-knit; to this day it is axiomatic among gentiles that the Jews look after their own. Jewish 'clannishness' could have looked very different to outsiders offered an opportunity to join the clan. The attractions of this close community life, this devotion to the idea of mutual aid, must have been the same as those exercised by the early Christian communities, the success of which we know.

We have mentioned the Mysteries, and indeed these aid us in understanding the position of the God-fearers in the synagogue. Vidman has pointed out[55] that initiation in the Mysteries, in the imperial age, was an expensive undertaking, so that Mystery adepts would in practice be members of exclusive clubs. As Nock remarks,[56] however, it was only in Mithraism that the initiates were co-extensive with the worshippers in a Mystery cult. Worshippers who were not *mystae*, we may assume, could attend public cult in the temples of Isis or Cybele or the like, could pray, could have a priest offer a sacrifice for them, could receive oracles, in a word could be present at and take part in all the usual pagan temple rites, but could not be privy to the Mysteries. The position is roughly that of catechumens in the Christian Church, who may attend church services, but not receive communion: we will remember that, in the fourth century A.D., when baptism was often delayed until maturity or the point of death, catechumens were a large proportion of the congregation in the churches. So it was, it seems, with the God-fearers in the synagogues; they are the outer circle, who may attend services and join in prayer, the Jews are the inner circle, the equivalent of initiates, who alone can read the scriptures to the assembly and comment on their meaning. Do God-fearers delay full conversion, including circumcision, until old age, as later Christians delayed baptism? Since circumcision was illegal, this could be one way of avoiding the full rigour of the law, but we have no evidence that this was ever done. It would, of course, be interesting to trace the historical connections between Mystery non-initiates, synagogue God-fearers, and Christian catechumens, but we are unable to imagine what evidence would point the way: who is imitating whom? The Christians, presumably, come last, but following which example?[57] What is clear, however, is that the 'of-but-not-in' stance of God-fearers towards Judaism was not an anomaly in Greco-Roman antiquity, but a familiar religious posture.

The adoption by the Greeks and Romans of oriental religions reciprocates the absorption by oriental élites of the culture of the Greeks, in the Hellenistic and Greco-Roman periods. What took place was, in a sense, an exchange of the 'higher' (more intellectually stimulating) culture for the 'higher' (more spiritually satisfying) religion. But how could the latter be practicable when Jewish religion was exclusivist (God insisted on having no other gods beside Him) and legalist (613 commandments at least)? What was needed was an adaptation of Judaism to pagan sensibilities. Such adaptations of oriental religions to Greek taste were common: they were adaptations made by Greeks, selectively stripping away whatever was repellent or bizarre, from an occidental point of view, and retaining the mysterious, the mystical and the exotic: Iranian religion without incestuous marriage, for example. Add a few popular aspects of Greek religion (e.g. the mystery initiation) and one has produced an oriental Mystery cult. This, of course, was never done with Judaism, with the possible exception of obscure syncretist groups like the Hypsistarii of Asia Minor and Tanais, who are most probably Greeks inventing a congenial adaptation of Judaism, doubtless with no encouragement from the Jews. Nevertheless the status of God-fearer, permitting the pagan to take an interest in Judaism without necessarily giving up his paganism, allowing him (apparently) to follow such Jewish laws and customs as he liked and to ignore all others, removed what was most repellent to the Greeks in Judaism. The theology and ethics of the stoicizing/Platonizing Pseudepigrapha provided the element of hellenization, in this case borrowing from Greek philosophy, which could make such an amalgam attractive, as well as non-repellent, to the Greek mind. These were Judaism's substitute for a mystery cult, and Judaism's entry in the race for the soul of the Roman empire.

Such are the possibilities raised by the high proportion of God-fearers on this inscription. Yet our evidence may not, in fact, point to conclusions of this kind. For so high a proportion of *theosebeis* is the reverse of the norm suggested by other Jewish inscriptions: in Rome, out of over five hundred Jewish funerary inscriptions, five refer to *theosebeis* (but they were found outside the catacombs, on the surface, where a much higher proportion of stones would be subject to re-use and consequently either wear or destruction); in Sardis, the great synagogue has yielded over eighty inscriptions, of which only six of those published so far refer to *theosebeis* (but most of the Sardian inscriptions are from individual donors of particular decorations in the building, which are more expensive than contributions to a building fund: this could skew the evidence). Therefore we need either special conditions in Rome and Sardis, or others in

Aphrodisias, to account for the discrepancy. In Aphrodisias the evidence may be skewed by conditions of time. If we again compare the phenomenon of the God-fearers to that of the oriental Mysteries in Asia and west of the Aegean, the latter appear in the literary record only in the first century A.D.; the second and third centuries see the appearance of inscriptions in significant quantity.[58] This is not unlikely to be a measure of the increasing popularity of the Mystery religions during the course of the principate: it indicates an intensification of interest in salvationist religion. The same, *mutatis mutandis*, ought to apply to pagan interest in Judaism. References to God-fearers occur from *c.* 200 B.C. (cf. p. 65). We know from the Book of Acts that there were God-fearers in many of the synagogues where Paul preached in the first century A.D., but our epigraphic evidence for θεοσεβεῖς does not begin until the second, and we now have a sizeable proportion of them in the Aphrodisian community in the early third. If this is the correct chronological sequence then we should be less surprised by the high proportion of God-fearers in our inscription; also, perhaps, less surprised by the acquisition in the third century by the Sardis community (see p. 21) of an unusually large synagogue (? to accommodate an increase in God-fearers), and certainly very careful about retrojecting this proportion to, say, the synagogues visited by Paul in the first century.

Finally, it is entirely possible that the discrepancy in numbers between God-fearers in Aphrodisias and elsewhere is an epigraphical one. Ours is the only list of its sort to be recovered from the ancient diaspora, whereas the inscriptional evidence elsewhere is from individual epitaphs and donations. A long list is an inclusive form of evidence, but epitaphs and donors' inscriptions are a scattered form, subject to archaeological chance: comparison between them cannot, perhaps, yield significant results. In that case, the proportion of God-fearers to Jews in Aphrodisias may not be atypical. We stress 'may': we are unable to speak of probability, in this connection.

What does, however, seem clear from our analysis of some of the other evidence for God-fearers is this: Commodian's polemical poems of the third century, seeking to persuade God-fearers to join the Church, John Chrysostom's sermons on judaizing Christians in the fourth century, the canons of the Council of Laodicea in the same century, forbidding Christians to attend synagogues, all indicate that the Church and the Synagogue are fighting over the same bodies, from the time of St Paul on.[59] Both seek not only to attract pagans, but to attract each other's new recruits. In this context it seems reasonable to take our inscription as possible evidence that Judaism was, by the third century, not only a rival, but a dangerous rival, to Christianity. This clearly has some bearing on the development of Christian antisemitism.

As for the implications of this Jewish inscription from Aphrodisias for the history of Christianity itself, *qui tacet, valet*.

NOTES

1 See *PG* I.1024–35.
2 On the Jewish source for this part of the *Const. Apostol.*, see M. Simon, *Verus Israel* (1964) 74–81.
3 Leisegang, *Index Verb.*, *s.v.*
4 As in G. Kittel, 'Das kleinasiatische Judentum in der hellenistischen-römischen Zeit', *TLZ* 69 (1944) 9–20; cf. F. Blanchetière, 'Juifs et non-Juifs: essai sur la diaspora en Asie-Mineure', *RPHR* 54 (1974) 367–82. A. T. Kraabel has therefore now been confirmed on this point, see *GRBS* 10 (1969) 81ff.
5 *Donateurs* 79 (*CIJ* II.1404).
6 *Donateurs* 28 (*CIJ* II.754).
7 Ch. Rabin, 'Hebrew and Aramaic in the first century', in Safrai/Stern II.1007–39; J. A. Emerton, *JThS* 24 (1973) 1–24.
8 *Donateurs* 10 (*CIJ* I.694); M. Hengel, 'Die Synagogeninschrift von Stobi', *ZNW* (1961) 145–83.
9 b Gitt. 59a, Gen.R. 49.10, cf. y Yeb. 12.7.13a, Gen. R. 81.1.
10 Epiphanius, *Adv. haer.* 30.4.11 (*PG* 41.409); cf. Pall. *Dial.* p. 90; Origen, *de princ.* 4.1.
11 Eusebius, *In Isaiam* 18.1f. (*PG* 24.213).
12 *C. Th.* 16.8.14 (A.D. 399), see A. H. M. Jones, *The later Roman empire* (1973) II.945.
13 On the *Nasi* see H. Mantel, *Studies in the history of the Sanhedrin* (1961); *id., HThR* 60 (1967) 90; S. Baron, *Social and economic history of the Jews*² II (1952) 191–209; v (1957) 38–46, 314; L. I. Levine, 'The Jewish patriarch (Nasi) in third century Palestine', *ANRW* II.19.2 (1979) 659–88; M. Goodman, *State and society in Roman Galilee* (1982) 112ff.
14 M. J. Jastrow, *Dictionary of the Targumim, the Talmud, etc.*, *s.v.*
15 b Meg. 18b (R. Me'ir); y Ḥag. 1.8.76b (R. Ḥiyya bar 'Abba').
16 y Meg. 3.1.74a (Syria); b Ber. 15a *et al.* (Babylonia); y M. Sh. 4.1.54d (Rome).
17 y Pe'ah 8.7.21a. On the office and duties of the *shaliaḥ*, see S. Krauss, 'Die jüdische Apostel', *JQR* 17 (1904–5) 370–83, still outstanding; H. Vogelstein, 'Die Entstehung und Entwicklung des Apostolats im Judentum', *MGWJ* 49 (1905) 427–9, and *id.,* 'The development of the Apostolate in Judaism and its transformation in Christianity', *HUCA* II (1925) 99–123, still questionable.
18 b Meg. 18b.
19 A. Oppenheimer, *Encycl. Jud.* XI (1971) 1241, *s.v.* 'Meir', citing Klein (ed.), *Sefer ha-Yishuv* (1939), *s.v.*
20 y Kil. 9.4.32c.
21 See tg Yer. and tg Ps.-Jon. *ad Num.* 34: 3–5; tg Onkelos *ad Num.* 24:14; m Git. 1.1; cf. A. Neubauer, *La géographie du Talmud* (1868) 11, 17, 21, app. II.
22 t Meg. 2.5.
23 S. Lieberman, in A. Altman (ed.), *Biblical and other studies* (1963) 129–30; b Hag. 15b, y Hag. 2.1.77b.
24 *Adv. haer.* 30.11.
25 When R. Me'ir was in Asia (late second century?), he found that there was no Hebrew text of Esther for him to read from in the synagogue service at Purim (t Meg. 2.5): this means that there was no complete Hebrew bible in whatever town he found himself in at the time. Writing and reading the bible in Greek are specifically permitted by the rabbis: whether, however, this was permitted in any other foreign language was a subject of debate (m Meg. 1.8, 2.1).
26 Better to have prayed in Greek than not to have prayed at all (y Sot. 7.1): see m Sot. 7.1–21 for earlier and more elaborate rulings.
27 S. Lieberman, *Hellenism in Jewish Palestine* (1950) 91ff.; H. Strack, *Introduction to Talmud and Midrash* (1931; repr. 1980) ch. 2.2; *contra,* H. Albeck, *Mavo' la Mishnah* (1960) = *id., Einführung in die Mischnah* (1971) 163–70. G. F. Moore suggests (*Judaism* I.98), probably correctly, that evidence for notebooks in the possession of individual scholars shows that notes

for private study and preparation were permissible, but manuscripts were not permitted in the classroom or court, and did not exist officially.
28 Augustine, *Adv. leg. et proph.* 2.1.2.
29 b Nidd. 69b: S. Lieberman ('Response to the introduction by Prof. Alexander Marx', *Rabbinical Assembly Proceedings* XII [1948] = Judah Goldin (ed.), *The Jewish expression* [1970] 121 n.) says that the idiom employed shows that the *baraita* is authentic. See also t Ket. 3.1, 4.9 and parallels, Alexandrian rabbis consulting the Palestinian *Beth Din ha-Gadol* before c. 225; and cf. y Yeb. 7.5, Ket. 4.6, Kid. 3.14. The tradition that Egyptian Jews brought religious questions to the sages and Hillel, their head, handed down solutions (t Kel. 4.9; y Yeb. 15.1; b BM 104a) may be a fictional retrojection of the power of the *Nasi'* to the time of the ancestor of the patriarchal house: cf. Gamaliel I sitting on the Temple Mount and dictating intercalary letters to the diaspora, at a time when the High Priesthood was still functioning (t Sanh. 2.2).
30 m AZ 3.7, Gitt. 4.7; t Nidd. 4.6.
31 t AZ 1.8, Nidd. 6.6, Par. 4.9.
32 A. J. Cowley, 'Notes on Hebrew papyrus fragments from Oxyrhynchos', *JEA* 2 (1915) 209ff., see also *CPJ* I, *Proleg.* 101–2 for text and discussion.
33 Cowley, *cit.* n. 32, 211; *CPJ* I, *Proleg.* 106.
34 See n. 27, *supra.*
35 De Boer, *VT* I (1951) 49ff. (for date see 57, n. 1).
36 y 'Erub. 3.21c, Kid. 3.64d.
37 b Pes. 53a–b (Theudas); b Sanh, 32b (Matya b. Ḥeresh).
38 *CIJ* I.611 and p. 439, n.
39 *CIJ* I.661 (Tortosa); *ibid.* 569–71, 584, 593–6, 599, 611, not counting several that consist simply of *shalom* (Venosa). Cf. *ibid.* 620–2 at Tarentum, said by Frey to resemble those from Venosa, and perhaps of the same date, and *ibid.* 633 from Bari, of which the same is said.
40 R. Mouterde, *Mel. Univ. Beyrouth* 17 (1933) 209–20; the possible explanations for this, however, are various and it may bear no relation to the use of the Hebrew language.
41 Justinian, *Nov.* 146 (A.D. 553): consult S. Krauss, *Studien zur byzantinisch-jüdische Geschichte* (1914) 61–2.
42 See the forthcoming corpus of late inscriptions from Aphrodisias edited by C. M. Roueché.
43 A. H. M. Jones, *The Greek city* (1940) 256–7; *C. Th.* 15.1.14 (A.D. 365), 26 (A.D. 397), 37 (A.D. 398).
44 *C. Th.* 16.8.1 (Constantine). 16.8.7 (Constantius II), 16.8.19 (Honorius), 16.8.26 (Theodosius II).
45 Constantine's law (*C. Th.* 16.8.1), however, threatens death *si quis uero ex populo ad eorum nefariam sectam accesserit*: we do not know what *ex populo* means; it could represent a ban on any conversion, it may mean *ex populo Dei*, therefore Christians; the latter seems likely, since all the subsequent laws deal with Christian converts to Judaism specifically; the former, however, is possible, and would be a repetition, in more general form, of the anti-circumcision legislation of the principate, of which we hear nothing thereafter (Theodosius II's anti-circumcision decree [*C. Th.* 16.8.26] applied only to Christians).
46 *C. Th.* 16.10.10, 11 (A.D. 391), 12 (392).
47 *Hom.* 1.1 (*PG* 48.845), 1.4 (*ibid.* 849), 2.2 (*ibid.* 859), 2.3 (*ibid.* 860–1), 4.2 (*ibid.* 881), 8.4 (*ibid.* 933).
48 Juster I.277ff., M. Simon, *cit.* n. 2, 391–2.
49 Mansi II, Laodicea: canons 16, 29, 37–8.
50 John of Ephesus, *Vitae Sanctor. Oriental.* 40, 43, 47 and *HE* 3.27ff.
51 Face *b*, ll. 58–9, ?51, 39, 60, 53 and ?46.
52 See section VII on Trade Designations, especially pp. 119–22 on the trades of the *theosebeis*.
53 A. H. M. Jones, *cit.* n. 43, 217–19; A. R. Hands, *Charities and social aids in Greece and Rome* (1968); H. Bolkestein, *Wohltätigkeit und Armenpflege im vorchristlichen Altertum* (1939).
54 Julian, *Epp.* 89b, 304b–c (J. Bidez and F. Cumont, eds., *Imp. Caesaris Flavii Claudii Iuliani epistulae, leges, poemata, fragmenta varia* [1922]).

55 L. Vidman, *Isis u. Sarapis bei den Griechen u. Römern* (*RVV* XXIX, 1970) 127.
56 A. D. Nock, *Conversion* (1933) 117.
57 Kazimierz Romaniuk, 'Die "Gottesfürchtigen" in NT', *Aegyptus* 44 (1964) 91, suggested that the God-fearers were the first step in the development of the Christian catechumenate, but did not elaborate further.
58 L. Vidman, *cit.* n. 55, 138.
59 See, for example, 'Martyrdom of Pionius' 13.1 in H. Musurillo, *Acts of the Christian martyrs* (1972); Pionius, in a speech to detained Christians and pagan visitors at a prison, says that he has heard the Jews had invited some of them to the synagogues, and warns against the anti-Christian propaganda they will encounter. (We owe this reference to the kindness of Prof. Martin Hengel.)

V COMMENTARY: THE PERSONAL NAMES

The observations which follow are based on the two briefly annotated lists of names given on pp. 97–111.

On face *a*, which contains a list comprising entries for thirteen born Jews, three proselytes and two *theosebeis*, names appear unquestionably in twenty-four places, with four possible additions, if εὔκολος in l. 16 and νεκτάρις in l. 25 are taken as second names rather than as descriptive tags, and if παλατιν. in l. 11 and ἀρχιδ. in l. 13 are taken as abbreviated patronymics rather than as status designations. With the evidence of the patronymics included in six, perhaps eight, of the entries, it gives names for twenty-three, perhaps twenty-seven, persons. Of these names eleven, perhaps as many as fifteen, used for twenty persons, have, or may have, Jewish connections. Thus eight are transliterated biblical names (used for twelve persons), four in the indeclinable form of the Septuagint and four with Greek case-endings, all but one ('Ιαηλ in l. 9) to be found in other Greek Jewish documents, although not always in the exact form in which they appear here.[1] One (used twice in slightly different forms) refers to Jewish tradition and is again readily paralleled.[2] Two are Greek names which Jews are generally believed to have regarded as translations of biblical names, and two more may be.[3] Yet another has a link with the history of Judaea in Roman times, if O. Masson's argument that 'Αντιπέος might be a development from 'Αντιπᾶς is accepted.[4] Ἑρμῆς or Ἑρμήας, although a Greek theophoric name, is unsurprising, since Jews do not seem to have been particularly sensitive to the religious implications of Greco-Roman names,[5] and this, with others referring to Hermes, is well-attested in Jewish use, perhaps recommended by a phonetic resemblance to Jeremiah. There remain two Greek and two transliterated Latin names, with the four possible additions (three of them Greek and one transliterated Latin) in which we have detected no Jewish connection. Of these Ἐμμόνιος, Εὔκολος, Εὐσέβιος, Νεκτάρις and Πολιτιανός imply qualities which would appeal to Jews as much as to pagans and Christians; 'Αντωνῖνος gained a special frequency throughout the Roman world from its use by the Antonine and Severan dynasties, but long outlived these; Παλατῖνος, whether it refers to the Palatine Hill or to the imperial court, presumably derived such popularity as it had in the imperial period from the glamour of Rome; 'Αρχίδημος comes from an older stratum of Greek names, but survived in use into late antiquity.

Only a limited number, six or possibly eight of the eighteen persons listed, are given patronymics. It is to be noted that one of these is a proselyte (l. 22), although, strictly, it would have been correct for him to drop reference to his natural father, as, we believe, the other two proselytes have done (ll. 13, 17; see also p. 9) – there was probably some tendency to retain the patronymic in the diaspora because of its obvious convenience. Everyone without a patronymic here has some other distinguishing designation.

On face *b* the upper list, in its present condition, comprises entries for fifty-five persons, all to be presumed Jews, and records what are unquestionably names in eighty-one places, with one possible addition if χιλᾶς in l. 29 is taken as a second name rather than as a trade designation. Including the evidence of the patronymics it gives names ostensibly for seventy-four persons (but it is possible that several of the fathers figure more than once, so that the total might be no more than seventy). Twenty-one names, used in forty-one places, have obvious Jewish connections: thus nine, used for twenty persons, are transliterated biblical names, five, perhaps six of them, in the indeclinable form of the Septuagint, three, perhaps four, with Greek case endings,[6] all but 'Ιωφ (l. 5) to be found in other Greek Jewish documents, although not always in the exact form in which they appear here;[7] three, perhaps four, used for twelve persons, relate to Jewish traditions and are again readily paralleled elsewhere; nine Greek and two transliterated Latin names, used for eleven persons, may have been regarded by Jews as equivalents of biblical names.[8] There remain eighteen, possibly nineteen Greek names, six transliterated Latin ones, one hybrid ('Αμφιανός), and one unexplained name (Εὐτάρκιος), as the residue in which we have detected no Jewish connections. A few of these, none of them very distinctive, are otherwise attested in use at Aphrodisias, but only four with any frequency.[9]

Only twenty-four of the fifty-five persons listed are given patronymics, but it is to be noted that, although homonymity in fathers and sons was contrary to Jewish tradition, there are two homonymous pairs here, one using a name with a Jewish connection and the other not.[10] Of those who lack patronymics, fifteen have no alternative distinguishing designation, perhaps because there were no homonyms within the community – it can at least be said that all those with homonyms in the list have a distinguishing designation.[11]

The lower list comprises entries for fifty-two persons, all described as *theosebeis*, which we interpret as judaizing gentiles (see pp. 48–66), and gives what are unquestionably, or very probably, names in sixty-nine places, with two more if γρύλλος and ψελλός in l. 52 are taken as second names rather than as descriptive tags. Two have obvious reference to Jewish traditions,[12] one may be Semitic,[13] one perhaps has a connection with Judaean history,[14] two belong to the group thought to be regarded by Jews as equivalents of biblical names,[15] but the great majority are Greco-Roman, without any Jewish connection that we can detect. These include a rather larger number of older-style Greek names than in the upper list (eighteen, perhaps nineteen, as compared with eleven)[16] and a much more obvious overlap with those found in other inscriptions at Aphrodisias (twenty-six, perhaps thirty, as compared with thirteen).[17] There are about the same number of transliterated Latin names as in the upper list[18] but the lower one may also contain two examples of Roman citizen nomenclature, Μ. Ἀνίκιος Ἄττα or Ἄττα(λος), l. 48, being more plausible than Ἰούν(ιος) Βαλος, l. 43.

As in both the earlier lists the use of patronymics is limited; they are given for fifteen, or perhaps seventeen, of the fifty-two persons listed. But there are perhaps as many as five pairs of homonymous fathers and sons.[19] Of those who lack patronymics all but six (seven if ΙΟΥΝΒΑΛΟΣ, l. 43, is included) have an alternative distinguishing designation; five (or six) of these have no homonyms in the list and the sixth, Ξάνθος, l. 40, is clearly enough distinguished from his homonymous son.

From the detail of this survey several general points emerge. In the first place there are clear differences (despite some overlap) between the name-list of Jews and that of *theosebeis*, above all the absence of biblical names from the latter and the presence of a wider range of Greco-Roman names instead. The differences are, we believe, sufficiently marked to provide a strong argument in favour of interpreting *theosebeis* as judaizing gentiles (see pp. 48f.). Secondly, among the Jews biblical names and Greco-Roman names which were certainly or probably taken to refer to Jewish traditions form a noticeable proportion of the total used (for nineteen of the twenty-two Jews named on face *a* and for forty-one of the eighty-one named on face *b*). It may even be right to argue that the proportion had been rising in the period before the inscriptions were cut, for in the thirty cases in which we know the names of both fathers and sons, twenty-five sons, but only fourteen fathers (at the outside), have names with certain or possible Jewish connections. About half of the biblical names appear in the indeclinable form of the Septuagint, but it is difficult to know how much to make of this except that, obviously, some of these Jews were less inclined to complete the hellenization of their names than others. Yet this was not a particularly introvert group. That is shown not only by the presence of the proselytes and *theosebeis*, but also by some features of the nomenclature, e.g. the use, albeit occasional, of homonymity for fathers and sons, of second names which are Greco-Roman alongside biblical ones,[20] of a number of names in use in Aphrodisias outside the Jewish community, of a number of transliterated Latin names beyond what has hitherto seemed the norm in the city, therefore perhaps drawing on sources of influence beyond its territory. There is also discernible, among both Jews and *theosebeis*, a penchant for a type of name found characteristically throughout the Roman empire from the later second century onwards, which is formed by the addition of the suffixes -ιος or -ιανός to simpler names, nouns or adjectives,[21] commonly ones which refer to admired or agreeable qualities. The aim was presumably to produce new meaningful names in place of old ones whose sense had been dulled by frequent use; and if so, analysis of the meaningful Greco-Roman names in the lists may throw some light on the aspirations of the community. Such analysis seems in fact to reveal a striking enthusiasm for names which refer to festivals – the Sabbath and an unspecified ἑορτή which is likely to be the Feast of Tabernacles. Probably the persons named for them were born on one of these Feast Days, but a degree of pietism seems to be implied by the practice, and that, no doubt, is also evident in the names derived from θεος – Θεόδοτος, Θεόδωρος, Θεόφιλος) and in Εὐσέβιος. It also produces a longish list of names relating to community virtues, several of them defined negatively. Among the Jews these stress peaceable dispositions (Ἀμάχιος, Ἀχόλιος, Πραοίλιος), consolation (Παρηγόριος), grace (Χαρῖνος), politeness (Πολιτιανός), seriousness (Σεβῆρος), agreeable personality, as cheerfulness (Ἰλαριανός), good-nature (?Εὔκολος), affections (Ἀμάντιος), sweetness (?Νεκτάρις); among the *theosebeis* absence of malice (Ἀδόλιος, Ἀπονήριος), faithfulness, endurance (Παράμονος, Ἐμμόνιος), good morals (Εὐτρόπιος), helpfulness (Ὀνήσιμος), hopefulness (Ἐλπιδιανός), judgment (Βραβεύς), obedience (Εὐπίθιος), sweetness (Μελίτων), watchfulness (Γληγόριος). Nevertheless others refer to qualities more commonly admired in the ancient world; thus to nobility and high spirit (Γοργόνιος, Εὐγένιος, Ὀξυχόλιος among Jews, Ὀξυχόλιος and Πατρίκιος among *theosebeis*), to luck (Εὐτύχιος among Jews, Εὐτυχιανός, Τυχικός among *theosebeis*), to success (Εὔοδος among Jews, Καλλίνικος, Προκόπιος, Στρατόνικος among *theosebeis*), to achievement (Ἀνύσιος, Καλλίκαρπος, both Jews), to leadership (Ἡγε(μονεύς?, Στρατήγιος, the father of a *theosebes* and a *theosebes*), to personal beauty (Ἡδυχροῦς, Καλλίμορφος, *theosebeis*), to long life (Πολυχρόνιος, *theosebes*). If it seems that there is a little more of this among the *theosebeis* than among the Jews, there is certainly not much to choose between them; Greco-Roman standards, and especially competitive spirit, have left a clear imprint.

Schedules of names

In the comments that follow we are especially indebted to Olivier Masson for advice on A, nos. 6, 25, 56; B, nos. 6, 12, 17, 18, 24, 28, 36, 53.

All indications of date of usage for individual names should be regarded with reserve, since our information is very limited and much of it not dateable with

PERSONAL NAMES 97

any precision; names may come into use long before our earliest dateable example and remain in use long after our latest dateable example.

Throughout, the easily accessible Roman evidence is constantly cited for social strata in which particular names occur; but, of course, names attested at Rome mainly or even wholly in modest circles often retained éclat in provincial cities.

We have found that the collection of H. Wuthnow, *Die semitischen Menschennamen in griechischen Inschriften und Papyri* (1930) is no longer very helpful.

(A) JEWS

(1) Αἰλιανός (*b*, ll. 29 twice, 30; cf. perhaps 42 for the father of a *theosebes*); transliterated Latin *Aelianus*; widely disseminated, both in the east and in the west,[22] especially after the reign of Hadrian whose *nomen* was Aelius; already attested in use at Aphrodisias.[23] For another Jewish example see *CIJ* I.82.

(2) Ἀμάντιος (*b*, l. 12); transliterated Latin *Amantius*, formed from *amans*, 'loving'; the Latin is attested in use both as a name and as a *signum*, and among both pagans and Christians,[24] commonly persons of modest status, although in late antiquity some of eminence, the earlier instances being mainly in the west. No other Jewish example found.

(3) Ἀμάχιος (*a*, l. 18); Greek, from ἄμαχος, 'uncontentious'; attested in use occasionally among pagans, more often, it seems, among Jews and Christians, usually persons of modest status, from the third century onwards, both in the east and in the west.[25] For other Jewish examples see *CIJ* I.86 (Rome) and *SEG* XXVI.1173 (a Catanate who died in Rome); its attraction for Jews might be comparable with that of names like Εἰρηναῖος, Ἡσύχιος which were also related to peaceable character and perhaps intended as translations of Solomon (*Shelomoh*, from 'peace');[26] cf. also Ἀχόλιος, no. 11, Πραοίλιος, no. 56.

(4) Ἀμμιανός (*b*, l. 29); on the face of it transliterated Latin *Ammianus*, from Ammius, but in the east perhaps attractive because of its apparent connection with names such as Ἄμμια, Ἀμμιας, common in Asia Minor;[27] already attested in use at Aphrodisias.[28] For another Jewish example, see *CIJ* II.776.

(5) Ἀμφιανός (*b*, l. 8); apparently Greek Ἀμφι- with a Latin suffix. No other example found. Perhaps a development from Amphio/Amphion, a common name in the Roman world, particularly for slaves.[29]

(6) Ἀντιπέος (*a*, l. 24, see also *b*, l. 37 for a *theosebes*); unattested and very surprising, perhaps (so O. Masson) to be explained as a variant of an also

unattested Ἀντιπαῖος (cf. κέ for καί), derived from Ἀντιπᾶς, the diminutive of Ἀντίπατρος. If so the name of Herod Ἀντιπᾶς provides a relevant parallel.

(7) **Ἀνύσιος** (*b*, l. 15); Greek from ἀνύω, accomplish; it seems to be rare in our evidence before late antiquity.[30] No other Jewish example found.

(8) **Ἀπελλί(ων)**, but there are other possible forms, e.g. Ἀπελλιανός (*b*, l. 20); Greek, from Ἀπελλᾶς; attested, but not very common, although the simpler forms Ἀπελλᾶς (see list B, no. 11), Ἀπελλῆς are frequent; the only example from Rome is a slave.[31] No other Jewish example found.

(9) **?Ἀρχίδημος** (*a*, l. 13, but see p. 9); common Greek name from early times; nine examples known at Rome, some of the Christian period.[32] No Jewish example found.

(10) **Ἀχιλλεύς** (*b*, l. 31); Greek hero's name; in use throughout the Roman period both in the east and in the west; of 79 cases known in Rome many are slaves, freedmen or uncertain in status, but there are some soldiers in the early third century and a few *equites*;[33] already attested in Aphrodisias.[34] For another Jewish example, see *CIJ* I.682.

(11) **Ἀχόλιος** (*b*, l. 22); Greek, from ἄχολος, 'lacking bile'; attested in use, both in the east and in the west, as a name and as a *signum*, probably from the later second century.[35] Perhaps influenced by Solomon (*Shelomoh*, 'peace'), although the common Εἰρηναῖος is the more direct and usual equivalent. For another Jewish example see *CIJ* II.910.

(12) **Βενιαμιν** (*a*, l. 15); transliterated biblical name in Septuagint form (Josephus has Βενιαμίς). For another example see *CIJ* I.376. See also Ἀλέξανδρος, list B, no. 5.

(13) **Βιωτικός** (*b*, l. 8); Greek adjective, 'fit for life, lively'; not a very common name in our evidence; of three cases at Rome two are freedmen, one a woman of uncertain status, the earliest of the first century A.D.[36] No other Jewish example found. For Jewish interest in names derived from words meaning 'life' see under Ζώσιμος, no. 29 below.

(14) **Γέμελλος** (*b*, l. 21); transliterated Latin *Gemellus*, 'twin'; quite common throughout the Roman period,[37] although in the east the Greek Δίδυμος is commonly preferred. For another Jewish example see *CIJ* II.993.

(15) **Γοργόνιος** (*b*, l. 31, also 46 for a *theosebes*); Greek from γοργός, 'vigorous';[38] quite common, both in the east and in the west, as a name and as a *signum*, from the third century onwards; of 45 cases at Rome, the earliest of the second century, most are of uncertain status.[39] For other Jewish examples cf. [Γ]οργονί(α) in *CIJ* I.14, Γοργονείς in *CIJ* I.30, with Lifshitz, *Prolegomenon* 26.

(16) **Δαμόνικος** (*b*, l. 22); Greek name, in Doric form, attested in use from early times; one case known at Rome in the first/second centuries, a man of

uncertain status;[40] in use at Aphrodisias for a magistrate.[41] No other Jewish example found.

(17) Διογένης (b, l. 18, twice; also in l. 35 for a *theosebes*); Greek theophoric name, 'descendant of Zeus'; widely disseminated both in the east and in the west; of 133 examples at Rome many are slaves, freed, or uncertain in status;[42] already attested in use at Aphrodisias;[43] Jewish tolerance of pagan theophorics is well known, and names referring to Zeus are thought to have been particularly acceptable.[44] For another Jewish example see *CIJ* II.787.

Εἰούδας, see Ἰούδας.

Εἰωσηφ, see Ἰωσηφ.

(18) Ἑορτάσιος/Ὁρτάσιος (b, ll. 7, 27, 31, 33; cf. 49 for a *theosebes*); Greek, from ἑορτάζω, 'keep a festival', here, no doubt, with reference to a Jewish festival, perhaps the Feast of Tabernacles; quite well attested as a name in the east, from the third century onwards, at any rate among Jews and Christians, but not at Rome where Solin only records the simpler Heorte, Heorticus, which are certainly used by pagans;[45] for use at Aphrodisias, although not by a born Aphrodisian, see *IG* II–III² 3169/70, l. 34, presumably pagan. Jews might, perhaps, regard it as a translation of Ḥaggai, 'festive'. For another Jewish example see *Donateurs* 76.

(19) Ἑρμῆς, Ἑρμή(ας?) (a, l. 24); Greek theophoric names known to have been tolerated by Jews;[46] widely disseminated throughout the imperial period, both in the east and in the west; of 133 cases of Hermias at Rome many are slaves, freedmen or uncertain in status;[47] already attested in use at Aphrodisias.[48] While the sense of luck given by Hermes may have been the predominant point favouring it, a Jew might, perhaps, have thought of it as an equivalent of the biblical name Malachi, 'my messenger'; or, since the pronunciation would be psilotic and the *eta* iotacised, Ἑρμήας might seem a phonetic parallel to Ἱερεμίας (Hebrew *Yirmeyahu*), 'Jeremiah'.

(20) Εὐγένιος (b. ll, 9, 24); Greek from εὐγενής, 'noble'; quite well attested both in the east and in the west, as a name and as a *signum*, from the later second century;[49] of 36 cases at Rome most are of uncertain status; already attested in use at Aphrodisias.[50] For another Jewish example cf. Εὐγενία, *CIJ* I.330.

(21) ?Εὔκολος (a, l. 16); Greek adjective, 'good-natured'; attested as a name, although not very commonly. No Jewish example found.[51]

(22) Εὔοδος (b, l. 14, twice); Greek adjective, 'successful'; well-attested throughout the Roman period, both in the east and in the west; of 80 cases at Rome most are slaves, freedmen or uncertain in status.[52] For another Jewish example see *CIJ* I.24 with Lifshitz, *Prolegomenon* 26.

(23) Εὐσαβάθιος, Εὐσαββάθιος (b, ll. 15, 16, 18, 24, 32; cf. 48 for a *theosebes*); Jewish Greek compound of εὖ with σαββαθ and the suffix -ios; cf. also Σαββάθιος, no. 59. For another Jewish example see *CIJ* I.379.
(24) Εὐσέβιος (b, l. 6; cf. a, l. 22 for the father of a proselyte); Greek from εὐσεβής, 'pious'; quite widely disseminated, both in the east and in the west, as a name and as a *signum*, from the second century; of 70 cases at Rome most are slaves, freedmen or uncertain in status;[53] already attested in use at Aphrodisias.[54] For another Jewish example see *Donateurs* 29.
(25) ?Εὐτάρκιος (b, l. 23); unattested and unexplained; Συτάρκιος is no easier; Αὐτάρκιος not really consonant with what survives on the stone.
(26) Εὐτύχιος (b, ll. 25, 27); Greek from εὐτυχής, 'lucky'; quite widely disseminated, both in the east and in the west, as a name and as a *signum*, throughout the imperial period; of 15 cases at Rome most are slaves, freedmen or uncertain in status.[55] For another Jewish example cf. Εὐτυχία, *CIJ* I.712.
(27) **Ζαχαρίας** (b, l. 20); transliterated biblical name in a form used both in the Septuagint and by Josephus. For another example see *Donateurs* 102.
(28) **Ζήνων** (b, ll. 4, 5, 28, ?33, and 34, 36 for *theosebeis*); Greek theophoric name; widely disseminated, both in the east and in the west, throughout the Roman period; of 51 cases at Rome many are slaves, freedmen or uncertain in status;[56] already attested in use at Aphrodisias.[57] For another Jewish example see *CIJ* I.116.
(29) ?Ζώσι(μος?), but Ζωσι(μιανός) is another possibility, (b, l. 28); Greek from ζωή, 'life'; widely disseminated throughout the imperial period; of 269 cases at Rome many are slaves, freedmen or uncertain in status;[58] already attested in use at Aphrodisias.[59] There is some indication that Jews were especially attracted to names with this root meaning, cf. also Βιωτικός, no. 13, Ζωτικός, no. 30, but presumably these are not, as one might be tempted to think, translations of standard Hebrew names such as Ḥayyim, 'life', or Ḥai, 'living', since the latter is not attested until the ninth century (in Babylonia), the former until an even later date (in the west) and neither appears in rabbinic literature until after the completion of the Babylonian Talmud. For a Jewish example see *CPJ* I.503.
(30) **Ζωτικός** (b, l. 33; cf. 52, twice for *theosebeis*); Greek from ζωή 'life'; widely disseminated, both in the east and in the west, throughout the imperial period; of 105 cases at Rome most are slaves, freedmen or uncertain in status;[60] already attested in use at Aphrodisias.[61] For Jewish interest in this type of name cf. Βιωτικός, no. 13, ?Ζώσι(μος) no. 29; but Ζωτικός itself might have been suggested by phonetic resemblance to Zedekiah. For another Jewish example see *CIJ* I.118, with Lifshitz, *Prolegomenon* 29.

(31) Θεόδοτος (*a*, l. 11); Greek, 'God-given'; quite widely disseminated, both in the east and in the west, throughout the Roman period; of 42 cases in Rome all are slaves, freedmen or uncertain in status;[62] possibly attested in use at Aphrodisias.[63] Known to have been favoured by Jews as an equivalent of the names Jonathan, Nathaniel, cf. Θεόδωρος, no. 32 and see p. 111, n. 3. For another Jewish example see *CIJ* I.358.

(32) Θεόδωρος (*a*, l. 23); Greek, 'gift of God'; widely disseminated, both in the east and in the west, throughout the Roman period; of 89 cases at Rome a significant proportion are slaves, freedmen or uncertain in status;[64] already attested in use at Aphrodisias.[65] Known to have been favoured by Jews as an equivalent of the names Jonathan, Nathaniel, see on Θεόδοτος, no. 31. For another Jewish example see *CIJ* II.879.

(33) Θεόφιλος (*b*, l. 19); Greek adjective, 'dear to God'; quite widely disseminated, both in the east and in the west, throughout the Roman period; of 66 cases in Rome most are slaves, freedmen or uncertain in status;[66] already attested in use at Aphrodisias.[67] It was popular among Jews[68] for whom it might have been an equivalent to Eldad, (?) 'God is a friend'. For another Jewish example see L. Robert, *Hellenica* III (1946) 101.

(34) Ἰαηλ (*a*, l. 9); transliterated biblical name in the form used by the Septuagint (Josephus has Ἰάλη for the feminine and would presumably have used Ἴαλος for the masculine). At first sight it evokes the woman Jael of Jdg. 4:18f., and has been taken as a woman's name by Brooten, 151; but although some women were highly honoured in diaspora communities, see p. 41, the lists here are otherwise demonstrably and consistently masculine; since the Septuagint uses the same form for a man at IV Ezra 10:43, cf. also at 10:26,[69] we believe that the feminine should be rejected in favour of the masculine here. No other example found in use.
Ἰακω, shortened form of Ἰακωβ, no. 35, *q.v.*

(35) Ἰακωβ (*b*, ll. 5, 13, 20); transliterated biblical name in the form used by the Septuagint (Josephus has Ἰάκωβος).[70] For other Jewish examples see *CPJ* 475 (Ἰακωβ), and *CIJ* II.787 (Ἰακω).

(36) Ἰάσων (*b*, l. 14); Greek hero's name; widely disseminated, both in the east and in the west, throughout the imperial period; of 32 cases at Rome an appreciable number are slave or freed;[71] already attested in use at Aphrodisias.[72] Thought to have been favoured by Jews because of a phonetic resemblance to biblical names such as Ἰησοῦς.[73] For another Jewish example see *Donateurs* 100.

(37) Ἰέσσεος (*a*, l. 14); transliterated biblical name in a form approximately that of Josephus (who has Ἰεσσαῖος). No exact epigraphic parallel found, but cf. Ἰέσουος, *Beth She'arim* 407, nos. 138, 139, Ἡσῆς, *Donateurs* 73*a*, and, rather later, Gesua at Venosa, *CIJ* I.614.

(38) Ἱλαριανός (a, l. 12); transliterated Latin *Hilarianus*, 'cheerful'. Several names developed from *hilarus*, ἱλαρός, are widely disseminated, both in the east and in the west, throughout the Roman period, but this particular form seems comparatively rare;[74] it is, however, of a type increasingly popular in and after the second century, see p. 96; already attested in use at Aphrodisias.[75] It may have attracted the attention of a Jew as a possible equivalent of Isaac.[76] For the nearest Jewish example found cf. Ἵλαρος, *CIJ* I.343.

(39) Ἰούδας/Εἰούδας (a. ll. 16, 23; b, ll. 6, 8, 10, 19, 22, 23, 27, 28); transliterated biblical name in the form used both by the Septuagint and by Josephus. It is a particularly common name in all Jewish communities, cf. L. Robert, *Hellenica* III (1946) 101. For another Jewish example see *CIJ* I.121.

(40) Ἰωσῆς (a, ll. 14, 17); hypocoristic form of the biblical Joseph, in very common use in Jewish communities. For another example see *CIJ* I.719.

(41) Ἰωσήφ/Εἰωσήφ (a, l. 22, b, ll. ?4, 26); transliterated biblical name in the form used by the Septuagint (Josephus has Ἰώσηφος). For another example see *CIJ* II.908.

(42) Ἰωσούας (a, l. 10); transliterated biblical name, although in a form used neither by the Septuagint nor Josephus. No exact epigraphic parallel found, but cf. Ἰέσουος, *Beth She'arim*, 407, nos. 138, 139, *Donateurs* 73a.

(43) Ἰωφ (b, l. 5); presumably a transliterated Jewish name, although in a form used neither by the Septuagint nor by Josephus, and not found elsewhere; most probably for *Job*, cf. Ἰακωφ for Ἰακωβ, *Arch. Chron.* in *Eph. Arch.* (1942–4) 16, no. 8.

(44) Καλλίκαρπος (b, l. 7); Greek adjective, 'rich in fruit'; attested as a name, although not in large-scale use, both in the east and in the west, in the early imperial period and into the third century; of 3 cases at Rome, 1 is a slave and 2 are of uncertain status;[77] It may have been attractive to a Jew as a possible equivalent of Ephraim, meaning 'doubly fruitful'.[78] No other Jewish example found, but cf. Εὔκαρπος, *CIJ* I.111.

(45) Κύρυλλος (b, l. 25); Greek, diminutive of κύριος, 'lord'; in the form Κύριλλος it is quite widely disseminated, especially in late antiquity; of 17 cases at Rome most are of uncertain status.[79] For other Jewish examples cf. Κύριλλος, *CIJ* I.922, Κυρύλλα, *CIJ* I.310.

(46) Λεόντιος (b, l. 21, twice); Greek, from λέων, 'lion'. Known already as a name in the fourth century B.C. and fairly widely disseminated, both in the east and in the west, throughout the imperial period, as a name, and later as a *signum*; of 108 cases at Rome many are of uncertain status, one a slave;[80] already attested, in the feminine form, at Aphrodisias.[81] No doubt attractive to Jews because it can be interpreted as having reference to the lion of Judah.[82] For other Jewish examples see L. Robert, *NIS* 45–7.

PERSONAL NAMES 103

(47) Μανασῆς (b, l. 5); transliterated biblical name approximately in the form used by Josephus (who has Μαναοσῆς; the Septuagint has Μανασση). For another example in use see *CIJ* II.941.

(48) Μίλων (b, l.16); Greek athlete's name well-known from the classical period and still current during the Roman period; of 9 cases at Rome all are slave, freed or uncertain in status;[83] already attested in use at Aphrodisias, but for a man of some social standing.[84] For another Jewish example see *CPJ* I.22.

(49) Μύρτιλος (b, l. 12); Greek, from μύρτος, 'myrtle'; attested from the classical Greek period and still current in the Roman; of 22 cases at Rome most are slaves, freedmen or uncertain in status.[85] No other Jewish instance found, but cf. Μυρτώ for Jewesses in Cyrenaica, Lüderitz, *Cyrenaika* nos. 13d, 31b, 44b, 52c, 59c.

(50) ?Νεκτάριος (a, l. 25, but see p. 47); Greek, from νέκταρ, 'nectar-sweet'; attested, both in the east and in the west, at least as early as the second century; of 11 cases known at Rome most are of uncertain status.[86] No other Jewish example found.

(51) Ὀξυχόλιος (b, ll. 11, 17, 31, 32; cf. 46 for the father of a *theosebes*); Greek from ὀξύχολος 'quick to anger' or, perhaps likelier in a name, 'spirited'; a scatter of examples occurs, both in the east and in the west, at least from the third century onwards, for Christians as well as pagans.[87] No other Jewish example found.

Ὁρτάσιος, see Ἑορτάσιος.

(52) ?Παλατῖν(ος) (a, l. 11); transliterated Latin *Palatinus*, which might be a name derived from that of the *Mons Palatinus*,[88] or a title derived from court service. On the latter sense see pp. 42–3.

(53) Παρηγόριος (b, l. 32); Greek, from παρήγορος, 'consoling, soothing'; quite widely disseminated, both in the east and in the west, as a name and as a *signum*, at least from the later second century; of 8 cases at Rome all are of uncertain status;[89] it is thought to have been regarded by Jews as an equivalent of Menaḥem, 'comforter'.[90] For another Jewish example, see *CIJ* II.926.

(54) Παῦλος (b, l. 19); transliterated Latin *Paullus*; widely disseminated throughout the Roman world;[91] the phonetic resemblance to the Greek form of the biblical Saul, Σαῦλος, may have led Jews with this name (which means, in Greek, 'with loose gait', *LSJ* s.v.) to adopt Παῦλος as a substitute; this may, for example, be what moved Saul of Tarsus to change his name to Paul (Acts 13:9).

(55) Πολιτιανός (a, l. 21);[92] transliterated Latin *Politianus*, from *politus*, 'polished, elegant';[93] the only example found is probably of the third or fourth centuries and may be Christian.[94]

(56) **Πραοίλιος** (*b*, l. 10, twice); apparently not attested, but perhaps a phonetic variant of Greek Πραΰλιος, which appears in a Christian inscription of the sixth century, and related to πραΰλος, a Greek adjective derived from πρᾶος, 'gentle'.[95] No other Jewish example found, but cf. Πραΰλος Σαμαρεύς, *I. Del.* 2616, a pagan, however, who participated in Egyptian cults.

(57) **Ῥουβην** (*b*, l. 26); transliterated biblical name in the form used by the Septuagint (Josephus has Ῥουβῆλος);[96] see also on Ῥοῦφος, no. 58 below. No precise parallel found, but cf. Ῥουβης in *IGR* IV.743.

(58) **Ῥοῦφος** (*b*, l. 11); transliterated Latin *Rufus*; very widely disseminated throughout the Roman empire;[97] thought to have attracted Jews because of its phonetic resemblance to Reuben.[98] For another Jewish example see *CIJ* I.145.

(59) **Σαβάθιος/Σαββάτιος** (*a*, ll. 18, 25); clearly derived from Σαββαθ, cf. Εὐσαββάθιος, no. 23; widely used by Christians as well as Jews. For another Jewish example cf. Σαβάτιος, *CIJ* I.263.

(60) **Σαμουηλ** (*a*, ll. 9–11 left margin, 13, 21, 26, *b*, l. 30); transliterated biblical name in the form used by the Septuagint (Josephus has Σαμούηλος); for another example see *Donateurs* 58.

(61) **Σεβῆρος** (*b*, l. 13); transliterated Latin *Severus*, 'serious'; widely disseminated, both in the east and in the west, throughout the Roman period.[99] For another Jewish example see Σεουῆρος, *Donateurs* 76. VII.

(62) **Σεραπίων** (*b*, l. 2); Greek theophoric name known to have been accepted by Jews and perhaps attractive because of its phonetic resemblance to the word *seraphim*;[100] widely disseminated throughout the imperial period; of 30 cases at Rome most are of uncertain status.[101] For another Jewish example see *Donateurs* 100.

(63) **Συμεών** (*b*, l. 33); transliterated biblical name in the form used both by the Septuagint and by Josephus; much less common than the Greek Σίμων, which Jews accepted as its equivalent.[102] For another example see *CPJ* 501.

(64) **Φίλανθος** (*b*, l. 30); Greek, 'lover of flowers'; attested as a name, but not, apparently, very common in our evidence; of 4 cases at Rome all are of the first or second centuries, and slave, freed or uncertain in status.[103] No other Jewish example found.

(65) **Φιληρ(?)** (*b*, l. 23); Greek; suitable names to fit the data are rare, but cf. Φιλήριφος, J. and L. Robert, *Bull. Ep.* 1942.32, 1959.184.

(66) **Χαρῖνος** (*b*, l. 12); Greek, from χάρις, 'grace'; attested from the classical Greek period and still current, but not, apparently, very common, in the Roman period; of 3 cases at Rome one is a slave, one uncertain in status and the third a soldier of the second/third centuries.[104] It could have been regarded as an equivalent of the Hebrew name Ḥanan, 'grace,

PERSONAL NAMES 105

favour', popular in Tanna'itic and 'Amora'ic times (Jastrow, *Dictionary of Targumim*, etc. *s.v.*, with examples).
(67) ?Χιλᾶς (*b*, 1. 29); Greek, rare, but apparently in use as a name at Corycus in late antiquity; it is cited by Pape-Benseler, *s.v.*, as the name of a Pythagorean philosopher in the list of Iamblichus, but O. Masson warns us that it would be rash to rely on this, since the list contains elements that are difficult to check.[105] It may be better taken here as a trade-designation, see pp. 118–19, no. 8.

(B) THEOSEBEIS AND THEIR FATHERS

(1) Ἀδόλιος (*b*, 1. 51); Greek, from ἄδολος, 'guileless', in the extended form which became popular in the later second century and thereafter; for the sentiment cf. Ἀπονήριος, no. 12 below and the quite common Ἀκάκιος;[106] rare in our evidence, but there are cases at Rome, some thought to be of the third century.[107] No Jewish example found.
(2) Ἀθηναγόρας (*b*, ll. 56, 60); Greek name known from the classical period, still current and widely disseminated in the Roman period, at any rate until the third century; of 7 cases at Rome 2 are senators and in fact originally resident at Aphrodisias.[108] No Jewish example found.
(3) Ἀθηνίων (*b*, 1. 42); Greek name known from the Hellenistic period, still current and found both in the east and the west in the Roman period; of 29 cases at Rome all are slaves, freedmen or uncertain in status.[109] For a Jewish example see *CIJ* 1.82.
(4) ?Αἰ(λιανός) (? 1. 42 for the father of a *theosebes*); see list A, no. 1.
(5) Ἀλέξανδρος (*b*, 1. 50); Greek name known from early times, with particularly wide dissemination after the campaigns of Alexander of Macedon; attested throughout the Roman period; 540 cases known at Rome;[110] in use at Aphrodisias;[111] thought to have been regarded by Jews as an equivalent of Benjamin;[112] but so common that serious meaning cannot be affirmed in any individual case. For a Jewish example see *Donateurs* 100.
(6) Ἀμαζόνιος (*b*, 1. 61); Greek, from Ἀμαζών; quite widely disseminated, both in the east (especially Egypt) and in the west, as a name and as a *signum*, from the later second century; the 6 cases known at Rome range from senator to slave;[113] in use at Aphrodisias.[114] No Jewish example found.
(7) ?Ἀνίκιος (*b*, 1. 47); could be a transliterated Roman *nomen*, *Anicius*, but see also Μανίκιος, no. 43.
(8) Ἀντίοχος (*b*, 1. 37); Greek name attested from the classical period; widely disseminated throughout the Hellenistic and Roman periods, both in the

east and in the west; of 299 cases at Rome a large number are slave, freed or uncertain in status, but there are also some senators;[115] in use at Aphrodisias.[116] No Jewish example found, but cf. the Samaritan, *CJI* 1.49, no. 635*a*.

(9) Ἀντιπέος (*b*, 1. 37); see list A, no. 6.

(10) Ἀντωνῖνος (*a*, 1. 20); transliterated Latin *Antoninus*, widely disseminated, both in the east and in the west, as a result of its employment by the Antonine and Severan dynasties, but still current in the Christian period.[117] For a Jewish example cf. *Antonina*, *CIJ* 1.236.

(11) Ἀπελλᾶς (*b*, 1. 47); Greek name attested from the classical period, widely disseminated in the Roman world, at least into the third century; of 28 cases at Rome the majority are slave or freed;[118] in use at Aphrodisias.[119] The poet Horace, *Sat.* 1.5.100, might suggest that it was a typical name for a Jew, but the epigraphical evidence does not support this; see also the discussion by Lüderitz, *Cyrenaika* 57–8. To Horace's Jewish Apellas one may add another at Ep. Rom. 16:10.

(12) Ἀπονήριος (*b*, 1. 38); Greek, apparently unattested, but easily understood as a combination of *alpha*-privative with πονήρος, giving 'free from malice'; for the sentiment see no. 1 above.

(13) Ἀππιανός (*b*, 1. 51); transliterated Latin *Appianus*, widely disseminated throughout the Roman world by the second century; in Asia Minor it may perhaps have been connected with local names in Ἀπφ- rather than with the *nomen Appius*, cf. Apphianus in the Roman name-lists.[120] No Jewish example found.

(14) ?Ἀρκά(διος) (*b*, 1. 56); Greek from Ἀρκάς, 'Arcadian'; fairly widely disseminated, although not particularly common in our evidence, in the Roman period; 4 cases known at Rome;[121] in use at Aphrodisias in the form Ἀρκάθιος.[122] No Jewish example found.

(15) ?Ἄττα or Ἄττα(ς) (*b*, 1. 48); native names in Asia Minor, notably in Phrygia;[123] one example of Attas known at Rome, a slave.[124] No Jewish example found.

(16) ?Ἄττα(λος) (*b*, 1. 48); Macedonian/Greek name, very popular in Asia Minor as a result of its employment by the Attalid dynasty of Pergamum, widely disseminated, both in the east and in the west, throughout the Roman period; of 68 cases at Rome many are slave or freed, but there are also senators, some Aphrodisian, from the late second century;[125] in use at Aphrodisias.[126] No Jewish example found.

(17) ?Βαλος (*b*, 1. 43); a rare native name, apparently attested only in Pamphylia;[127] if it occurred it was as a *cognomen* with the Roman *nomen* Ἰούν(ιος) (no. 37 below), or as a second name with Ἰουν (no. 35 below); but see also under Ἰουνβαλος (no. 36 below). No Jewish example found.

PERSONAL NAMES 107

(18) Βραβεύς (b, 1. 49); Greek, 'umpire'; attested from the classical period but rare in our evidence.¹²⁸ No Jewish example found.
(19) Γληγόριος (b, l. 44); Greek Γρηγόριος, with a common change from *rho* to *lambda*, from γρηγορέω, 'be wakeful, watchful'; widely disseminated, both in the east and in the west, as a name and as a *signum*, from the later second century onwards; of 54 cases at Rome a few are men of status, most uncertain.¹²⁹ For a Jewish example cf. Γληγορία, *CIJ* II.927.
(20) Γοργόνιος (b, 1. 46); see list A, no. 15.
(21) ?Γρύλλος (b, l. 52); Greek, 'pig, porker', and 'comic figure', cf. Pliny, *HN* 35.114; attested as a name from the classical period, but not at all common in the Roman period; one case only, and that from the literary evidence, in Rome.¹³⁰ No Jewish example found.
(22) Διογένης (b, 1. 35); see list A, no. 17.
(23) Ἐλπιδιανός (b, l. 54); Greek, from ἐλπίς, 'hope', *via* Ἐλπίδιος, with a Latin suffix; names expressive of good hope are common enough in the Greek and Roman world, but this particular form seems comparatively rare; of the examples found there is one at Rome, said to be Christian and of the later third century.¹³¹ No Jewish example found.
(24) Ἐμμόνιος (a, l. 19); Greek, from ἔμμονος, 'steadfast'; apparently very rare; we have only found one other example (in Bithynia).¹³² It might be possible to relate it to Hebrew אֱמוּן, *'emun*, 'faithful', which appears at Prov. 13:17, 14:9, 20: 6, where the LXX text has πιστός, and as a personal name in the OT, e.g. II Kgs. 21:18–25, II Chron. 33:20–5.
(25) Εὐπίθιος (b, ll. 39, 53 twice, once for a father); Greek, from εὐπειθής, 'obedient'; not common; there are none at Rome, although the simple form Εὐπειθής is found for a freedman of the first/second centuries;¹³³ attested in use at Aphrodisias.¹³⁴ For another Jewish example see *Donateurs* 44, 55. In a Jewish context obedience to the Law may be intended.
(26) Εὐσαββάθιος (b, 1. 48); see list A, no. 23.
(27) Εὐσέβιος (a, l. 22, father of a proselyte, possibly but not necessarily a *theosebes*); see list A, no. 24.
(28) Εὕρετος (b, 1. 56); Greek, 'discoverable'; comparatively rare in our evidence, but there are 9 cases at Rome (with 6 more unaspirated), dated from the first to the third century, many slave or freed.¹³⁵ No Jewish example found, but cf. Εὕρεσις, Lifshitz, *Prolegomenon*, no. 650e.
(29) Εὐτρόπιος (b, 1. 55); Greek, from εὔτροπος, 'morally good'; quite well disseminated, both in the east and in the west, as a name and as a *signum*, from the later second century; of 7 cases at Rome all are of uncertain status.¹³⁶ For a Jewish example see *CIJ* I.418.
(30) Εὐτυχιανός (b, 1. 58); Greek, from Εὐτύχιος (see list A, no. 26), with a Latin suffix, 'fortunate'; widely disseminated, from the first/second cen-

turies onwards; of 73 cases at Rome most are slaves, freedmen or of uncertain status;[137] attested in use at Aphrodisias.[138] For a Jewish example cf. [E]ὐθυχιανός, *CIJ* I.110.

(31) **Ζήνων** (*b*, ll. 34, 36); see list A, no. 28.
(32) **Ζωτικός** (*b*, l. 52 twice); see list A, no. 30.
(33) **Ἥγε** (?) (*b*, l. 47); Greek, from ἡγέομαι, 'lead'; a number of old Greek names, as well as newer formations, could be restored here; of these only Ἡγεμονεύς is attested in use at Aphrodisias (in the third century).[139] No Jewish example found.
(34) **Ἡδυχροῦς** (*b*, ll. 48, 54, 55); Greek, 'sweet-complexioned'; attested Greek name, although not very common in our evidence; of 8 cases at Rome, all thought to be of the first or second centuries, most are slave or freed.[140] No Jewish example found.
(35) **?Ιουν** (*b*, l. 43); transliterated biblical name, presumably for Jonah, but not in the form used by the Septuagint or Josephus (which is Ἰωνᾶς), cf. Ιουν, *Beth She'arim* nos. 7, 9; Ιεων at Sardis, *NIS* 54; if it is correct, it is used with Βαλος, no. 17, as a second name. But see also Ἰουνβαλος, no. 36, Ἰούν(ιος), no. 37, for other possibilities.
(36) **?Ἰουνβαλος** (*b*, l. 43); perhaps, as O. Masson suggests, transliterated from the biblical name Jubal, which appears in the Septuagint as Ἰουβαλ, Ἰωβελ, with insertion of *nu* before *beta*,[141] as well as the addition of a Greek case-ending; for a parallel to the insertion of *nu*, cf. Ἱερομβαλος = Ἱεροβααλ, a Jewish priest named in a passage of Philo Byblius which is quoted at Eusebius, *Praep. Eu.* 1. 9.
(37) **?Ἰούν(ιος)** (*b*, l. 43); would be the transliterated and abbreviated Latin *nomen*, *Junius*, and, if correct, was used with Βαλος, no. 18, as the *cognomen*; but cf. Ιουν, no. 35, Ἰουνβαλος, no. 36, for other possibilities.
(38) **Καλλίνικος** (*b*, l. 55); Greek, 'gloriously triumphant'; quite well-attested as a name in the Roman period; of 37 cases at Rome, the earliest of the first century A.D., most are slaves, freed or of uncertain status;[142] attested in use at Aphrodisias.[143] For a Jewish example see *CIJ* II.834.
(39) **Καλλίμορφος** (*b*, l. 43 twice, ?50 for a father); Greek, 'handsome'; attested as a name, although not very common in our evidence, during the Roman period; of 22 cases at Rome, dated from the first century A.D. onwards, all are slave, freed or of uncertain status;[144] in use at Aphrodisias.[145] No Jewish example found.
(40) **Κλαυδιανός** (*b*, l. 50); transliterated Latin *Claudianus*, widely disseminated, both in the east and in the west, during the whole Roman period, and at all social levels;[146] in use at Aphrodisias.[147] No Jewish example found.
(41) **?Λευ(?)** (*b*, l. 51, for a father); a number of old Greek names are known, formed from λευκ-, 'white', many still current in the Roman period.

(42) Λογγι(ανός), ?Λογγῖ(νος) (b, l. 36, for a father); transliterated Latin *Longianus* or *Longinus*; the former seems preferable because already attested in use at Aphrodisias,[148] although Longinus is widely disseminated, both in the east and in the west, throughout the Roman period.[149] For a Jewish example cf. Λογγ[- - -, *CIJ* I.589.

(43) ?Μανίκιος (b, l. 48); unattested, but cf. Mannacius in *CIJ* I.222, Μανικός reported in Pape/Benseler *s.v.* from a dubious source, and Μανικων, perhaps Thracian, on the Black Sea coast.[150] See also under Ἀνίκιος, no. 7.

(44) Μελίτων (b, l. 61, ? also 41, for fathers); Greek from μέλι, 'honey'; widely disseminated, both in the east and in the west; of 16 cases at Rome, the earliest of the Augustan period, most are slaves, freed or of uncertain status;[151] in use at Aphrodisias.[152] For a possible Jewish example see Lüderitz, *Cyrenaika*, appendix nos. 23*f*, *l*, and cf. Μελίτιον, *CIJ* I.141.

(45) Ξάνθος (b, l. 40 three times, twice for a father); Greek adjective, 'golden-haired', attested as a name from an early date and still current in the Roman world, at least into the third century; of 18 cases at Rome all are slaves, freed or of uncertain status.[153] No Jewish example found but cf. Ξανθίας, *CIJ* I.70.

(46) Ὀνήσιμος (b, l. 36); Greek adjective, 'helpful'; widely disseminated as a name in the Roman period; for obvious reasons common as a slave name, but not confined to slaves; of 449 cases at Rome 174 are certainly slave or freed;[154] in use at Aphrodisias.[155] For a Jewish example see *CIJ* II.761.

(47) Ὀξυχόλιος (b, l. 46, for a father); see list A, no. 51.

(48) Ὁρτάσιος (b, l. 49); see list A, no. 18.

(49) Παράμονος (b, l. 57); Greek adjective, 'trusty, enduring'; attested as a name from the classical period and quite widely disseminated in the Roman world; of 9 cases at Rome all are slave, freed or uncertain in status.[156] For a Jewish example cf. Παραμόνη, *CPJ* III.4, l. 19.

(50) Πατρίκιος (b, l. 53); transliterated Latin *Patricius*; quite well attested in the later Roman period, although not very common in our evidence.[157] For a Jewish example cf. Πατρικία, *CIJ* I.266.

(51) Πολυχρόνιος (b, ll. 42, 45); Greek adjective, 'long-lived', quite widely disseminated, both in the east and in the west, from the later second century; of 19 cases at Rome, the earliest thought to be of the second/third century, all are of uncertain status;[158] in use at Aphrodisias.[159] For a Jewish example see *CIJ* I.383 as corrected by H. Solin.[160]

(52) Προκόπιος (b, l. 58); Greek, from προκοπή, 'progress'; not very common in our evidence but attested, both in the east and in the west, as a name and as a *signum*, at least from the early third century; of 4 cases at Rome all are of uncertain status and thought to be of the third century;[161] attested

in use at Aphrodisias.[162] For a Jewish example see *Beth She'arim* 88, no. 200.

(53) **Προυνίκιος** (*b*, l. 59); Greek, from προύνικος, 'porter'; in the simpler form it occurs as a name occasionally in respectable circles; and 5 men with 1 woman are known at Rome, from the first to third centuries, all of uncertain status.[163] This is a secondary development and the only examples we have found are Christian, *IG* xvi.163 (Syracuse, from Bechtel *HP* 519) and *MAMA* iii.670 (Corycus).

(54) **?Πυ** (?) (*b*, l. 50, for a father); a number of old Greek names could be restored here, of which Πυθέας and Πύρρος are attested in use at Aphrodisias.[164]

(55) **'Ρωμανός** (*b*, l. 38); transliterated Latin *Romanus*; widely disseminated, both in the east and in the west, throughout the Roman period;[165] attested in use at Aphrodisias.[166] For a Jewish example see perhaps *CIJ* i.154.

(56) **Στρατήγιος** (*b*, l. 39); Greek, from στρατηγός, 'general'; attested examples are all from later antiquity; none in Rome except the feminine Στρατηγία, thought to be of the late second century.[167] No Jewish example found.

(57) **Στρατόνικος** (*b*, l. 59); Greek name attested from the classical period and widely disseminated in the Roman period, both in the east and in the west; of 23 cases at Rome most are slave, freed or uncertain in status;[168] attested in use at Aphrodisias.[169] There may be a Jewish example in *CIJ* i.176.

(58) **Τατιανός** (*b*, l. 46); perhaps to be associated with the local name Τατα, to which a Latin suffix has been given, rather than taken as transliterated Latin *Tatianus*; disseminated quite widely in the Roman period;[170] in use at Aphrodisias.[171] For a Jewish example cf. Τατιανή, *CIJ* ii.774.

(59) **Τέρτυλλος** (*b*, l. 35); transliterated Latin *Tertullus*; a quite widely disseminated name, both in the east and in the west, throughout the Roman period;[172] attested in use at Aphrodisias.[173] For a Jewish example see Acts 24:1.

(60) **Τυχικός** (*b*, l. 44, three times, twice for a father); Greek, from τύχη, 'luck'; one of many variants with the sense of 'fortunate', widely disseminated, both in the east and in the west, throughout the Hellenistic and Roman periods; of 15 cases at Rome the majority are slaves and freedmen;[174] attested in use at Aphrodisias.[175] For a Jewish example see *CIJ* i.412.

(61) **Ὑψικλῆς** (*b*, l. 41); old Greek name attested from the classical period and still current in the Roman period in the east; attested in use at Aphrodisias.[176] No Jewish example found.

(62) **Χρύσιππος** (*b*, l. 45); old Greek name attested from the classical period and quite widely disseminated, both in the east and in the west, during the Roman period, at any rate into the third century; of 15 cases at Rome all are slave, freed or uncertain in status;[177] in use at Aphrodisias.[178] No Jewish example found.

(63) ?Ψελλός (b, l. 52); attested as a nickname (see p. 13); we have not found it used as a name before the Byzantine period, but cf. Ψελλίων noted by L. Robert, *Noms Indigènes* 301, n. 1.

NOTES

1 Indeclinable – Βενιαμιν, Ἰαηλ, Ἰωσηφ, Σαμουηλ (used three times); with case endings – Ἰέσσεος, Ἰωσῆς (used twice), Ἰωσούας, Ἰούδας (used twice). Within the Roman period, the tendency seems to be to use case endings more often than not in the high empire, and indeclinable forms more often than not in late antiquity; but the time of the change in practice is not clearly defined because few of the relevant inscriptions are dated, and even the number of dated papyri is limited. The influence of the Septuagint, which used the indeclinable forms, might surely be felt at any date; and the papyri do in fact show some indeclinables quite early, cf. Ἀζακιελ in the second century (*CPJ* III.464), and some case-endings quite late, cf. Αὐρήλιος Ἰωσήφιος of A.D. 542 (*CPJ* III.508).
2 Σαβάθιος/Σαββάτιος, see list A, no. 59.
3 In general, for the existence of these equivalents, see the rabbinical reference at Lev.R. 32.5 (Hebrew edition of Mirkin); in the translation of J. J. Slotki (in the Soncino edition), R. Huna, citing Bar Kappara (c. A.D. 200–220), said that the Hebrews in Egypt were liberated by God because 'they did not change their names...they did not call Judah "Leon", nor Reuben "Rufus"...nor Benjamin "Alexander"'. On Θεόδοτος and Θεόδωρος for Jonathan and Nathaniel, see G. Mussies in Safrai/Stern II.1050, cf. also Lüderitz, *Cyrenaika* 65; on Ἀμάχιος and Ἰλαριανός see list A, nos. 3, 38.
4 See list A, no. 6.
5 See Mussies, *cit.* n. 3, 1051–2.
6 Indeclinable – Ἰακωβ/Ἰακω (used three times), Ἰωφ, Ἰωσηφ, Ῥουβην, Σαμουηλ, ?Συμεών; with case endings Ἰούδας (used eight times), Μανασῆς, Ζαχαρίας; see also n. 1. It will be seen that the majority of persons with a biblical name in fact used one with a case ending. The frequency of appearances of the name Ἰούδας accords with evidence elsewhere, cf. L. Robert, *Hellenica* III (1946) 101.
7 Ἑορτάσιος/Ὁρτάσιος (used four times), Εὐσαββάθιος (used five times), Λεόντιος (used twice), and perhaps Κύρυλλος.
8 Βιωτικός, Ζώσι(μος?), Ζωτικός, Καλλίκαρπος, Ἰάσων, Παρηγόριος, Σεραπίων; perhaps, Ἀχόλιος, Θεόφιλος, Παῦλος and Ῥοῦφος.
9 Αἰλιανός, Ἀμμιανός, Δαμόνικος, Διογένης, Εὐγένιος, Εὐσέβιος, Ζήνων, Ζώσι[μος?), Ζωτικός, Θεόφιλος, Ἰάσων, Λεόντιος, Μίλων; but the only ones known in common use are Ἀχιλλεύς, Διογένης, Ζήνων, Μίλων.
10 Λεόντιος Λεοντίου, l. 21, Αἰλιανὸς Αἰλιανοῦ, l. 29; R. Hachlili, *BASOR* 235 (1979) 53, notes that in Judaea this was a foreign custom, prevalent in the first century A.D. only among the local aristocracy (reference owed to O. Masson).
11 Αἰλιανός, l. 30; Εὐσαββάθιος, l. 16; Εὐτύχιος, ll. 25, 27; Ζήνων, l. 28; Ἰακω, Ἰακωβ, ll. 13, 20; Ἰούδας, l. 28; Ἰωσηφ, l. 26; Ὀξυχόλιος, ll. 11, 17.
12 Εὐσαββάθιος, l. 48, Ὁρτάσιος, l. 49.
13 ΙΟΥΝΒΑΛΟΣ, l. 43, see list B, no. 36; other explanations are available, see nos. 17, 35, 37.
14 Ἀντιπέος, l. 37, see list A. no. 6.
15 Ἀλέξανδρος, but it is so widely used that it seems rash to hold that it must be so used here; Ζωτικός, see list A, no. 30.
16 In the lower list Ἀθηναγόρας, Ἀθηνίων, Ἀλέξανδρος, Ἀντίοχος, Ἀπελλᾶς, Βραβεύς, ?Γρύλλος, Διογένης, Ἡδυχροῦς, Ζήνων, Καλλίμορφος, Καλλίνικος, Μελίτων, Ξάνθος, Ὀνήσιμος, Παράμονος, Στρατόνικος, Ὑψικλῆς, Χρύσιππος; in the upper list Ἀπελλί(ων?), Ἀχιλλεύς, Δαμόνικος, Διογένης, Εὔοδος, Ζήνων, Ἰάσων, Μίλων, Μύρτιλος, Φίλανθος, Χαρῖνος.

17 In the lower list Ἀθηναγόρας, Ἀλέξανδρος, Ἀμαζόνιος, Ἀντίοχος, Ἀπελλᾶς, ?Ἀρκάθιος, ?Ἄτταλος, Βαλεριανός, Διογένης, Εὐπίθιος, Εὐσέβιος, Εὐτυχιανός, Ζήνων, Ζωτικός, ?Ἡγεμονεύς, Καλλίνικος, Καλλίμορφος, Κλαυδιανός, ?Λονγι(ανός), Μελίτων, Ὀνήσιμος, Πολυχρόνιος, Ῥωμανός, Στρατόνικος, Τατιανός, Τέρτυλλος, Τυχικός, Ὑψικλῆς, Χρύσιππος; for the upper list see n. 9.
18 In the lower list ?Αἰλιανός, Ἀππιανός, Βαλεριανός, Κλαυδιανός, Λονγι(ανός) or Λονγῖ(νος), Πατρίκιος, Ῥωμανός, Τέρτυλλος, cf. also the hybrids Ἐλπιδιανός, Εὐτυχιανός, probably Τατιανός, and the *theosebes* Ἀντωνῖνος on face *a*: in the upper list Αἰλιανός, Ἀμάντιος, ?Ἀμμιανός Γέμελλος Παῦλος, Ῥοῦφος, Σεβῆρος, cf. also the hybrid Ἀμφιανός and on face *a* Ἰλαριανός, Πολιτιανός, perhaps Παλατῖνος.
19 Ἀπονήριος Ἀπονηρίου, l. 41; Εὐπίθιος Εὐπι(θίου), l. 53; Καλλίμορφος Καλ(λιμόρφου?), l. 43; Ξάνθος Ξάνθου, l. 40; Τυχικὸς Τυχι(κοῦ), l. 44.
20 Ἰακωβ ὁ κὲ Ἀπελλί(ων?), *b*, l. 20; Ἰούδας ὁ κὲ Ζώσι(μος?), *b*, l. 28; Αἰλιανὸς ὁ καὶ Σαμουηλ, *b*, l. 30.
21 For the development see L. Robert, *NIS* 40; Solin, *OL* 138–9. For the results cf. face *a*, Ἀμάχιος, Ἐμμόνιος, Εὐσέβιος, Σαβάθιος (Σαββάτιος), Ἰλαριανός, Πολιτιανός; face *b*, upper list, Ἀμάντιος, Ἀνύσιος, Ἀχόλιος, Γοργόνιος, Ἑορτάσιος/Ὀρτάσιος, Εὐγένιος, Εὐσαββάθιος, Εὐσέβιος, ?Εὐτάρκιος, Εὐτύχιος, Λεόντιος, Ὀξυχόλιος, Πραοίλιος; lower list Ἀδόλιος, Ἀμαζόνιος, Ἀπονήριος, Γληγόριος, Γοργόνιος, Εὐπίθιος, Εὐσαββάθιος, Εὐτρόπιος, Ὀρτάσιος, Πολυχρόνιος, Προκόπιος, Προυνίκιος, Στρατήγιος, Αἰλιανός, Ἀμμιανός, Ἀμφιανός.
22 Kajanto, *LC* 139, records 128 examples.
23 C. M. Roueché, *JRS* 71 (1981) 108, no. 5, l. 3, probably in the second half of the third century.
24 Kajanto, *LC* 255, *Supernomina* 76; Solin, *OL*, 106.
25 Solin, *GP* 831, has four examples at Rome, two of them Jews; for a certainly pagan example see K. Kostoglou-Despini, *AAA* 4 (1971) 202–6.
26 See Lüderitz, *Cyrenaika* 168.
27 Zgusta, *KP* 59, 57, 16f.
28 *MAMA* VIII.451 for instance.
29 Solin, *GP* 459–61, has 53 slaves or freedmen out of a total of 93 cases in Rome.
30 Solin, *GP*, has no examples at Rome, although Anytus, Anyte are found.
31 Solin, *GP* 255.
32 Solin, *GP* 31.
33 Solin, *GP* 464–6.
34 *MAMA* VIII.559 for instance.
35 Kajanto, *Supernomina* 76, Solin, *GP* 771.
36 Solin, *GP* 816.
37 Kajanto, *LC* 295.
38 For the meaning of the adjective when applied to ephebes, see L. Robert, *Hellenica* I (1940) 128.
39 Kajanto, *Supernomina* 83; Solin, *GP* 534.
40 Solin, *GP* 35.
41 *BMC Caria* 663.
42 Solin, *GP* 236–8.
43 *MAMA* VIII.417 for instance.
44 So Mussies, *cit*. n. 5.
45 Solin, *GP* 1037–8; see also the note by L. Robert, *Noms Indigènes* 284.
46 See n. 5.
47 Solin, *GP* 338.
48 *MAMA* VIII.413 for instance.
49 Kajanto, *Supernomina* 81; Solin, *GP* 983–4.
50 L. Robert, *Hellenica* IV (1948) 133.
51 *IG* IX.2, 549, cited by Bechtel, *HP* 172; B. Petrakos, in *Acts of the Athens epigraphic congress, 1982* (1985) 335.

PERSONAL NAMES   113

52 Solin, *GP* 852.
53 Kajanto, *Supernomina* 81; Solin, *GP* 1227–9.
54 Appendix I.9 which may be Jewish, and a graffito, as yet unpublished, on a theatre seat.
55 Kajanto, *Supernomina* 82; Solin, *GP* 811.
56 Solin, *GP* 240–1.
57 *MAMA* VIII.409 for instance.
58 Solin, *GP* 819.
59 *MAMA* VIII.545 for instance.
60 Solin, *GP* 827.
61 R. Noll, *Griechische und lateinische Inschriften der Wiener Antikensammlung* (1962) no. 67.
62 Solin, *GP* 71–2; cf. n. 3 above.
63 *MAMA* VIII.490 for instance.
64 Solin, *GP* 74–6.
65 *MAMA* VIII.477 for instance.
66 Solin, *GP* 81–2.
67 Inscription from Aphrodisias as yet unpublished.
68 V. Tcherikover, *Hellenistic civilisation and the Jews* (1959) 523, n. 5.
69 Here we have drawn heavily on the help of Professor Martin Hengel and Dr Nicholas de Lange.
70 On the variant form Ἰακω see L. Robert, *RPh*. 32 (1958) 39, n. 5, 40, n. 1.
71 Solin, *GP* 489–90.
72 *MAMA* VIII.488 for instance.
73 So e.g. Mussies, *cit*. n. 3, and cf. Lüderitz, *Cyrenaika* 31.
74 Kajanto, *LC* 260.
75 Lebas-Waddington 595 for instance.
76 A suggestion from Dr de Lange; it is commonly thought that Γελάσιος was so regarded, see Mussies, *cit*. n. 3.
77 Solin, *GP* 91.
78 A suggestion from Dr de Lange.
79 Solin, *GP* 409.
80 Kajanto, *Supernomina* 84; Solin, *GP* 1052–4.
81 *MAMA* VIII.586 for instance.
82 L. Robert, *NIS* 46–7.
83 Solin, *GP* 256.
84 *MAMA* VIII.413 for instance.
85 Solin, *GP* 1096–7.
86 For a collection of instances and discussion see L. Robert, *Documents de l'Asie Mineure Méridionale* (1966) 63–4; cf. also Solin, *GP* 880.
87 Kajanto, *LC* 284; Solin, *GP* 778.
88 Kajanto, *LC* 50.
89 Kajanto, *Supernomina* 87, *LC* 243; Solin, *GP* 1248.
90 Mussies, *cit*. n. 3.
91 Kajanto, *LC* 243.
92 For this use of the suffix -ianus from the second century onwards see Solin, *OL* 138–9.
93 Kajanto, *LC*, only has *Politus*.
94 *CIL* VI.13287 (*ICVR* I.1286).
95 For Πραΰλιος see W. H. Buckler, *JHS* 37 (1917) 95 (whence Grégoire, *Byzantion* 2 [1925] 330, W. M. Calder and H. Grégoire, *Bull. Acad. Belgique* [1952] 163, J. and L. Robert, *Bull. Ep.* 1954.211, where there is a printer's error giving Πραΰλλιος, and also G. Daux, *BCH* 89 [1965] 302).
96 For discussion see L. Robert, *Hellenica* XI–XII.414f., especially 422, N. G. Cohen, *JSJ* 7 (1976) 112f.
97 Kajanto, *LC* 30.
98 See Cohen, *cit*. n. 96, 118–19.
99 Kajanto, *LC* 256–7.

100 See Mussies, *cit.* n. 3.
101 Solin, *GP* 377–8.
102 Cohen, *cit.* n. 96, 112–16; cf. also Lüderitz, *Cyrenaika* 29.
103 Solin, *GP* 157; but see also *TAM* III.525 of the third century.
104 Solin, *GP* 1298.
105 *MAMA* III.492B, 536B for Corycus; *Vit. Pythag.* §267 for Iamblichus.
106 *SEG* XXVII.1268, for instance.
107 Solin, *GP* 731.
108 Solin, *GP* 13, cf. *MAMA* VIII.517.
109 Solin, *GP* 267.
110 Solin, *GP* 186–94.
111 *MAMA* VIII.414, for instance.
112 Cohen, *cit.* n. 96, 119.
113 Kajanto, *Supernomina* 76; Solin, *GP* 528.
114 *MAMA* VIII.414, for instance.
115 Solin, *GP* 201–6.
116 *MAMA* VIII.565, for instance.
117 Solin, *OL* 107.
118 Solin, *GP* 253–4.
119 *MAMA* VIII.559, for instance.
120 Kajanto, *LC* 172; Solin, *GP* 954.
121 Solin, *GP* 570.
122 *MAMA* VIII.536.
123 Zgusta, *KAP* 119.7 and 119.9.
124 Solin, *GP* 954.
125 Solin, *GP* 209–11.
126 *MAMA* VIII.413, for instance.
127 Zgusta, *KAP* 141.1, cf. also *SEG* XXXI.1526c; for a possible connection between the Aphrodisian synagogue and Pamphylia see p. 42 on ll. 9–17, left margin.
128 Bechtel, *HP* 517 records an example of the fifth century B.C. at Maroneia.
129 Kajanto, *Supernomina* 59–61; Solin, *GP* 764–6.
130 Solin, *GP* 1046, cites Martial I.59.3.
131 Solin, *GP* 1212, cites *ICVR* 12936.
132 Zgusta, *KAP* §§333–4 cites G. Perrot, J. Delbot, *Exploration archéologique de la Galatie et de la Bithynie* (1862) 60, no. 45, probably of the third century.
133 Solin, *GP* 477.
134 Inscription as yet unpublished.
135 Solin, *GP* 1275, with 1271.
136 Kajanto, *Supernomina* 82; Solin, *GP* 1278–9.
137 Solin, *GP* 807–8.
138 *CIG* 2801.
139 Reynolds, *Aphrodisias* 132.
140 Solin, *GP* 691.
141 See W. Schulze, *Kleine Schriften* 281–96; A. Buturas, *Glotta* 5 (1914) 175.
142 Solin, *GP* 834.
143 Inscription as yet unpublished.
144 Solin, *GP* 92.
145 *MAMA* VIII.451.
146 Kajanto, *LC* 144.
147 *MAMA* VIII.517, for instance.
148 *MAMA* VIII.418.
149 Kajanto, *LC* 231.
150 Zgusta, *Die Personennamen griechischer Städte der nördlichen Schwarzmeerküste* (1955) 293.
151 Solin, *GP* 1290–1.

PERSONAL NAMES 115

152 *MAMA* VIII.478, for instance.
153 Solin, *GP* 693–4.
154 Solin, *GP* 913–19.
155 *MAMA* VIII.413 (freedman), 560 (citizen), for instances.
156 Solin, *GP* 762–3.
157 Kajanto, *LC* 313.
158 Solin, *GP* 948–9.
159 *MAMA* VIII.457, for instance.
160 Solin, *Arctos* 11 (1977) 122.
161 Kajanto, *Supernomina* 88; Solin, *GP* 1250.
162 *IGCA* 247.
163 *LSJ* cite *IG* 3.1100, l. 12 (Athens) of the second century A.D., *IG* 12.8.484 (Thasos); see also Solin, *GP* 1030.
164 *MAMA* VIII.409, 492, for instances.
165 Kajanto, *LC* 182.
166 Inscription as yet unpublished.
167 Solin, *GP* 1254.
168 Solin, *GP* 145.
169 *BMC Caria* 131.
170 Kajanto, *LC* 156.
171 *MAMA* VIII.576, for instance.
172 Kajanto, *LC* 292.
173 Inscription as yet unpublished.
174 Solin, *GP* 446–7.
175 Inscription as yet unpublished.
176 *MAMA* VIII.408, for instance.
177 Solin, *GP* 251.
178 *CIG* 2774, for instance.

VI COMMENTARY: THE TRADE-DESIGNATIONS

On face *b* a number of names are followed by trade-designations which are of interest beyond their significance in this particular text. Elsewhere, at any rate in the eastern provinces, such designations seem to be commoner in the late Roman than in the earlier evidence; but they are certainly not excluded at any date, as is shown, for instance, by a text of the fourth century B.C. at Ephesus which includes trade-designations beside a number of names in a list of sacrilegious Sardians.[1] It is the comparative rarity of texts concerned with persons of modest status in the earlier evidence which has surely distorted the picture – many men must always have been known by their trades. If a particular explanation seems needed for the number in this inscription it might have to be sought in the civic status of some of the persons listed, who may have been resident aliens without γῆς ἔγκτησις, and so very obviously dependent on, therefore associated with, a craft or trade, see further pp. 124–5. It is unfortunate that in the text here the designations are all abbreviated, except in ll. 8 and 50, and sometimes so sharply as to leave it in doubt whether a name, trade-designation or other description was intended, and, if a trade-designation, which of several possibilities is the right one. Nevertheless there is sufficient information to justify a brief discussion based on the two annotated lists given on pp. 117f. and 119f.

Twenty-two persons are described, certainly or very plausibly, by trade-designations and a further five possibly so, ten of these twenty-seven being Jews and seventeen *theosebeis*. We have no explanation for the discrepancy in numbers and feel that they are too small to justify speculation. The trades named are paralleled from other evidence, often also from other evidence concerning Jews; but although only one trade, that of bronze-smith, appears on both lists, it is clear that there is nothing particularly Jewish about those in which the Jews were engaged. We may assume that Jews concerned in food trades will have respected the dietary laws; in principle, however, there is no trade in either list in which pagans and Christians are not also known to have been engaged (where any identifiable practitioners are recorded). The *theosebeis* are shown in a wider range of occupations, which may include some that might be thought surprising for a Jew, see p. 57; but that is the most that can be said.

The information can be tabulated in much the same way and with much the same results as in recent work on similar documentation elsewhere, notably at

Corycus, Tyre and Narbonne.² Social and economic considerations are discussed on pp. 124–31.

N.B. in the following table the less certain designations are preceded by a question-mark; some designations appear under more than one heading.

 a. Production and sales of food: 'charcutier', confectioner (2), greengrocer, ?grocer, ?poulterer, ?sheep-rearer.
 b. Production and sales of textiles: carder/fuller (3), ?linen-worker, purple-dyer, rag-picker (second-hand clothes dealer), ?sheep-rearer, ?stitcher (braider, plaiter).
 c. Production of leather-goods: ?boot-maker, ?harness-maker, ?sheep-rearer.
 d. Production of metal goods: ?armlet-maker, bronze-smith (2, ?3), goldsmith, ?missile-maker.
 e. Woodworking: carpenter, ?tablet-maker, ?knob-turner.
 f. Stoneworking: stone-cutter/carver, ?image-maker, ?marble-worker.
 g. Building construction: carpenter, ?plasterer, ?stone-cutter, ?marble-worker.
 h. Other crafts: ?ink-maker, ?painter (of images).
 i. Miscellaneous services: ?customs'-collector, ?dealer in horse-fodder, ?door-keeper, money-changer, ?treasurer.
 j. Others: ?athlete, ?boxer.

In the lists below we are grateful for information, particularly linguistic information, contributed by Olivier Masson on nos. A, 1–8; B, 2, 4, 5, 8, 13, 19, 21.

(A) *For Jews*
 (1) **Γρυτ(οπώλης?)**, *b*, l. 28, 'rag-picker, rag-dealer, ?second-hand clothes dealer'; in a recent discussion of the term, Marcel Hombert has noted its rarity in all categories of source material;³ to his assembly of evidence one case may be added from the cemetery at Tyre.⁴ It is clear that this was a low-status occupation, but its members were sometimes organised, as at Cos in the Augustan period,⁵ where they were able to contribute to a public monument; and, given the probable importance of the second-hand cloth and clothing trade in antiquity,⁶ some of its dealers, although lacking in interest to literary writers, doubtless made a fair living. In comment on the inscription at Cos, Maiuri suggested that its dedicators were Jews (despite their dedication to Hermes); Hombert observes that Jews have no particular association with the trade in antiquity, although one Jewish rag-dealer is already known, *CIJ* II.928, an Alexandrian whose son was buried at Joppa. The addition of this Aphrodisian case does not undermine his argument.

(2) Λαχα(νοπώλης?), l. 15, 'greengrocer'; quite a well-attested term (also in the shortened form λαχανᾶς, and cf. too λαχανευτής, λαχανοπράτης),[7] although commoner in papyri than in inscriptions, no doubt because of the modest status normally involved. But an inscribed censer, the offering of a Christian greengrocer, acquired for the Collection Froehner in Smyrna,[8] shows that donations were within the reach of some. No other Jewish example found.

(3) Μονο(πώλης?), l. 20, ?'retailer', ?'grocer';[9] a rare term known only from one inscription recording a Carpus, *monopoles*, citizen of Ancyra and Tavium, who dedicated Θεῷ Ὑψίστῳ;[10] given his double citizenship and his dedication he can hardly have been a really poor man. (It is just possible that he was a *theosebes* – not, however, a Jew (see pp. 64–5) – but there is no clear indication of it, and many dedications to Θεὸς Ὕψιστος are wholly pagan.)[11]

(4) Ὀρν(ιθοπώλης?), l. 27, 'poulterer'; another rare term;[12] the alternative ὀρνιθᾶς may be confined to Egypt and seems to correspond rather to an ὀρνιθοτρόφος.[13] No other Jewish example found, but because of Jewish slaughtering laws it is likely that this kind of trade within a Jewish community would always be handled by a Jew. See p. 57.

(5) Παστι(λλάριος?), l. 26, twice, 'confectioner'; this term, and its shortened form παστι(λλᾶς), which would provide an alternative restoration here, are quite well attested both in inscriptions and papyri, the earliest known in an inscription of the third century A.D. at Hierapolis.[14] No other Jewish example found.

(6) Προβατον(όμος?), l. 13, 'shepherd', ?'sheep-rearer'; compounds with πρόβατον are known, thus προβατο-βοσκός, προβατο-κτηνο-νόμος, but none is attested in which the second element has initial *nu*; what O.Masson has proposed is unattested but plausible on the analogy of μηλο-νόμος, αἰγι-νόμος etc. There was certainly sheep-rearing in the territory of Aphrodisias and one tombstone for a shepherd has been found;[15] but shepherds were usually men of very modest means, and even a master-shepherd would lead an isolated life, so that a sheep-rearer, i.e. owner of a flock, seems more likely here.

(7) Χαλκο(τύπος?), ll. 25, 53 and perhaps 46, the second and third cases being *theosebeis*, 'bronze-smith'; a common term (cf. also χαλκεύς, χαλκουργός), well known in inscriptions and papyri as well as in literature, the earliest known inscription being of the sixth century B.C.[16] We have chosen the form of the word thought to be in commonest use in the imperial period.[17] For another Jewish smith cf. Alexander the smith, referred to as an influential figure in his community in the Epistles to Timothy.[18]

(8) ?Χιλᾶς, l. 28, unattested but perhaps a 'dealer in horse-fodder' or a

'stitcher', 'braider', 'plaiter'; for the first sense it would be related to χίλος, 'forage', as κυμινᾶς to κύμινον, μαραθᾶς to μάραθος, πρασᾶς to πράσον etc.:[19] for the second it would be a form of χηλᾶς, cf. Hesychius, χηλᾶς; ῥάπτης, πλέκτης...and χηλεύει: ῥάπτει, πλέκει; discussed by P. Chantraine, *Dictionnaire étymologique de la langue grecque*, *s.v.* χηλή. For its rare use as a name, see p. 105, no. 67.

(9) **Χρυσοχόος**, l. 9, 'goldsmith'; a well-attested term throughout antiquity and one implying a respectable status, as this man's place in the list shows; cf. the goldsmith who was a city-councillor at Mutina in the second century A.D. (*L'Ann. Ep.* 1981, 387).

Goldsmiths are also known at Aphrodisias from as yet unpublished inscriptions in the stadium, which show that an organisation of αὐράριοι had reserved seats there. For other Jewish goldsmiths see *CIJ* II.805, 1006.

(B) *Theosebeis*

(1) ?'**Ἀθλη(τής?)**, l. 54, 'athlete'; it is difficult to see how else to resolve the abbreviated word, but an athlete is unexpected in this company, and in any case this man comes rather low in the list for the status of his profession. Since he is a *theosebes* he would presumably have felt no religious scruples (see also p. 57); moreover it is now thought possible that diaspora Jews were not always completely opposed to athleticism.[20]

(2) ?'**Ἀρκά(ριος?)**, l. 56, 'treasurer'; Greek transliteration of Latin *arcarius*, attested for men in imperial service throughout the empire and in the west also in civic and private employment; normally slaves.[21] An imperial slave might be expected to appear rather higher up this list; and at Aphrodisias the city and most private households would surely have used a Greek word, ?οἰκονόμος. So if this is an occupational designation, it suggests a treasurer in the household of one of the Aphrodisians who were Roman senators (there were at least two by the early third century), where nomenclature might well be romanized.

(3) ?**Βελ(οποιός?)**, l. 45, 'missile-maker'; an attested term, but very rare;[22] the area of Aphrodisias would have been good hunting country and is also likely to have needed patrolling against brigands, so that there would be demand.

(4) **Γναφ(εύς)**, ll. 58–9, three cases; 'fuller' or 'carder'; a well-attested term for men performing essential functions in the production of cloth; the earliest example cited by *LSJ*[9] is probably of the sixth century B.C.[23] Fulling establishments (*fullonicae*, κναφεῖα) are designed to carry out a variety of specialised operations both to new cloth and to soiled clothing, among others cleaning, bleaching, combing and shearing the nap. A number of water-basins and cleaning-tubs were required (examples have been found

at Pompeii), as well as instruments, and, in consequence, a sizeable material investment was involved.²⁴ The three men here, since they are placed near the bottom of the list and in a proximity to each other which perhaps suggests a workshop group, are, then, far more likely to be employees – whether slave, freed or free and paid – than owners of establishments. For a Jewish example see *CIJ* 929 (Joppa), but the occupation is naturally widespread.

(5) Ἰκονο(γράφος?), ἰκονο(ποιός?), l. 57, 'image-painter', 'sculptor'; ἰκονογράφος is only known in restored form, [εἰκονο]γράφος, in Diocletian's Price Edict, where it corresponds to Latin *pictor imaginarius*²⁵ – he would presumably paint portraits, or images of live, dead or mythological characters; ἰκονο(ποιός) implies sculpture or modelling of some kind; Jewish Law concerning graven images seems to have tolerated painting or drawing or other representation in the flat (so mosaic), see p. 57. This was in any case a *theosebes* who did not necessarily feel bound by the Jewish Law; see also on λατύπος. The status of the craft varied, but might be higher than this man's place in the list suggests, cf. a summary of some recent discussion in *SEG* xxix.1206.

(6) Ἰσικιάριος, l. 51, 'charcutier', 'maker of mincemeat'; transliterated Latin *isiciarius*, a term adequately attested in late antiquity but no doubt current earlier since the *insicia* which the *isiciarius* made and sold were already mentioned by Varro.²⁶ The man was a *theosebes* and may not have felt bound by the Jewish dietary laws; but in any case Diocletian's Price Edict lists *isicia bubula* as well as *porcina*, so that he could have conformed to Jewish standards if he had wished (see also p. 57).

(7) ?Καλ(ιγάριος?), l. 50, 'boot-maker'; transliterated Latin *caligarius*, known from a number of examples in the eastern provinces, the earliest perhaps of the third century. For a Jewish example see *CIJ* ii.787.

(8) Λατύ(πος?), l. 49, 'stone-cutter/carver'; a term quite well-attested in inscriptions from at least the second century A.D. (sometimes in the form λαοτύπος) for men who sometimes seem of quite high local status;²⁷ the man might cut and dress stones or carve figures, including portraits. His occupation is a very natural one at Aphrodisias because of its marble-quarries; other inscriptions there suggest that a stone-carver making figures might be more likely to call himself ἀγαλματοποιός, but it is not known whether that would also apply to one who carved in relief. On the implications for θεοσεβεῖς and Jewish Law, see under ἰκονογράφος, ἰκονοποιός, and p. 57.

(9) ?Λευ(κουργός?), l. 51, 'marble-worker'; a trade particularly suitable at Aphrodisias; the term is reasonably well-attested and used of a workman at nearby Heraclea Salbake.²⁸

(10) ?Λευ(κωτής), l. 51, 'plasterer'; the term is quite well-attested in a trade naturally needed everywhere, and clearly not necessarily without some standing.

(11) ?Λι(νουργός?), or perhaps λι(νοξόος), λι(νοπώλης), λι(νυφαντάριος), λί(νυφος), l. 42, 'linen-worker'; an occupation well-documented throughout the ancient world and certainly suitable in Aphrodisias where there was an organised group of λινουργοί; but if correct here its position suggests a higher status than might have been expected.[29]

(12) ?Μελ(ανουργός), l. 41, presumably 'ink-maker'; the word appears as the equivalent of Latin *atramentarius* in late Glossaries, see G. Loewe, G. Goetz, *Corpus Glossariorum Latinorum* III (1965) 308.47, 529.82, but neither word seems to be otherwise attested.

(13) ?Πενα(κᾶς?), l. 47, 'maker of wooden tablets'; a trade quite well-attested in antiquity and a term attested for it in a Christian inscription at Athens; it must correspond to πινάκια, wooden writing tablets.[30]

(14) Πορφυρ(ᾶς), l. 39, 'purple-dyer', 'purple-seller', a well-known ancient trade for which πορφυρεύς, πορφυροπώλης were also used – we have chosen πορφυρᾶς because it is already attested in use at Aphrodisias.[31] The value of the dye would suggest that a respectable status was likely and that accords with the position of this man in the list; cf. H. W. Pleket's recent citation of a πορφυροπώλης who was a member of the city council at Hierapolis (probably third century).[32]

(15) ?Πύ(κτης?), l. 50, 'boxer'; a word found often enough in inscriptions and papyri (see *LSJ s.v.*); it does not seem particularly suitable in this context, but since the man is a *theosebes* it may be right. For other possibilities see nos. 16, 17 below and List B of names, no. 54.

(16) ?Πυ(λουρός?), l. 50, 'door-keeper'; the word appears at Athens in the first century A.D. for citizens on duty at the gate of the Acropolis (*IG* II².2292), their function perhaps to be gauged from the evidence for the πυλωρός at the gate of the Acropolis of Pergamum, who received a sum of money in respect of sacrifices offered on it (*I. Pergamon* 255 [*Sylloge*³ 982], cf. E. Ohlemutz, *Die Kulte und Heiligtümer der Götter in Pergamon* [1940] 52–4); it is clearly most unlikely that a man employed in such cult-related activity would become a *theosebes*; it also occurs at Dura-Europos in the later second century, again for freeborn men performing a public function (P. V. C. Baur and M. I. Rostovtzev, *The excavations at Dura-Europos, preliminary report on the second season of work* [1931] 138–9, nos. 102, 103, with discussion pp. 156–8) – Jotham Johnson, who published the texts, connected it with the use of πύλη for a customs-house in *P. Teb.* 1.5.34–5, of πῶρτα in the same sense at Dura and of ὁ σατράπης ὁ ἐπὶ τῶν μεγάλων πυλῶν at Babylon, in Philostratus, *V. Apollonii* 1.27, and inclined to

interpret it as a customs'-collector; in late Glossaries (*cit.* under B, no 12 above) it is given with the Latin equivalents *ianitor, portitor*, where *portitor* again means customs'-collector. A customs'-collector in the Roman world might denote either a contractor who bought the contract to collect a particular tax or group of taxes, or a member of his staff (who, of course, actually did the work of collection and who might well be a slave). The alternative sense of 'janitor' would apply to one employed in a public building (e.g. a bath building) or a private house, both very likely to be slaves. This man's position in the list may seem rather high for a slave, but a slave employed in collection of customs duties or as a door-keeper might achieve some prosperity through extortion or receipt of tips, so that it is perhaps not unreasonably so.

(17) ?Πυ(ρηνᾶς?), l. 50, 'knob-turner'; unattested in the singular number, but there was a trade-organisation of πυρηνάδες at Ephesus.[33]

(18) Τέκτω(ν), l. 60, 'carpenter'; a well-attested term at all periods – there are three in the cemetery at Tyre; social status varied from slave upwards.[34]

(19) Τρα(πεζίτης?), l. 58, 'money-changer'; a widely-attested term at all periods, covering a variety of social statuses.[35] For a Jewish example see *CIJ* 1010.

(20) ?Χαλ(ινουργός?), l. 46, 'harness-maker'; a term given in a late Glossary as an equivalent for Latin *lorarius*, and perhaps attested in abbreviated form, χαλινου(ργός), in *Sammelbuch* 5124.684 of the second century.[36]

(21) Χαλκο(τύπος?), l. 53, ?l. 46, 'bronze-smith'; see A, no. 7.

(22) ?Ψελ(οποιός), ψελ(ιοποιός), l. 52, 'armlet-maker'; a term known only from a late Glossary where it appears as an equivalent of Latin *armillarius*.[37]

NOTES

1 *I. Eph.* 1.1.
2 E. Patlagean, *Pauvreté économique et pauvreté sociale à Byzance* (1977) 158f. (Corycus); Rey-Coquais (*cit.* n. 4) 152–61 (Tyre); M. Gayraud, *Narbonne antique des origines à la fin du IIIe siècle* (1981) 479–91. See also K. Hopkins in D. Abrams and E. A. Wrigley (eds.), *Towns in societies* (1978) 52f.
3 M. Hombert, in A. E. Hanson (ed.), *Collectanea papyrologica...in honour of H. C. Youtie* (1976) 621–6.
4 J.-P. Rey-Coquais, *Bulletin du musée de Beyrouth* 29 (1977) 56, no. 95.
5 A. Maiuri, *Nuova silloge epigraphica di Rodi e Cos* (1925) 168, no. 466; the connection he makes with luxury toilet articles is mistaken.
6 H. Granger Taylor by letter, with reference to an article in preparation for *JRS*.
7 For λαχανοπώλης, λαχανᾶς see O. Masson, *ZPE* 11 (1973) 7–9; for λαχανευτής P. Oxy. 1139.2, λαχανοπράτης P. Amh. 148.2.
8 A. Mondésert, *Syria* 37 (1960) 122–3, with correction by J. and L. Robert, *Bull. Ép.* 1961, 71.
9 *LSJ*[9] translate 'monopoly holder' which is not very helpful. It is probably better interpreted as approximately equivalent to the commoner παντοπώλης on whose wares (which might

include pickles, paints, drugs) the glossaries throw some light, see L. Robert, *Hellenica* 11–12 (1960) 40, 46.
10 G. Iacopi, *Dalla Paflagonia alla Commagene* (1936) 13f., J. and L. Robert, *Bull. Ep.* 1938, 487.
11 See A. T. Kraabel, *GRBS* 10 (1969) 87–93.
12 *LSJ*[9] cite only Pollux 7.198.
13 Discussed by O. Masson, *CE* 49 (1974) 177–8.
14 For a discussion and collection of cases see L. Robert, *Noms indigènes* I (1963) 242. The third century example is in *I. Hier.* no. 222.
15 J. M. R. Cormack, *ABSA* 59 (1964) 29, no. 42, L. Robert, *AC* 35 (1966) 383.
16 *SEG* XII.364 (Camirus). For a collection of later inscribed instances see L. Robert, *Études Épigraphiques et Philologiques* (1938) 195.
17 J. and L. Robert, *Bull. Ep.* 1962, no. 307.
18 II Tim. 4:14.
19 For a list of these words see L. Robert, *Hellenica* 11–12 (1960) 43, and for discussion O. Masson, *ZPE* 11 (1973) 1–19.
20 H. A. Harris, *Greek athletics and the Jews* (1976).
21 Ch. Habicht, *Altertümer von Pergamon* VIII.3, 99 and 125 (imperial slaves); *CIL* x.1495 (Naples, a civic slave); *CIL* VI.9146 (private slave).
22 *LSJ*[9] cite only Philo Mechanicus, Βελοποιική 58 (*Abh. Berl. Akad.* 1918, no. 16, p. 25), Pollux 7.156.
23 *IG* I².436 (Athens); for a later example see *MAMA* III.361 at Corycus.
24 Daremberg-Saglio, *Dictionnaire des Antiquités* II.2 (1896) *s.v. Fullonica*, cols. 1349–52 making use of the remains of *fullonicae* found at Pompeii in the nineteenth century and sculptured reliefs of them from Italy and Gaul.
25 S. J. Lauffer, *Diokletians Preisedikt* (1971) 119 (ch. 7, l. 9).
26 See P. Ryl. IV.640.10, 641; P. Strassb. 46; Varro, *De Lingua Latina* 5.110; for an early third century example see now D. Knibbe, *JOAI* 56 (1986) 71, no. 2.
27 For a collection of examples see L. Robert, *Hellenica* 11–12 (1960) 30–1, note especially J. and L. Robert, *La Carie* II.210, no. 146 (of A.D. 155–6), G. Radet, *BCH* 11 (1887) 448, no. 7.
28 For examples see L. Robert, *Ét. Anat.* 107, J. and L. Robert, *Bull. Ep.* 1949.234, *La Carie* II.182, no. 162, Th. Reinach, *BCH* 32 (1908) 500f. where the man must have had some status to appear in this kind of text.
29 The Aphrodisian evidence is as yet unpublished; on the probably low social status of linen-workers in general see H. W. Pleket, *Acta of the Athens epigraphic congress, 1982* (1985), 140, 141.
30 *CIA* III.3459, see also J. S. Creaghan and A. E. Raubitschek, *Hesperia* 16 (1947) 8, 19, no. 107, and the discussion by O. Masson, *ZPE* 11 (1973) 5–7.
31 *MAMA* VIII.562, perhaps of the second century A.D.
32 Lauffer, *cit.* n. 26, 187, 189 for the value of the dye; cf. also J. P. Rey-Coquais, *cit,* n. 4, 158–9; and for some recent discussion Pleket, *cit.* n. 29, 141–2.
33 *I. Eph.* VI.2079.
34 For the meaning see J. and L. Robert, *Bull. Ep.* 53.279; and for Tyre, Rey-Coquais, *cit.* n. 4, nos. 11*b*, 65, 143; for a slave see *SEG* XXIX.1186 at Saittae.
35 For a definition see R. Bogaert, *Banques et banquiers dans les cités grecques* (1968) 39–41 and for examples the list on pp. 429–30.
36 *LSJ*[9] *s.v.* and cf. H. V. Petrikovits, *ZPE* 43 (1982) 301.
37 *LSJ*[9] *s.v.* and cf. Petrikovits, *cit.* n. 36, 304.

VII THE SOCIETY AND ECONOMY OF APHRODISIAS

The stone presents a part of the Jewish community at Aphrodisias (two parts, at two different periods, for those not convinced of the contemporaneity of the two inscribed faces), together, we believe, with a group of associated gentiles; in all seventy-one active Jews (including the three proselytes) and fifty-four associated *theosebeis*. Although the gentile group (the *theosebeis*) certainly covered a wide social and economic range (from city-councillors down to fullers, who were probably employees and possibly slaves), and the Jews may well have done so too, it would be rash to assume that either is representative of the city as a whole; we do not have anything that we can safely take as a cross-section of the total population. Nevertheless some light is thrown not only on the life of the Jews but on the society and economy of the city as a whole, if this evidence is examined with caution. Caution is called for, above all, by the omissions from the lists, especially those of most synagogue officials and senior members of the Jewish community, of all women (with one possible exception, see p. 101, no. 34), and, if face *b* contains a donors' list, as we believe (see p. 22–3), of any really indigent persons; but we also lack relevant indications of the civic status of most of those listed. That being said, however, there is information worth discussing.

In the first place, the Jews of Aphrodisias, unknown before Professor Erim's excavation began, and glimpsed only in a very small way before the discovery of this stone (see Appendix), can now be seen as a coherent unit and a significant element in the life of the city, at any rate from the beginning of the third century A.D. They form a group whose origins are unknown. It could have been a comparatively recent development at the time of the inscription, resulting from the voluntary immigration of individuals attracted by favourable conditions at Aphrodisias;[1] but many Jewish communities in Asia Minor are known to have been in existence in the second and first centuries B.C.,[2] and the Aphrodisian may have been one of them. Some originated in colonies established by Hellenistic kings;[3] and although we have no positive reason for thinking that there was such a colony in the territory of Aphrodisias, neither do we have any grounds for excluding it. The civic status of Jewish colonists and their descendants is controversial, but those descendants would surely inherit, as their own property, land allotments and installations built on them; voluntary immigrants to a Greek city, on the other hand, would have no right to own real property within its territory unless given the privileges either of γῆς ἔγκτησις or of local citizenship.[4] We do not, at present, know with certainty whether any Jew resident at Aphrodisias had either privilege; all may have been free resident aliens without the right to own real estate there, while some may even have been slaves, since the absence of patronymics with a number of names could, although it need not, have that implication. We may of course be sure that the nine *theosebeis* who were city councillors were free-born and Aphrodisian citizens; but there may well be immigrants or freedmen among the remaining *theosebeis* too, again, in that case, with the status of resident aliens, and equally, perhaps some slaves. One man in the list of Jews may be from Perge in Pamphylia (*a*, ll. 9–17, left margin), one (*b*, l. 16) is described as ξένος, which we have taken to mean 'immigrant' (pp. 47–8); others on either list may be so without proclaiming it, and the presence of a number of persons with transliterated Latin names may be a sign of this. Transliterated Latin names are not unknown in the other evidence from Aphrodisias, but the number here is unexpectedly large[5] and perhaps points to influence, and visitors, from outside, especially from the provincial capital of Ephesus, with its Roman officials and soldiers and its Jewish community well attested in the literary evidence.[6]

Of the Jews it may be said that they showed a serious interest in their own traditions, by what we take to have been study of Judaic Law, and, more simply, by adoption of biblical names, quite often in indeclinable form unadapted to Greek usage, as well as of Greco-Roman names which were associable with biblical ones, or which emphasised pacific, moral and cooperative qualities (see p. 96). But it is clear that they had, in many ways, adapted themselves to their Greek setting. They spoke Greek, were on sufficiently close terms with their 'Greek' neighbours to engage the interest of some in their religion and community activities, sometimes, at least, may have worked alongside them, sometimes took names from the general onomastic tradition of the Greco-Roman world and may have accepted something of the *mores* which these often embodied (e.g. admiration for competitive qualities); in all this, of course, resembling many other communities of the western diaspora, in so far as we know them.

Of the *theosebeis* the major feature is that a group which shows comparatively little trace of semitic connections in its names, and which reaches at the top into the lower echelons of the civic office-holding class, was sufficiently interested in Judaism to make donations to a Jewish foundation, while two of its members seem to have studied Judaic Law (*a*, ll. 19, 20) and three became proselytes (*a*, ll. 13, 16, 22) – for it is surely from among the *theosebeis* that these converts were drawn. Both proselytes and *theosebeis* have accepted public inscription of their connection with the Jews on stone (which *a priori* must have been accessible to non-Jews, even if placed within the synagogue). The existence of the nine city-councillors among them may have seemed to be a guarantee of security; but there would surely have been no city-councillors in the list if the Jews had not been an established, and, by and large, an accepted element in the city's population. In fact there seem to be no signs here of strong, or at least of open, antisemitism in Aphrodisian society at this date – which is not, of course, to say that Jews might not sometimes be the subject of tensions.

Given the focus of Aphrodisias on the goddess Aphrodite, who has hitherto seemed predominant in the city's life,[7] this gives us an interesting new feature of its history. It is one for which a good parallel can be found at Sardis, where the Jewish community (attested by Josephus as well established in the first century B.C.)[8] had, at least from the third century A.D., a grandly-appointed synagogue; and, if the word *theosebeis* had the same meaning there as at Aphrodisias (and we believe that it should do), had attracted the association of gentiles of substance who made donations to its buildings.[9] We cannot at present document these gentiles in numbers comparable with those now known at Aphrodisias, and do not know of any proselytes there; but that is explicable as an accident of the evidence so far discovered (see p. 89). We do not happen to have from Sardis a monument which is comparable with this one at Aphrodisias. Conversely we do not have at Aphrodisias inscriptions such as do occur at Sardis, recording Jews who had local and/or Roman citizenship, and who held civic office, of which they were clearly proud; in the Aphrodisias inscription, at any rate as it has survived, there is no reference either to local or to Roman citizenship, and all the city-councillors named are *theosebeis*, not Jews. The reason for the apparent difference may be, at least in part, chronological, for the Sardian inscriptions concerned are all probably later, many of them demonstrably later, than the Antonine Constitution of A.D. 212,[10] while we have proposed a date a little earlier than that for the Aphrodisian (see pp. 19–22).

Ever since the Sardis synagogue was excavated, it was predictable that more, flourishing, third-century Jewish communities would be discovered in Asia Minor; this is the first major piece of new evidence to appear. We still need much more information if we are to make a serious evaluation of their importance to the particular cities in which they existed, and to city-life in general. At present we can hardly say much more than that when the emperors Severus and Caracalla agreed, sometime between 198 and 211, that Jews might be admitted to city councils,[11] they implied, obviously enough, that there were Jews who had, or might be given, local citizenships, and who could meet the local property-qualifications for this office. They also implied, of course, that some cities were feeling quite acutely the problem, well known to have been developing during the second century, of a shortage of men from the traditional sources to undertake the burdens of office.[12] Aphrodisias was highly favoured with exemptions from Roman levies and taxation;[13] she might not be among the first to feel this shortage. We still do not know whether she ever felt it to the extent of recruiting Jews into her council; it might be thought that the existence of the nine *theosebeis* now attested as council members could imply some extension of recruitment into unfamiliar areas. This is a hypothesis to be treated with reserve, however, since we are ill-informed about the membership of her council apart from this text; we can make no precise statements about the earlier sources of recruitment, and are equally ignorant of the family backgrounds of the nine *bouleutai* who were *theosebeis* – they might, quite well, come from perfectly normal bouleutic strata, despite the appearance among them of unexpected, including transliterated Latin, names (*b*, ll. 35, 36, 37, 38).

Jews and *theosebeis* between them commanded resources to set up a monument with certain pretensions (although not necessarily of great size), judging from the use of marble and the height of the stone published here. They seem to have included in their numbers quite prosperous men (cf. the goldsmith and the purple-dyer [*b*, ll. 9, 39]), as well as more modest ones; and it is, perhaps, unlikely that the Jews would have attracted into association the nine gentiles who were city-councillors, consequently able to meet a property-qualification and to command a degree of social recognition in the city as a whole, unless they themselves included a number of men of comparable substance (even if that substance did not include real property). The evidence for the sources of their income is manifestly inadequate but allows of some conjectures.[14]

We have already given a commentary on the trade-designations which appear beside the names of perhaps ten Jews and seventeen *theosebeis* (pp. 116–22). The low proportion of those with them to those without conforms to the pattern in all periods of Greek and Roman antiquity.[15] Nevertheless it seems to us that from the archaic period onwards, in the Greek as well as in the western world, there were areas of society in which manual skill and successful achievement with it, even a little notoriety derived from the activity of a retailer or small-scale entrepreneur of a specific type, were felt to be matters deserving record, despite their disparagement by the élite.[16] This might be especially natural in a community of resident aliens, lacking the right to own real property and so peculiarly dependent on their trades (see also p. 125). But some of those whose trades are given here are certainly men of quite high status – above all the goldsmith among the Jews and the purple-dyer among the *theosebeis*, the latter ranking immediately after the city-councillors (*b*, l. 39), in a position in which it would be surprising, we think, to find a resident alien.[17] The inscription perhaps shows us, in the list of *theosebeis*, an area of society where a trade (or some trades) might be regarded with a certain satisfaction even by a citizen.

The number of trades recorded here is, of course, very small, but sufficient to show Jews variously employed and in the same ways as gentiles. Taking the evidence for the Jews and the *theosebeis* together, the overall picture accords with that of other relevant inscriptions from Aphrodisias, and with that of other ancient areas which have produced larger bodies of information.[18] It points, very obviously, to production of basic consumer goods for local consumption, with particular emphasis on food, textiles and metal goods. Like the Aphrodisian evidence as a whole it lays an unusual emphasis on marble-working which is very natural there, but also, less expectedly, stresses cloth processing; it offers less indication in the trade names of the very detailed craft specialisation that is commonly found elsewhere; and it makes no reference to corn, oil and wine or to earthen-wares of which there are strong traces elsewhere. It seems worth remarking that there is also no mention of inn-keepers, although it is certain that visitors needing their services were attracted to the city by the asylum and rites of Aphrodite and, increasingly in the second and third centuries, by agonistic festivals held there. It is possible that the Jews stood aside from provision of these services because of the dietary laws; it is not clear that the *theosebeis* would do so, or if either would withdraw from the provision of objects to be sold to visitors to the sanctuary of Aphrodite for dedication there (see p. 57). But that is a point that serves as a reminder of our extensive areas of ignorance on these issues.

It might be easier to assess the place of the Jewish community and its associates in the life of the city if we could estimate the scale of operations of the tradesmen listed; but only guess-work is possible. The probable Jewish sheep-rearer (*b*, l. 13) may have operated in a large or moderately large way, since he stands quite high in the list as we have it, although below the goldsmith (*b*, l. 9); but the value of the goldsmith's stock, assuming that he was his own master, would, presumably, have given him the economic edge, just as the value of the purple-dyer's stock would help to account for his position among the *theosebeis* immediately after the city-councillors (*b*, l. 39). On the other hand we might presume small-scale activity for those near or at the bottom of the lists – among the Jews for the two confectioners, the poulterer, the second-hand clothes dealer and the χιλᾶς who may have been a dealer in hay or a 'stitcher' (?tailor) or 'plaiter' (*b*, ll. 26–9); while among the *theosebeis* the fullers, the money-changer and the carpenter (*b*, ll. 58–60) are likely to have been employees rather than independent tradesmen (see p. 120, 122). If we accept that the lists are hierarchical in order, as we believe that they are, one conclusion to be drawn is that an occupational designation by itself may seem to convey implications that are in fact misleading, just because it says nothing of the scale of operations involved. Here, since the money-changer rubs shoulders with fullers at the bottom of the list (*b*, ll. 58–9), and since the fullers are a three-some suggesting a group of employees rather than owners of establishments (see p. 120), we seem to have some indication at the lower end of the scale, but none of the gradations between that and the upper end. The picture may also be confused by issues of legal status; if it is right to see a doorkeeper and a treasurer among the *theosebeis* (*b*. ll. 50, 56, see pp. 119, 121) they are quite likely to be slaves, but they are well above the bottom of the list and there is strong indication, in what we have interpreted as patronymics (*b*, ll. 53, 55, 56, 61), that free-born men appear below them. Slave status too, then, may mislead, since a slave's status certainly depended in part on his owner's status, as well as on his own function in his owner's household.[19]

A large majority of the men listed, however, both Jews and *theosebeis*, have no trade-designation with their names and must be presumed either to have preferred to omit mention of their trade or to have lived without one. For Cicero, to be a merchant was only acceptable if the operation was on a large enough scale (especially, of course, if the profits were invested in land);[20] and it may be that some unproclaimed merchants who shared his views are listed here. But it is also reasonable to consider whether some on the lists derived an income from rural or urban property (which would necessarily have been rented if they had no right to own real estate) and/or from money loaned at interest. It has hitherto seemed natural to suppose that the territory of Aphrodisias was divided into a few very large estates, cultivated by a rural population, possibly dependent, which was descended from the native ἔθνη of the area; but there is almost no evidence. The existence of smaller farms, whether owned or tenanted by those who worked them, is entirely possible. Some of the men on these lists may have farmed in this way. On the other hand the development of the group of *theosebeis* is likely to have been an urban phenomenon; and many of the trades which appear among the trade-designations also belong essentially in an urban context and suggest that the community as a whole is urban rather than rural.[21] Those who lived on income from property might be owners, or tenants, of urban property which they let, or sublet, for rent. Quite apart from the general probability, we know that the city itself derived income from urban property so let, and can name at least one member of its governing class who did the same.[22] Alternatively, or in supplement, some of these men may have lived on the interest of loans, whatever the original source of their money. There is a considerable body of evidence at Aphrodisias for income from loans, some of which were made within the city's territories, some in that of neighbouring cities.[23]

We cannot as yet go beyond hypothesis and we have pushed hypothesis as far as seems desirable. The problems raised, however, suggest new issues on which evidence must be sought in the material constantly accumulating from the site. It may indeed be reasonably expected that the rich soil of Aphrodisias will, in due course, give us more and clearer evidence on the Jews and God-fearers of the city and their place in its society and economy.

NOTES

1 Cf. Reynolds, *Aphrodisias*, document 8, especially ll. 29ff., 51ff.
2 Cf. I Maccabees 15:23 for Caria in general, Cnidos, Halicarnassus and Myndos in particular, in the later second century B.C.; Josephus, *AJ* XIV.224ff., for Ephesus, Halicarnassus, Laodiceia, Miletus, Pergamum, Sardis, Tralles in the first century B.C.
3 Cf. Josephus, *AJ* XII.148–53, for settlements of Jews from Babylonia ordered by Antiochus III.
4 On *enktesis* evidence is exiguous after the Hellenistic period (for which see briefly M. I. Rostovtzeff, *Social and economic history of the Hellenistic world* [1941] 204–5, C. Marek, *Die Proxenie* [1984] 158f.), but it seems improbable that Greek cities changed their principles thereafter, even if an increasing willingness to grant their citizenship to others may have removed most occasions for the smaller grant; and *Fouilles de Delphes* IV.4, nos. 94, 103 appear to be of the imperial period. On grants of citizenship to Jews in Greek cities the evidence is often unclear (but the letter of Claudius to the Alexandrians shows conclusively that they did not have it, as a general rule, in Alexandria, see E. M. Smallwood, *Documents of Gaius, Claudius and Nero* [1967] no. 370); for recent discussion see V. Tcherikover, *Hellenistic civilization and the Jews* (1961) 296–332, S. Applebaum in Safrai/Stern i.420–83, Tessa Rajak, *JRS* 74 (1984) 107–23. The probable solution is that the communities as a whole had resident alien status, while certain individuals were given citizenship, no doubt for services rendered; cf. the small number of Jews at Sardis who described themselves as Sardians, in a manner which suggests that this was a distinguishing title, L. Robert, *NIS*, nos. 14–17.
5 See the index of names to the Aphrodisian section of *MAMA* VIII, where we reckon that there are only 29 transliterated Latin names in approximately 300 local entries (N.B.: it is not quite a straightforward operation to extrapolate local entries from others), compared with 20 in a total of 97 names here.
6 See Josephus, *AJ* XIV.234; Acts 19:34.
7 See, for instance, Reynolds, *Aphrodisias* 3–4, 38, and the references to Aphrodite in imperial letters, documents 17, 18, 21.
8 Josephus, *AJ* XIV.232.
9 See A. R. Seager and A. T. Kraabel, 'The synagogue and the Jewish community', in G. M. A. Hanfmann (ed.), *Sardis from prehistoric to Roman times* (1983) 168–90, with L. Robert, *NIS*, nos. 37–58 (N.B. he rejected the interpretation of the *theosebeis* as gentiles).
10 Robert, *cit*. n. 9, nos. 53f.
11 *Digest* 50.2.3.3; see also pp. 66–7.
12 A. H. M. Jones, *The Greek city* (1940) 190.
13 Reynolds, *Aphrodisias* 76, on document 8, ll. 30f.
14 For some more general discussion of the economic activities of diaspora Jews, see Tcherikover, *cit.* n. 4, 333–43, S. Applebaum in Safrai/Stern II.701–27.
15 A. Burford, *Craftsmen in Greek and Roman society* (1972) 12, 27.
16 Some of the evidence is collected and discussed by Burford, *cit*. n. 15, 11–27.
17 We do occasionally hear of city councillors who had connections with trade, cf. Burford, *cit*. n. 15, 150–1; add a goldsmith at Mutina (p. 119, on no. 9), a purple-dyer at Hierapolis (p. 121, on no. 14), and there is, of course, the well-known weaver at Apthungi who was a duumvir, Optatus, *de schismate Donatistarum*, App. II.26a, 27b, cf. A. H. M. Jones, ed. P. A. Brunt, *The Roman economy* (1974) 357.
18 Cf. the works cited p. 112, n. 2, together with *MAMA* III (for the cemetery of Corycus).

19 That is clear, for example, at Pompeii, cf. *ILS* 6381, where precedence is given to the slave of Agrippa (probably Agrippa Postumus).
20 *De officiis* I.151.
21 Compare the presence of patently rural designations, especially γεωργός in P. Lond. II.257, 258, 259 from a village in the Arsinoite nome of Egypt.
22 Inscription as yet unpublished.
23 For instance *MAMA* VIII.413; and cf. Reynolds, *Aphrodisias*, document 57.

APPENDIX:
OTHER JEWISH INSCRIPTIONS AND GRAFFITI AT APHRODISIAS

(A) INDISPUTABLE CASES

1. Graffiti roughly incised within partially smoothed areas on seats in the odeum,[1] probably to be dated in the Byzantine period along with a number of similar non-Jewish texts; *a* published by A. Cameron;[2] *a* and *b* to appear also in Roueché, ch. 10.

Letters, irregular: 0·012–0·045; E, Ϲ, Ⱳ, cursive *alpha*, and ligatured *nu* and *pi* in *a*; lunate *epsilon*, *sigma*, *omega* in *b*. In both texts the letters show signs of wear, and in *b* the first three letters of Ἑβρέων seem to have been chiselled out (but can be read in a cross-light).

a Seating block *d*, row 6: Τόπος Βενέτων
   Ἑβρέων τῶν παλειῶν
b Seating block *b*, row 5: Τόπος Ἑβρέων

a. The use of Ἑβραῖοι rather than Ἰουδαῖοι in inscriptions is thought to be late (perhaps beginning in the sixth century A.D.).[3]

On the Blue Faction, see Cameron.[4] That some Jews attended pagan public entertainments seems clear, cf. the reservation of seats for them in the theatre of Miletus, cited above p. 54, and, as reported recently, in the Hippodrome of Tyre. The reservation here in the block occupied by the Blues seems to support the view that there was a connection between Jews and Blues; the evidence for this has been discussed by Cameron and rejected,[5] but subsequently Rey-Coquais has announced new and confirmatory evidence at Tyre.[6]

Παλειῶν is presumably for παλαιῶν; παλαιοί appear in another Greek Jewish inscription found near Chalcedon,[7] where they are usually taken to be πρεσβύτεροι; and it is worth noting that a short distance away from the Aphrodisian text is another, τόπος νεοτέρω[ν] (sic), which could, perhaps, be associated with it – implying there a provision of seats also for Jewish younger men (for Jewish νεώτεροι there is evidence in an inscription at Hypaepa, Ἰουδα[ί]ων νεωτέρων,[8] which was connected by S. Krauss with separation of old and young in the synagogues,[9] by S. Applebaum with a Jewish gymnasium).[10]

For the erasures cf. the removal of the faction names in the Hippodrome at Tyre

(J. and L. Robert, *cit.* n. 2); the reason for them here is beyond recovery, but anti-semitism is obviously possible.

2. Graffiti representing two seven-branched lampstands (*menoroth*), one with associated but unidentified objects, as well as a short text, incised on a marble block, perhaps part of a door-jamb which has been cut down for re-use (*c.* 0·43 × 1·29 × 0·41); found with other re-used material in the theatre,[11] apparently part of the rubble with which the *cavea* was filled in the seventh century.

Letters, irregular and not closely dateable, ave. 0·01; ⨆.

    . . .]ωρα *vac.* τῷ οἴκῳ
             τούτῳ
           [.]ΝΑΙ
           [. . .

Line 1. There may have been here a prayer to God to protect this house, or a statement that He has done or does do so (e.g. Θεὸς ἐνωρᾷ τῷ οἴκῳ, cf. *CIJ* I.696 [with Lifshitz, *Prolegomenon* 79], where the *menorah* stands above the text which Frey interpreted as ἐνορῶ(ντος) Θεοῦ); but too little survives for effective restoration. The *menorah* was a characteristic indicator of Judaism, found in diaspora Jewish art at least from the second century A.D., but it may be used also to symbolize the image of God and the light of the Law, and for apotropaic value.[12] The house could, in principle, be a private one, but the word is sometimes used for the assembly hall of a synagogue;[13] the use of a large block of marble in fact rather suggests a public building.

Line 3. Possibly from ἰνδικτιών, and if so unlikely to be earlier than the last quarter of the fourth century;[14] but a date is not particularly relevant here, so that a verb (?ἐνδιαιτᾶται) might be considered more probable.

3. Part of a neatly-carved relief of a seven-branched lampstand (*menorah*) on a fragment of marble found in the débris of modern houses a little to the north of the museum; it must derive from a formal context, very possibly the synagogue itself. There is no evidence for its date. For the significance of the *menorah* see no. 2.

4. Graffito of a seven-branched lampstand (*menorah*) on a three-footed base, probably with schematic representations of a palm-branch (*lulab*) and ceremonial ram's horn (*shofar*), one on each side of the stem, neatly incised on a column beside the entry to one of the *tabernae* in the south portico of the imperial cult building known as the sebasteion.[15] The graffito must date from the period after the cessation of cult activities there, when the building seems to have been

converted for use as shops, but before the early seventh century, when it was destroyed in an earthquake. For the significance of the *menorah* see no. 2. Another column in the same portico carries a graffito of a cross. See also nos. 5, 6.

5. Graffiti representing a variety of Jewish symbols, at least two, probably four, seven-branched lampstands (*menoroth*) on three-footed bases, one jug, ram's horns (*shofarim*), citrons (*ethrogim*), palm-branches (*lulabim*), and an item of a type interpreted by Frey as a torah cupboard,[16] roughly incised on a damaged marble block re-used to close the entry to one of the *tabernae* in the south portico of the imperial cult building known as the sebasteion (see nos. 4, 6). It is not clear whether the graffiti were cut when the stone was already in this position or at an earlier stage when it may have stood in a wholly Jewish context – perhaps not the synagogue itself in view of their crudity, but possibly in its forecourt.[17]

6. Graffito of a seven-branched lampstand (*menorah*) on a three-footed base, with unidentifiable objects on either side of the stem, neatly incised on a column in the north portico of the imperial cult building known as the sebasteion, beside the entry to one of the *tabernae* (see nos. 4, 5).

B. POSSIBLY JEWISH

7. Graffiti incised on marble panels in a threshold within the bath-building beside the extra-mural nymphaeum;[18] while *a* may be complete on its stone, *b* is certainly not, and must originally have extended onto flanking panels; but it is not clear whether the texts were cut in their present position, in which case the flanking panels must have been subsequently replaced with the blank ones which now lie beside them, or whether the inscribed panels that we have are in secondary use now.

Rough letters, not dateable; 0·03–0·04; lunate *epsilon*, *sigma* and *omega* except in the second hand of *a*, cursive *delta* and *mu* in *a*, cursive *alpha* in *b*.

(*a*) *first hand*   νικᾷ ἡ τύχη τῶν ὅδε
                     Εὐσεβίου γράμματα *vac.*
    second hand (rather larger and inserted between the end of l. 1 and the right edge).
                                ΚΕ*v.*

(*b*) [νικᾷ ἡ τύχ]η τῶν ὅδε   *vac.*
      . . .] Ζηνᾶς   *vacat*
      . . .] Νόννος   *vacat*

...] Θε[όδ]ωρ(ο)ς   vac.
...] Σαββάτιο[ς]
...] Κάλλιστος   v.

The case for regarding the texts as Jewish rests essentially on the name Σαββάτιος; but this might also be pagan or Christian.

b, l. 1 is restored from *a*, l. 1. Formulae with νικᾷ and especially νικᾷ ἡ τύχη τῶν --- are assembled and discussed by E. Peterson, ΕΙΣ ΘΕΟΣ (1926) 152–63, and A. Cameron, *Porphyrius* 74–80. Jews accepted the concept of τύχη (cf. *CIJ* I.123, τῇ τύχῃ σου in a funerary text), but we have not found a certainly Jewish use of the νικᾷ formula. Also relevant is a text found in an Egyptian quarry – Ἀπολλώνιος Ἰσιδώρου εὐχαριστῶ τῇ τύχῃ τῶν ὧδε;[19] that suggests that these may be the graffiti of workmen and even perhaps of marble-workers. If so, one Jew (or more), or one Christian (or more), might be included in a group of gentiles or pagans.

At the end of *a*, l. 1, the added KE could be κέ for καί, meant as a link with the name of Eusebius in l. 2, although it makes nonsense of the word γράμματα there (perhaps, therefore Κ(ύρι)ε). With or without it, 1. 2 was presumably intended to associate the writer with his acclamation, cf. *IGCEg*. 37 at Alexandria, νικᾷ ἡ τύχη Εὐτοκίου καὶ τῶν Βενέτων καὶ τοῦ γράψαντος. For the use of γράμματα cf. Καίσαρος γράμματα below an inscribed copy of a letter of Octavian at Aphrodisias (cut in the third century) and γράμμ(ατα) Κωνσταντίνου ὑποδιακ(όνου) below a Christian building inscription on Samos:[20] the more normal language in which to claim responsibility for a scribble is ἔγραψα (ἔγραψεν) or χειρί followed by the name in the genitive.

Of the names, Εὐσέβιος is used by Jews, Christians and pagans, and attested in our main inscription both for a Jew and for a gentile (father of a proselyte), see p. 100, list A, no. 24; Ζηνᾶς is comparable with Ζήνων, a pagan theophoric name used by Jews, and in our main inscription by Jews and *theosebeis*, see p. 100, list A, no. 28; Νόννος is widely disseminated, in the east especially, and above all in Egypt, at least from the later second century (for discussion see Lüderitz, *Cyrenaika* 78) – for a Jewish example see *Donateurs* 56; for Θεόδωρος as a name favoured by Jews and found in our main inscription, see p. 101, list A, no. 32; Κάλλιστος is widely disseminated and has no Jewish connections, but for a Jew so named see *CIJ* I.587; for Σαββάτιος see p. 104, list A, no. 59.

8. Small marble column-base (0·50 × 0·88 × 0·48) inscribed on one face with a text which cannot be related to the original purpose of the monument; found *in situ* in the north colonnade of the portico east of the theatre.[21] To be published also in Roueché, ch. 11.

Letters uneven, but cut rather than scratched: 0·023–0·045.

> Ἑορτασίου Κο-
> νιορτοῦ
> τόπος

The case for regarding this text as Jewish rests on the name, which occurs several times for Jews in the main text and once for a *theosebes*, see p. 99, list A, no. 18; it is certainly attested elsewhere for Christians, while pagans without Judaizing sympathies seem to have used it too, as they did its simpler forms such as Ἑορταῖος.

The date is not easily assessed from the lettering, which might be as early as the second century and as late as the sixth; but since the monument was originally part of a civic complex and the text apparently marks it as Heortasios' place of business,[22] it should be at any rate after the area was remodelled in the mid fourth century (but the portico may have been in use as late as the seventh century).

Κονιορτός, 'dust', may be a name or a nickname;[23] here it is perhaps a nickname, since if it were a patronymic the article τοῦ ought, in the phrase as presented, to stand immediately before it. That accords with the evidence of the main inscription, where a number of men have the name Heortasios (see p. 99), so that distinguishing designations for each would be desirable. It would be satisfactory if this nickname could be related to the nature of the man's work – but only too obviously many trades make a man dusty.

9. Marble panel, slightly concave, reconstructed from two pieces (together, 1·35 × 0·53 × 0·24; excavation inventory no. 74.262), inscribed on one face. Found loose in the area east of the museum, in proximity to the stone carrying the main text; now in the museum. To appear also in Roueché, ch. 2.

Letters, capitals quite well cut and aligned, necessarily, but not very obviously, fourth century at the earliest: 0·03.

> [.]θε[.]ῷ ἐπηκόῳ Φλ(άβιος)
> Εὐσέβιος ἀπὸ πριμι-
> πιλαρίων ἐκ τῶν
> τοῦ θεοῦ δομάτων
> 5 τὸ πρῶτον καὶ τρίτον
> διάστυλον ἐποίησεν

Line 1. The first word, cut in an erasure which is too large for it, is presumably intended for Θεῷ. We have no satisfying explanation of what was erased; Κυρίῳ would occupy the space, but its removal would be surprising.

The case for suggesting that this text might be Jewish rests partly on the findspot (but since it is not certain that either this or the stone carrying the main text were in, or very near, their original location, that is not at all a conclusive argument), largely on the formula used in ll. 3–4. The concept of gifts given to God from God's gifts to man seems to be essentially Jewish and Christian; for a good Jewish example quite recently published see the text from the Sardis synagogue (perhaps third century A.D.), --- ἔδ]ωκα ἐκ τῶν δωρεῶν τοῦ παντοκράτορος Θ(εο)ῦ τὴν σκούτλωσιν πᾶσαν.[24] For δόματα in the sense of 'gifts' see J. and L. Robert, *Bull. Ep.* 1968, 478. On the other hand we have not found either an unequivocally Jewish example, or even a Christian one, for the dedicatory formula Θεῷ ἐπηκόῳ; in two Jewish texts from Hellenistic Egypt, where it is commonly printed, it is largely or wholly restored,[25] while a third, possibly Jewish, from Panticapaeum, of A.D. 306, where it is complete, does not appear in *CIJ, CJI* or *Donateurs*.[26] It was of course extensively used by pagans.[27]

The personal name of the dedicator is one used by Jews, but also by pagans and by Christians, see p. 100, list A, no. 24; his title and the name Flavius (see below) imply a career and a date which, if this stone does come from a Jewish context, might be more suited to a *theosebes* than to a full Jew.

Ἀπὸ πριμιπιλαρίων indicates a man who is retired from service as a *primipilaris*, and therefore served as such after the word ceased to denote a retired *primus pilus* in consequence of the military reforms of Gallienus;[28] the name *Flavius* is likely to have been acquired at earliest under Constantine.[29] The work of a *primipilaris* was administrative rather than military, but it might be difficult for a practising Jew to observe the Law strictly while carrying out the duties of this office; it could be, however, that Eusebius' office was honorary rather than actual.

A διάστυλον is an intercolumniation; it is attested at Aphrodisias in connection with a set of stoas, cf. the interesting series of texts from Ephesus in which a benefactor records provision of one or more *diastyla* for the use of particular trade organizations,[30] and the τετράστοον (presumably a colonnaded court) mentioned in conjunction with the synagogue at Stobi.[31] It is not at all clear where this inscription would be placed in such a structure, nor why Eusebius provided the first and the third rather than the first and the second *diastyla*. An intercolumniation was presumably a unit which could be separately priced, and was within the means of donors who were not outstandingly wealthy.

10. Rectangular marble panel ($0.57 \times 0.52 \times 0.18$; excavation inventory number 75.5) inscribed on one face; found during preparation of the site for the Aphrodisias museum in proximity to the stone carrying the main text. To be published also in Roueché, ch. 8.

Letters, post-classical, perhaps fifth century, but not precisely dateable:

0·055–0·07; lunate *sigma* in ll. 3, 4, varied in l. 4 by a rectangular one; abbreviation mark in the form of s at the end of l. 1.

 Εὐχὴ Φλ(αουίου)
 Δαμοχά-
 ριδος κούρ-
 vac. σορος

The case for regarding this as possibly Jewish depends partly on the findspot (but see our comment on no. 9), partly on the presence of the formula εὐχή[32] without any associated Christian symbol such as might have been expected at the likely date; but there is nothing distinctive in the name, and the implied career might suggest that at the most the man was *theosebes*, for a *cursor* was an official messenger and it might be difficult for a practising Jew to observe the Law strictly while carrying out the duties of this office. The date follows from the name *Flavius* which is likely to have been acquired at earliest during service under Constantine.[33]

11. Small altar reconstructed from two pieces, crudely moulded at the top and the bottom on three sides (0·10 × 0·26 × 0·10; excavation inventory nos. 65·337 + 67·199), inscribed on two adjacent faces. Stray find, now in the museum.

Letters, very irregular and poorly cut, not dateable: 0·015–0·025; lunate *sigma*, cursive *alpha*.

	Face a	Face b
	Μα-	ὑψίσ-
	ρκια-	τοι ε[ὐ]-*sic*
	[v]ὸς	χή
sic	θεῷ	

This text may be due to a *theosebes*, see p. 64 f.–5, since θεὸς ὕψιστος was a formula sometimes associated with the Jewish God;[34] but it is also attested in pagan cult so that there can be no certainty.[35] The name is, of course, transliterated Latin, and without Jewish connections.

12. Upper right corner of a marble altar, the upper moulding chiselled away and the face damaged, perhaps by burning (0·12 × 0·135 × 0·09; excavation inventory no. 65.433), inscribed on one face. Found in the odeum, re-used; now in the museum.

Letters, late Hellenistic, perhaps I cent. B.C.–I cent. A.D., neat but unevenly sized: ave. 0·015; lunate *epsilon*, *sigma* and *omega*.

...]Τατας
... θ]εῷ ὑψίστῳ
[...

For the possible Jewish connections of this category of dedication see on no. 11. The name of the dedicant is without Jewish content and in fact indigenous to Asia Minor.[36] Since we cannot assess how much of the stone is lost to the left, we must allow that a specific god's name may have appeared at the beginning of l. 2 (cf. ῞Ηλιος Θεὸς ῞Υψιστος, *I. Pergamum* II, no. 330).

NOTES

1 On the building see K. T. Erim, *AS* 14 (1964) 26, 16 (1966) 37-8.
2 A. Cameron, *Porphyrius the charioteer* (1973) 276, *Circus factions in the Roman world* (1976) 315, with 79 and 150; cf. J. and L. Robert, *Bull. Ep.* 1977, 82.
3 See R. Mouterde, *Mélanges de l'Université de Beyrouth* 17 (1933) 209–10, and L. Robert, *NIS* 38, n. 6. A late date, although not necessarily as late as the sixth century, would be suitable to the whole group of graffiti to which these two belong.
4 *Cit.* n. 2.
5 *Circus factions, cit.* n. 2, 149–52.
6 J. P. Rey-Coquais, *RA* 1979, 167.
7 *CIJ* II.800, see now *I. Chalcedon* 75.
8 *CIJ* II.755.
9 S. Krauss, *Synagogale Altertümer* 231.
10 S. Applebaum in Safrai/Stern I.478.
11 For the building see K. T. Erim, *National Geographic Society Research Projects* (1973) 89, (1976) 79.
12 For discussion see E. R. Goodenough IV.71–98.
13 L. Robert, *NIS* 51.
14 See O. Seeck, *RE* 9, col. 1332.
15 On the building see K. T. Erim, *AS* 30 (1980) 205–6, 32 (1982) 10–13, 33 (1983) 231–4.
16 *CIJ* I.682, 730; this interpretation is questioned by Goodenough II.9.
17 Crude graffiti do of course occur on the sacred monuments of pagans and Christians, but we have not found a satisfying parallel from the interior of a synagogue.
18 On the building see K. T. Erim, *AS* 19 (1969) 16.
19 Cited by L. Robert, *Hellenica* 11–12 (1960) 27–8, from F. Preisigke, *Gebel Selsile* (1915) no. 195 (Preisigke, *Sammelbuch* 4071).
20 Reynolds, *Aphrodisias* 43, doc. 6, l. 53, *IGCA* 147.
21 On the building see K. T. Erim, *AS* 23 (1973) 19–23.
22 For this use of τόπος cf. J. and L. Robert, *Bull. Ep.* 1962, 307 and L. Robert, *Journal des Savants* (1971) 83–4.
23 See the discussion by L. Robert, *Noms Indigènes* 301, arising from a graffito in the Priene gymnasium (*I. Priene* 313.721, ὁ τόπος Κονιορτοῦ).
24 See L. Robert, *NIS* 49; J. and L. Robert, *Bull. Ep.* 1968.478; and, for earlier discussion, Leclerq in *DCAL* IV, col. 1507, citing LXX, I Chron. I.29:14 --- ὅτι σὰ τὰ πάντα καὶ ἐκ τῶν σῶν δεδώκαμεν.
25 *Donateurs* 86, 87; in the latter it was rejected by D. M. Lewis, *CPJ* III (1964) 139–40; the concept is Jewish, however, cf. LXX, II Chron. 6:4 and 7:15, καὶ τὰ ὦτά μου ἐπήκοα τῇ προσευχῇ τοῦ τόπου τούτου. M. Avi-Yonah, *IEJ* 9 (1959) 5f. knew no more satisfactory Jewish instance. A parallel has now been discovered at Silifke (an altar showing ears in relief as well

as a [five-branched] candlestick); we are most grateful for permission to refer to its forthcoming publication in G. Dagron et D. Feissel, *Inscriptions de Cilicie*, no. 14.

26 *CIRB* 64 (IGR I.873). M. Avi-Yonah, *cit.* n. 25, regards it as judaizing rather than Jewish, but we have found no detailed argument for this view; we are not convinced by the suggestion in *PLRE* I, *s.v.* Aurelius Valerius Sogous, that it was the dedication of a judaizing Christian (as C. M. Roueché has pointed out to us, it seems unlikely that a Christian would be making a dedication in the east in A.D. 306, even in an area which was strictly client rather than annexed).

27 O. Weinreich, ΘΕΟΙ ΕΠΗΚΟΟΙ, *MDAI(A)* 34 (1912) 1–68.

28 B. Dobson, *Die Primipilares* (1978) 139–45, J. Le Carrié, *ZPE* 35 (1979) 212–24; we are grateful for advice here from Professors Frank Gilliam and M. P. Speidel. For a very brief account of the general development of titles indicating former service (and so, often, current privilege) see F. G. B. Millar, *JRS* 73 (1983) 94–5.

29 J. G. Keenan, *ZPE* 11 (1973) 33–63.

30 *MAMA* VIII.498 for Aphrodisias; see also *I Eph.* II.444, 445, 2076–82 and now the discussion by D. Knibbe, in *JOAI* 56 (1986) 72–77.

31 *Donateurs* 10, cf. J. and L. Robert, *Bull, Ep.* 1968.325, noting that this was likely to be a feature associated with the synagogue rather than the synagogue itself.

32 For Jewish uses cf., for instance, *Donateurs* 4, 5, 7.

33 See Keenan, *cit.* n. 29, 59, for two Egyptian *cursores* with the nomen Flavius (late fifth and sixth centuries).

34 *Donateurs* 4, 5, 6, 87, 95; see also p. 65.

35 A. T. Kraabel, *GRBS* 10 (1969) 81ff.

36 Zgusta, *KP* 1517.3, 17, 21; it is used both for men and for women.

7. Appendix 1*a*.

8. Appendix 1*b*.

9. Appendix 2.

10. Appendix 3.

11. Appendix 4.

12. Appendix 5.

13. Appendix 7a.

14. Appendix 7b.

15. Appendix 8.

16. Appendix 9.

17. Appendix 10.

18. Appendix 11, face *a*.

19. Appendix 11, face *b*.

INDEX OF GREEK WORDS USED IN THE INSCRIPTIONS

INDEX OF NAMES IN THE GREEK TEXTS

'Αδόλιος, b. 51
'Αθηναγόρας, b. 56, 60
'Αθηνίων, b. 42
Αἰλιανός, b. 29 (twice), 30, ?42
'Αλέξανδρος, b. 50
'Αμαζόνιος, b. 61
'Αμάντιος, b. 12
'Αμάχιος, a. 18
'Αμμιανός, b. 29
'Αμφιανός, b. 8
'Ανίκιος, ?b. 48
'Αντίοχος, b. 37
'Αντιπέος, a. 24, b. 37
'Αντωνῖνος, a. 20
'Ανύσιος, b. 15
'Απελλᾶς, b. 47
'Απελλί(ων), ?b. 20
'Απονήριος, b. 38, 41 (twice)
'Αππιανός, b. 51
"Αττα(λος), ?b. 48
'Αττα(ς), ?b. 48
'Αχιλλεύς, b. 31
'Αχόλιος, b. 22

Βαλεριανός, b. 47, 56
Βαλος, ?b. 43
Βενιαμιν, a. 15
Βιωτικός, b. 8
Βραβεύς, b. 49

Γέμελλος, b. 21
Γληγόριος, b. 44
Γοργόνιος, b. 31, 46

Δαμόνικος, b. 22
Δαμόχαρις, app. 10
Διογένης, b. 18 (twice), 35

Εἰούδας, see 'Ιούδας
Εἰωσηφ, see 'Ιωσηφ
'Ελπιδιανός, b. 54

'Εμμόνιος, a. 19
'Εορτάσιος, b. 7, 31, 33, app. 8, see also 'Ορτάσιος
'Ερμή(ας), ?Έρμης, ?a. 24
Εὐγένιος, b. 9, 24
Εὔοδος, b. 14 (twice)
Εὐπίθιος, b. 39, 53 (twice)
Εὐσαββάθιος, b. 15, 16, 18, 24,·32, 48, app. 9
Εὐσέβιος, a. 22, b. 6, app. 7b
Εὔρετος, b. 56
Εὐτάρκιος, ?b. 23
Εὐτρόπιος, b. 55
Εὐτυχιανός, b. 58
Εὐτύχιος, b. 25, 27

Ζαχαρίας, b. 20
Ζην(?), b. 33
Ζηνᾶς, app. 7a
Ζήνων, b. 4, 5, 28, 34, 36
Ζωσι(?), b. 28
Ζωτικός, b. 33, 52 (twice)

Ἡδυχροῦς, b. 48, 54, 55
Ἡγε(μονεύς), ?b. 47

Θεόδοτος, a. 11
Θεόδωρος, a. 23, app. 7a
Θεόφιλος, b. 19

'Ιαηλ, a. 9
'Ιακω, b. 13
'Ιακωβ, b. 5, 20
'Ιάσων, b. 14
Ἰέσσεος, a. 14
'Ιλαριανός, a. 12
'Ιούδας, a. 16, 23, b. 6, 8, 10, 19, 22, 23, 27, 28
'Ιουν, ?b. 43
'Ιουνβαλος, ?b. 43
'Ιούν(ιος), ?b. 43
'Ιωῆς, a. 14, 17
'Ιωσηφ, a. 22, b. 4, 23, 26

147

INDEX OF GREEK WORDS

Ἰωσούας, *a.* 10
Ἰωφ, ?*b.* 5
Καλλίκαρπος, *b.* 7
Καλλίμορφος, *b.* 43 (twice)
Καλλίνικος, *b.* 55
Κλαυδιανός, *b.* 50
Κύρυλλος, *b.* 25

Λεόντιος, *b.* 21 (twice)
Λονγι(ανός), ?*b.* 36
Λονγῖ(νος), ?*b.* 36

Μανασῆς, *b.* 5
Μανίκιος, ?*b.* 48
Μαρκιανός, *app.* 11
Μελ(?), *b.* 41
Μελίτων, *b.* 61
Μίλων, *b.* 16
Μύρτιλος, *b.* 12

Νόννος, *app.* 7*a*

Ξάνθος, *b.* 40 (three times), 42

Ὀνήσιμος, *b.* 36
Ὀξυχόλιος, *b.* 11, 17, 31, 32, 46
Ὀρτάσιος, *b.* 27, 49

Παράμονος, *b.* 57
Παρηγόριος, *b.* 32
Πατρίκιος, *b.* 53
Παῦλος, *b.* 19
Πολιτιανός, *a.* 21

Πολυχρόνιος, *b.* 42, 45
Πραοίλιος, *b.* 10 (twice)
Προκόπιος, *b.* 58
Προυνίκιος, *b.* 59
Πυ(?), ?*b.* 50

Ῥουβην, *b.* 26
Ῥοῦφος, *b.* 11
Ῥωμανός, *b.* 38

Σαβάθιος, *a.* 25
Σαββάτιος, *a.* 18, *app.* 7*b*
Σαμουηλ, *a.* 9–11, 13, 21, ?26, *b.* 30
Σεβῆρος, *b.* 13
Σεραπίων, *b.* 2
Στρατήγιος, *b.* 39
Στρατόνικος, *b.* 59
Συμεών, *b.* 33

Τατας, *app.* 12
Τατιανός, *b.* 46
Τέρτυλλος, *b.* 35
Τυχικός, *b.* 44 (three times)

Ὑψικλῆς, *b.* 41

Φιληρ(?), *b.* 23
Φλ(άουιος), *app.* 9, 10

Χαρῖνος, *b.* 12
Χιλᾶς, ?*b.* 29
Χρύσιππος, *b.* 45

SELECTED GREEK WORDS IN THE TEXTS

ἀθλη(τής), ?*b.* 54
ἀπενθησία, *a.* 6
ἀρκ(άριος), ?*b.* 56
ἀρχιδ(έκανος), ?*a.* 13
ἄρχων, *a.* 10

βελ(οποιός), ?*b.* 45
Βένετοι, *app.* 1*a, b*
βοηθός (θεός), *a.* 1
βουλ(ευτής), *b.* 11, 34–8 (nine times)

γέρων, *b.* 11
γναφ(εύς), *b.* 58, 59 (twice)
γράμματα, *app.* 7*b*
γρύλλος, ?*b.* 52
γρυτ(οπώλης), ?*b.* 28

δεκανία, *a.* 3
διάστυλον, *app.* 9
δόμα, *app.* 9

Ἑβρεοι, *app.* 1*a*
ἐπήκοος, *app.* 9
εὔκολος, ?*a.* 16
εὐχή, *app.* 10, 11

θεός – βοηθός, *a.* 1
ἐπήκοος, *app.* 9
ὕψιστος, *app.* 11, 12
θεοσεβής, *a.* 19, 20, *b.* 34

ἱερεύς, ?*a.* ?26
ἰκονο(γράφος), *b.* 57

INDEX OF GREEK WORDS

ἰνδ(ικτιών), ?*app.* 2
ἰσικιάριος, *b.* 51

κονιορτός, *app.* 8
κούρσωρ, *app.* 10
κτίζω, *a.* 7

λατύ(πος), ?*b.* 49
λαχα(νοπώλης), ?*b.* 15

μνῆμα, *a.* 8
μονο(πώλης), ?*b.* 20

νεκτάρις, ?*a.* 26
νεώτερος, *b.* 17

ξένος, *b.* 16

οἶκος, *app.* 2
ὀρν(ιθοπώλης), ?*b.* 27

παλατῖνος, ?*a.* 11
παλεοί, *app.* 1a
παντευλογ(?), *a.* 5
παστιλλάριος, *b.* 26 (twice)
πάτελλα, *a.* 1
πενα(κᾶς), ?*b.* 47
Περγειους, *a.* ll. 15–17
πλῆθος, *a.* 7

πορφυρ(ᾶς), ?*b.* 39
προβατον(όμος), ?*b.* 13
πρεσβευτής, *a.* 12–14, ?26
πριμιπιλάριος (ἀπὸ πριμιπιλαρίων), *app.* 9
προστάτης, *a.* 9
προσήλ(υτος), *a.* 13, 17, 22
πύ(κτης), ?*b.* 50
πυ(λωρός), ?*b.* 50
πυ(ρηνάδης), ?*b.* 50

τέκτω(ν), *b.* 60
τόπος, *app.* 1a, b, 8
τρα(πεζίτης), ?*b.* 58
τύχη, *app.* 7a, b

ὑποτάσσω, *a.* 2
ὕψιστος, *app.* 11, 12

φιλομαθής, *a.* 4

χαλ(ινοῦργος), ?*b.* 46
χαλκο(τύπος), ?*b.* 25, 46, 53
χιλᾶς, ?*b.* 29
χρυσόχοος, *b.* 9

ψαλμο(λόγος), ?*a.* 15
ψελ(λός), ?*b.* 52
ψελ(οποιός), ?*b.* 52